'An invaluable addition to the literature on terrorism that examines the profound impact of 9/11 on the discipline of criminology and elaborates the theoretical and empirical contributions that criminology can make to our understanding of the "new" terrorism. Its provocative and engaging approach challenges the reader to question common assumptions about what terrorism is, who its perpetrators are and what combatting it requires. Wide-ranging substantive analysis and insightful exploration of key concepts like risk, pre-emption, preparedness and resilience render this a must-read book for all students and scholars of terrorism and security.'

Lucia Zedner, Professor of Criminal Justice, Faculty of Law, University of Oxford, UK

'This critical, multilayered and multifaceted discussion of the concepts of risk, security, resilience and vulnerability is theoretically sophisticated and empirically rich. The book's insightful analysis of the way the discourse of "new terrorism" has constructed vulnerable individuals and communities as risky, cast them as targets of pre-emptive interventions, and the consequences this has for targeted groups, delivers fully on its promise to uncover the many contradictions of contemporary terrorism and counter-terrorism. A must-read for anybody working in the field of risk analysis and security management.'

Lasse Lindekilde, Associate Professor, Department of Political Science, Aarhus University, Denmark

CONTRADICTIONS OF TERRORISM

Over the last 15 years there has been a significant growth in literature dealing with terrorism. Nevertheless, scholars within mainstream criminology have only recently begun to grapple with the problem of terrorism in a sustained fashion. In this provocative book the authors provide both an exposition of the contradictions that have emerged around the regulation of terrorism and an incisive analysis of the questions that the management of terrorism poses for the discipline.

Focusing primarily on the processes and practices that have emerged in the United States and the United Kingdom, the book provides a critical account of the political construction, mediation and regulation of the terrorist threat since the events of 9/11. The authors explore the ways in which new institutional modes of risk assessment based on the principle of pre-emption have impacted on individuals targeted by them. Noting the dilemmas produced by the pre-emptive turn, the authors also elucidate more recent moves to develop the idea of resilience in counter-terrorism and security policy.

This book will be suitable for academics and students interested in political violence, terrorism, geopolitics and risk, as well as for practitioners and experts working in the security industries.

Sandra Walklate is Eleanor Rathbone Chair of Sociology and **Gabe Mythen** is a Reader in Sociology. Both are based in the Department of Sociology, Social Policy and Criminology at the University of Liverpool. The authors have established an international reputation for their joint work on risk, security and victimization, which appears in a range of esteemed journals.

NEW DIRECTIONS IN CRITICAL CRIMINOLOGY

Edited by Walter S. DeKeseredy, West Virginia University, USA

This series presents new cutting-edge critical criminological empirical, theoretical and policy work on a broad range of social problems, including drug policy, rural crime and social control, policing and the media, ecocide, intersectionality and the gendered nature of crime. It aims to highlight the most up-to-date authoritative essays written by new and established scholars in the field. Rather than offering a survey of the literature, each book takes a strong position on topics of major concern to those interested in seeking new ways of thinking critically about crime.

CONTRADICTIONS OF TERRORISM

Security, risk and resilience

*Sandra Walklate and
Gabe Mythen*

Routledge
Taylor & Francis Group

LONDON AND NEW YORK

First published 2015
by Routledge
2 Park Square, Milton Park, Abingdon, Oxon, OX14 4RN

and by Routledge
711 Third Avenue, New York, NY 10017

Routledge is an imprint of the Taylor & Francis Group, an informa business

British Library Cataloguing in Publication Data
A catalogue record for this book is available from the British Library

Library of Congress Cataloging-in-Publication Data
Walklate, Sandra.
   Contradictions of terrorism: security, risk and resilience/Sandra Walklate
   and Gabe Mythen.
   pages cm. – (New directions in critical criminology ; 7)
   1. Terrorism – Prevention. 2. Internal security. 3. National security.
   4. War on Terrorism, 2001–2009. I. Mythen, Gabe. II. Title.
   HV6431.W347 2014
   363.325—dc23
   2014005492

ISBN: 978-0-415-62652-1 (hbk)
ISBN: 978-0-415-62653-8 (pbk)
ISBN: 978-0-203-10261-9 (ebk)

Typeset in Bembo and Stone Sans
by Florence Production Limited, Stoodleigh, Devon, UK

MIX
Paper from
responsible sources
FSC
www.fsc.org FSC® C013604

Printed and bound in Great Britain by
CPI Group (UK) Ltd, Croydon, CR0 4YY

CONTENTS

ACKNOWLEDGEMENTS

We would like to acknowledge a debt of gratitude to the innumerable colleagues who have shaped our thinking on risk, victimization and security over recent years. You know who you are. We would also like to say a big thank you to Heidi Lee at Routledge for her flawless advice and boundless patience and to Tom Sutton for cajoling us into writing a book we probably ought to have written much sooner.

ABBREVIATIONS

BME	black and minority ethnic
CBRN	chemical, biological, radiological and nuclear
DHS	Department of Homeland Security
ETA	*Euskadi Ta Askatasuna*
FBI	Federal Bureau of Investigation
GWOT	Global War on Terrorism
IRA	Irish Republican Army
MMG	Muslim minority group
OCO	Overseas Contingency Operation
PLO	Palestine Liberation Organization
PTSS	Post Traumatic Stress Syndrome
RAID	Rapid Assessment and Initial Detection
SNFCR	Strategic National Framework on Community Resilience
WAT	War against Terrorism
WMD	Weapons of Mass Destruction
WOT	War on Terror

INTRODUCTION

Terrorism is always a provocation. The question is, how do we respond to a provocation?

(Rehn, 2003: 56)

We would like to begin with an anecdote that raises to the surface some of the paradoxes that have captured our interest over the past few years and which we will wrestle with further in the pages of this book. Back in 2009 one of the authors was speaking at a Festival of Human Rights in Stavanger on the topic of terrorism and the risk society. Throughout the talk the audience was generally genial, yet a certain sense of bemusement hung in the air. In the question and answer session that followed, a gentleman at the back of the lecture theatre raised his hand and quizzically asked: 'If risk society is the thesis, what is the anti-thesis?' Having pondered for a moment the speaker responded: 'You would have to say the safe society, I suppose.' 'Yes', replied the questioner nodding eagerly. 'We already have it. It is called Norway.' Of course, the objection being – very politely – made here was well founded. Why, in one of the safest and most secure places in the world, would we want to get hung up on the risk of terrorism? Is the penchant for focusing on high impact but low probability events tantamount to indulging in gratuitous fear seeking? While these are searching questions to contemplate, after the terrible events in Oslo and Utoya less than two years later, Norway began to look like not such a safe society after all.

In many respects what happened in Norway in the summer of 2011 underscores the point about the risk society that Beck (1996: 32) has been making for over twenty years: there are no bystanders anymore. Given the mobility of people, capital, products, ideas and technologies, the notion of the safe haven – where one can be securely tucked away from harm – is no more than a faint memory of modernity, a museum piece, if you will. Certainly, in the context of debates about terrorism, much has been made of the global nature of the threat and the vulnerability of all nations to attack. Yet, in the spirit of contradiction that is central to this book, we would invite the reader to think again. Rather than committing to the dominant view that the terrorist threat is ubiquitous and universal, we should perhaps heed the advice given by Nassim Nicholas Taleb (2010). Taleb believes that extraordinary events such as the attacks in Norway occur from time to time and are impossible to predict or legislate for. For Taleb, such 'Black Swans' can only be rationalized with the benefit of hindsight rather than routinely foreseen or anticipated. As such, we might not be able to predict highly irregular occurrences with any degree of accuracy, but we do have to learn to live with them. If we cannot, the risk of over-responding after the event is likely to produce ruptures and ripples that are as big, if not bigger, than the initial happening.

Before we become disorientated by the ambiguities let us bring in some clarity and say something about our objectives and motivations. In searching for a solid compass we have been both captivated and inspired by a book about a somewhat different subject, Daniel Bell's (1979) *The Cultural Contradictions of Capitalism*. In this well-respected text, Bell offers a provocative commentary on, and analysis of, what he sees as the cultural struggle between tradition and modernity that took place between the 1920s and the 1960s. His analysis of this struggle suggested that, while liberalism would not have a problem with the notion of personal freedom in art and imagination, to embrace such freedom as a feature of *lifestyle* (his emphasis) was problematic. He went on to observe that:

> Liberalism finds itself uneasy in trying to say why. It approves a basic permissiveness, but cannot with any certainty define the

bounds. And this is its dilemma. In culture, as well as in politics, liberalism is now up against the wall.

(Bell, 1979: 79)

First published in 1976, Bell's book offers a thought-provoking and, in its time, controversial analysis of what he saw to be the increasing disarray in the relationship between liberalism and capitalism. In the Foreword to the second edition of this book he comments, tellingly, on the burgeoning presence of single dimensional analyses of complex social problems. Here he suggests that such analyses are to be found in the desire 'to find a tag which can locate the author into the comfortable niches of the marketable vocabularies of conversation' (ibid.: xi). Read in retrospect, these comments – taken along with his analysis of the tensions between liberalism and capitalism – presage some aspects of the dilemmas faced today in understanding and responding to terrorism.

In the second edition of this book Bell comments that:

> The foundation of any liberal society is the willingness of all groups to compromise private ends for the public interest. The loss of *civitas* means either that interests become so polarized, and passions so inflamed, that terrorism and group fighting ensues, and political *anomia* prevails; or that every public exchange becomes a cynical deal in which the most powerful segments benefit at the expense of the weak.

(Ibid.: 245)

Read in the aftermath of two occurrences that have had, and continue to have, global consequences – namely the terrorist attack in New York in September 2001 and the financial crisis of 2008 – such comments foretell much of the present. Indeed, it could be argued that Bell's comment might only be amended to include both of the outcomes that he points to – rather than the either/or possibility he suggests – to give us a sense of the predicaments for liberalism in the present moment. Moreover, in the Introduction to the second edition of this book, Bell argues that for him 'religion is the fulcrum' (ibid.: xxviii).

He suggests, 'a culture [i.e. capitalism] which has become aware of the limits in exploring the mundane will turn, at some point, to the effort to recover the sacred'. Given the contemporary political, policy and social challenges posed by international terrorism – activities assumed to be fuelled in part by religious radicalism – this is an interesting observation.

In this book we do not intend to engage in a discussion of the efficacy or otherwise of Bell's analysis for the time at which it was written, or indeed for the contemporary moment. What we do intend to do is to pick up some of the threads of his thinking to make sense of the problems and issues associated with political violence in the modern world. Thus, our title is *The Contradictions of Terrorism*. Our interest lies primarily with the ways in which the challenges posed by terrorism for Western liberal capitalist countries have been managed, politically and culturally, with a view to considering the ways in which these responses belie the economic dilemmas that underpin them. In choppy times in which neoliberal capitalism finds its 'back against the wall', hegemonic visions and geopolitical aspirations become all the more vital. We are also motivated to assess the general effectiveness of social scientific responses in making sense of the contradictions of terrorism and the specific contribution made by criminologists. Our focus is thus twofold. First, we are committed to making sense of terrorism as a social construct as well as a physical act. Second, we wish to cogitate on the dual impacts of the material and the social construction of terrorism in the academy and wider society. All of which begins with 9/11. Or does it?

9/11 and all that?

Finnane (2013) comments that the first decade of the twenty-first century has, without doubt, been conceived as the decade of terrorism. In some respects this observation is accurate insofar as across a number of jurisdictions, terrorism now has a much higher profile on policy and political agendas than it did prior to 9/11. Indubitably, terrorism receives much wider coverage in the social science and criminological literature than at any point previously. As Hogg (2007: 98) asserts, thinking about terrorism has long transcended the narrow confines of maintaining national security and filtered into a range of policies and practices:

> The terrorist threat now inflects and intensifies popular and political discourse on everything from the acceptability of religious modes of dress to street crime in the suburbs to the future of multiculturalism and the policing of national loyalties through teaching and enforcing commitment to 'Australian values'.

Such observations are not unique to Australia and would not seem out of place if they were made about Denmark, Canada or France. While for many that are able to feed off the fruits of capitalism life may seem relatively secure, the threat of terrorism has become a worrisome motif of the twenty-first century that both signifies, and is a signifier of, a preoccupation with security at every level – from the security of the State to our own feelings of ontological security. Despite declaring firm doubts about the relative scale of the terrorist threat in relation to other social harms, Jackson and Sinclair (2012: 1) concede that we live in a 'terrorism-saturated world'. This is probably the case – at least as far as mediation of the threat in the West is concerned – but what exactly was it about 9/11 that piqued the political, policy and public imagination?

This question can be answered in a number of ways, but let us begin with some comparative observations from recent history. Woods (2011) posits that the narrative of the terrorist threat now has a presence in both the public and political mindset in the United States in ways that were not evident post the first attack on the World Trade Center in 1993 or the Oklahoma bombings of 1995. Why so? Was it the spectacular multi-mediated nature of the attacks? The number of fatalities/casualties? The unusual method of attack? Finnane (2013) reminds us of the longevity of the international dimensions of the terrorism, making reference to the taking of hostages at the Munich Olympics in 1972. This incident – which took place over forty years ago – did much to focus minds from the United Nations and beyond, on the intent of groups such as Palestine Liberation Organization (PLO) to both engage with and threaten international communities to draw attention to the plight of oppressed peoples. Reinforcing Finanne's (2013) reminder not to forget the past, the United Kingdom had, by 2001, become well used to responding to and dealing with specific acts and threats posed by the rather euphemistically dubbed 'troubles' stemming from dispute about the sovereignty of Northern Ireland. So too had Spain and Germany, in relation to the respective threats presented by Euskadi Ta Askatasuna (ETA) and the Baader-Meinhof Group.

So, from a point of view, these respective internal security agendas meant that many jurisdictions already had the means in place, exceptional or otherwise, to enable their States to respond to, and manage threats to, their security. This is evidenced by the introduction of internment before and during the Second World War alongside recourse to other such legal and policy repertoires since that time. Yet the presence of such continuities between the past and the present in respect of responses to terrorism, do not fully answer the questions posed by the response to 9/11. What was it about *these* events that provoked such a concentrated and momentous reaction? One way of developing a fuller answer to the circumstances surrounding and the reasons behind the 'the 9/11 effect' (Roach, 2011) is to think about geography. Aas (2012) suggests that when we look at the world it is important to think about what kind of maps we operate with. She poses this question particularly for criminology, but it is also a useful yardstick when trying to make sense of the 9/11 moment.

The Munich Olympics, the Irish 'troubles' and the Oklahoma bombing are just some of the events that serve to remind States of their vulnerabilities. Despite the embedded cultural memory of Pearl Harbour, the United States is not a country inured to the experience of external attack. As McMillan (2004: 383) observes of the aftermath of 9/11, 'suddenly the national identity of each American was reappraised as inherently dangerous, an invitation for victimization'. This imagery of national hurt and national harm, invoked not only a threat to the national body of America but also individual reassertions of patriotism. So, in the face of victimization, the search was on to re-establish non-vulnerability. As Altheide (2004: 290) points out, 9/11 invoked a cultural currency that extended way beyond the problem of violence. Terrorism became a perspective, an orientation, a discourse for 'our time', the 'way things are today' and an expression of 'how the world has changed'. This was the case not only in the United States. In other countries such as the UK the traces and shadows of terrorism have lingered long. Worcester (2001), for instance, cites a MORI poll that suggested 73 per cent of people in England and Wales believed that 'the world would never be the same again'. Further grist to this mill can still be found over a decade later with half of the respondents to a large-scale survey believing that terrorism was 'the biggest threat to the British way of life' (Chatham House/YouGov, 2012). Betwixt these times a survey conducted in October 2007 by the Mental Health Foundation for England and Wales reported that 70 per cent of respondents defined terrorism as the global issue that they found to be most worrying. The inescapable multi-mediated vision of harm done to the American body – and by implication the potential for such harm to be done elsewhere – reverberated around the world in such a way as to facilitate the reassertion of wider moral, political and also economic imperatives. On this basis, Howie (2012) argues that 9/11 has become emblematic of the risks and uncertainties of the twenty-first century, producing consequences that have been, paradoxically, both exceptional and mundane. As we will underscore in subsequent chapters, the impact of 9/11 was both synchronic and diachronic. Alison Young (2010: 106), for instance, reports that a year on from 9/11: 'twenty-two per cent of those living within a kilometre radius of the World Trade Center were said to be suffering from Post Traumatic Stress Syndrome (PTSS), a two hundred per cent increase affecting some 422,000 individuals'. Indeed, the sustained representation of this event as a *collective* trauma has served to fix its status as a historical watershed (Pollard, 2011). Yet, this collective trauma has acted as a lever for institutional attempts to reinforce social control (Jackson, 2005: 97; Mythen and Walklate 2006). Somewhat ironically, in seeking a consensus around security, proactive military actions have ironically served to expose the vulnerability and frailties of Western nation States, graphically illustrated by failed military actions in Iraq and Afghanistan.

So, if we return to the question of geography foregrounded by Aas (2012) in relation to 9/11 we are led to ask 'who and where is the "subject at risk" and who and where is the "risky subject"' (ibid.: 12). The responses to these prickly and textured questions do indeed depend greatly on 'who is talking' (ibid.) and what kind of 'security' is being sought. The government of the United States clearly did not see itself – nor was it commonly seen – as a vulnerable target or a subject at risk. Yet in the aftermath of 9/11, as a State doing a good deal of the 'talking' it has certainly been involved (with others) in both defining the risky subject and setting the parameters of and limits to debates about security. It not only matters who is talking, it also matters what that talk presumes. The events of 9/11 exposed the vulnerability and inherent riskiness of the most powerful State in the world, yet they also provided a moment at which hegemonic aspirations and geopolitical fancies could be pursued. As such, it is important to acknowledge that talk about risk and security is culturally and geographically specific. Moreover, as with this offering, it is invariably uttered through the voice-box of the Western metropole.

With direct reference to the work of Connell, Aas (2012) asks us to consider what risk and vulnerability would look like if they were not perceived from a metropolitan perspective. Reflecting on the way in which particular modes of thinking about the world dominate politics, policy and the academy, Connell (2007) has made some astute observations about the nature and impact of 'Northern theorising'. In particular, she observes that the ubiquitous narrative that 'we are all in this together', combined with the presumption of the irreversibility of globalization – and for our purposes we are situating the phenomenon labelled as 'international terrorism' within the frame of globalization – implies a shared knowledge about the world and our existence in it that is questionable. Here, Connell is discussing the particular way in which presumptions about globalization are performed theoretically and practically. She goes on to suggest that these presumptions about globalization lead commentators such as Giddens (2002) to resort to an analysis that invokes the 'dark side' of globalization to explain terrorism. Such analyses tend to overlook the 'systemic violence of the metropole' (Connell, 2007: 378). This reification of the metropole in sociological theorizing presents the world as existing in a simple linear progression moving from industrial society to a world risk society: a reification found to a greater or lesser extent in the writings of Beck, Giddens and Bauman. For Connell, such sociological theorizing is representative of a normative structure that reproduces globalization 'as a fact rather than something to be debated' (ibid.: 370). These assumptions have three consequences; the exclusion of other voices, the erasure of non-metropolitan experiences, and the gathering of data from the 'periphery' framed by Northern concepts (ibid.: 380).

However, it is not only in sociological/criminological theorizing that it is possible to discern the consequences of Northern theorizing. They can be traced in the political rhetoric and policy practice that have flowed from the events of 9/11. Presumptions that 'we are all in this together' have emanated not just from the United States 9/11 agenda but also from wider Westo-centric thinking. Such thinking has driven both foreign policy and international security agendas, from efforts to tighten security at airports to the invasion of Iraq and the war in Afghanistan. Our purpose in the chapters that follow is to tease out and trace the influence of this kind of thinking and its presence in the policy and academic narratives around terrorism that have flowed from the 9/11 moment.

Mapping the terrain

Following on from the discussion above, we should add in the customary riders and caveats. Although we will be offering some comparisons along the way, this book does not seek to offer a detailed history of terrorism over time or place. Instead, we are foremostly concerned with examining the nature of contemporary terrorism and the institutional responses to the threat posed by Islamic fundamentalist groups in particular. We should also say that while we are motivated to illuminate the drivers for and the effects of political violence, we also wish to engage with adjacent problems and issues. This is not only a book about terrorism. It is a book about how terrorism is vectored through and connected to power, inequality and (in)justice.

Having touched upon some of the areas of thematic interest to us and offloaded our disclaimers, it is worth offering a capsule synopsis of the structure of the book. Chapter 1 provides the theoretical context for the book as a whole. In this chapter we examine government responses to 9/11 through the lens of the increasing presence of risk as a driver for social, political and legal responses. Situating these responses within a critical assessment of the analytical frameworks established by Beck, Furedi and Bauman, we consider the extent to which the perceived threat from terrorism can be placed within a wider culture of fear, and reflect upon the kinds of strategies that have variously framed States' responses within the assumed cultural context of the risk society. As Giddens (1999: 5) observes:

> A good deal of political decision-making is now about managing risks – risks which do not originate in the political sphere, yet have to be politically managed. If anyone – government official, scientific expert or lay person – takes any given risk seriously, he or she must proclaim it. It must be widely publicized because people must be persuaded that the risk is real – a fuss must be made about it. However, if a fuss is indeed created and the risk turns out to be minimal, those involved will be accused of scaremongering. Paradoxically, scaremongering may be necessary to reduce risks we face – yet if it is successful in this sense, it appears as just that, scaremongering. We cannot know beforehand when we are actually scaremongering and when we are not.

Since 9/11, the dilemma posed by Giddens above is one that has confronted governments in managing their respective security agendas: how to convey risks effectively. Having considered the impact of dominant theoretical frames of risk, fear and security, in Chapter 2 we question the foundational premises of the discourse around 'new terrorism'. In particular we shall consider what is 'new' about contemporary forms of terrorism and question the extent to which the discourse of new terrorism obscures both the complexities of political violence and its causes. In other words, following Bell's instruction, we wish to question the proclivity for searching for unidimensional analyses. Looking underneath and behind dominant discourses, in Chapter 2 we draw attention to the ideological interests involved in defining and representing terrorism. Building on this analysis, in Chapter 3 we situate events such as 9/11 and 7/7 not as random happenings but as events that have occurred within the wider tapestry of economic and political change in Europe, the Middle East and elsewhere. In putting power relationships to the fore, this chapter places the 'war on terror' in an appropriate cultural context. Here we will be concerned to ask, what work the 'war on terror' narrative does and for whom? In exploring this question we pursue the role of an unflective State, in its involvement in a number of *risk hypocrisies* – from indefinite detention to extraordinary rendition and torture – as policies that in and of themselves present terrorism as a uniform and unifying concept, not dissimilar to predominant policy uses of risk. These risk hypocrisies form the backcloth against which pre-emptive practices of all kind have become normalized in the maintenance of State power.

Chapter 4 furthers our understanding of pre-emption. Here we argue that the 'war on terror' has resulted in a raft of pre-emptive legislation, particularly in the United States and the United Kingdom. Using the UK as a case study of such strategies – and drawing on original data – we consider the consequences that concentrated pre-emptive strategies have had on groups that are targeted. Our analysis returns us to some rudimentary questions. Security for whom and under what conditions? After Bell (1979), how much freedom should be compromised for security? The data we present illustrates the capacity of State security strategies to produce deleterious consequences. Of course, appreciation of these consequences belies the fact that in discussing freedom and security in a cultural context in which a 'war on terror' has such a prominent role, some voices are heard and some are silenced. We will argue that this results in a sense of *partial security* for some ethnic minority groups, demonstrating that security is not a zero sum game and leading us to emphasize the question of voice. Who is heard and listened to, and who is not, reminds us of the salience of the challenges posed by Aas (2012) and Connell (2007) referred to earlier. Answers to the questions that these challenges pose depend upon who is considered to be the risk. Chapter 5 pays some detailed attention to these issues and situates the responses of the UK and the US within a wider international setting. The chapter considers how the risky have been constructed and what the unintended consequences for those constructions might be for States as well as the individuals labelled as 'risky'. In situating constructions of the risky in a comparative context, not only do the role and influence of the metropolitan voices become apparent if expressed somewhat differently in different cultural settings, the shared presumptions around what causes political violence also become apparent. At this juncture the influence of particular criminological voices can also be heard. However, some of these voices have done little to challenge or contest the construction of those considered 'suspect'.

In Chapter 6 we consider the changing nature of the contemporary policy agenda. As the first decade of the twenty-first century unfolded, the risk agenda – so discernible within responses to 'new terrorism' – transmuted into one that is increasingly concerned with preparedness and resilience. Consequently, in many ways risk and resilience have become intimately connected with one another through their joint reliance on assumptions of vulnerability. This chapter explores these interconnections and excavates the issues that have been elided in the policy drive to build resilience. In this final chapter we explore the central contradictions and tensions that are embedded in the construction, representation and regulation of terrorism. These contradictions lead to a consideration of the disjunctions between religion and culture (*qua* Bell, 1979). Such contradictions pose external and internal dilemmas all at the same time. These dilemmas are suggestive of the need for a critical, multilayered and multifaceted appreciation of not only the concepts of risk, security, resilience and vulnerability, but also the issues that have become glossed politically in the policy processes that have been focused on terrorism: namely poverty, exclusion and economic exploitation. Thus, when we speak of globalization in this book, we will be presuming that we are not 'all in it together'. On the contrary, we are concerned to demonstrate that geography and voice frame both how we understand this moment and our responses to it. The desire to use risk, security, resilience as uniform and unifying categories is endemic in political and policy domains and the academy carries some of the responsibility for this being the case. Using these concepts as uniform and unifying categories obscures not only the hegemonic purposes to which they are put in the interests of the State and capital but also our ability to develop answers to the very simple questions that the 9/11 moment has posed for criminology. What is crime, who is the victim, who is the offender, and how do we make sense of the relationship between them and the particular outcomes that they generate? In the conclusion to the book, we endeavour to consciously muddy these particular conceptual waters and create some space for differently nuanced understandings to emerge within criminology. If we fail to create and protect an alternative discursive space, our quest to understand terrorism will remain as elusive as ever.

References

Aas, K. (2012) The earth is one, but the world is not: Criminological theory and its geopolitical divisions. *Theoretical Criminology*, 16(1): 5–20.

Altheide, D. L. (2004). Consuming terrorism. *Symbolic Interaction*, 27(3): 289–308.

Beck, U. (1996) Risk society and the provident state. In B. Szerszinski, S. Lash and B. Wynne (eds) *Risk, Environment and Modernity: Towards a New Ecology*. London: Sage, pp. 27–43.

Bell, D. (1979) *The Cultural Contradictions of Capitalism*. London: Heinemann.

Chatham House/You Gov (2012) *Hard Choices Ahead: British Attitudes Towards the UK's International Priorities*. London: Chatham House.

Connell, R. (2007) The northern theory of globalization. *Sociological Theory*, 25(4): 368–85.

Finnane, M. (2013) Terrorism and government: Between history and criminology. *Australian and New Zealand Journal of Criminology*, 46(2): 159–77.

Giddens, A. (1999) *Runaway World: How Globalization is Reshaping Our Lives*, 1st edition. London: Profile.

Giddens, A. (2002) *Runaway World: How Globalisation is Reshaping Our Lives*. London: Profile.

Hogg, R. (2007) Criminology, crime and politics before and after 9/11. *Australian and New Zealand Journal of Criminology*, 40(1): 83–105.

Howie, L. (2012) *Witnesses to Terror*. London: Palgrave-Macmillan.

Jackson, R. (2005) *Writing the war on terrorism: Language, politics and counterterrorism.* Manchester: Manchester University Press.

Jackson, R. and Sinclair, S. (2012) *Contemporary Debates on Terrorism.* London: Routledge.

McMillan, N. (2004) Beyond representation: Cultural understandings of the September 11 attacks. *The Australian and New Zealand Journal of Criminology,* 37(1): 380–400.

Mythen, G. and Walklate, S. (2006a) Criminology and terrorism: Which thesis? Risk society or governmentality? *British Journal of Criminology,* 46(3): 379–98.

Mythen, G., and Walklate, S. (2006b) Communicating the terrorist threat: Harnessing a culture of fear? *Crime, Media, Culture,* 2(2): 143–58.

Pollard, J. (2011) Seen, seared and sealed: Trauma and the visual presentation of September 11. *Health, Risk and Society,* 13(1): 81–101.

Rehn, E. (2003) Excessive reliance on the use of force does not stop terrorism. In T. Hoeksema and J. ter Laak (eds) *Human Rights and Terrorism.* Holland: NHC/OSCE, pp. 45–57.

Roach, K. (2011) *The 9/11 Effect: Comparative counter-terrorism.* Cambridge: Cambridge University Press.

Taleb, N.N. (2010) *The Black Swan: The impact of the highly improbable.* London: Penguin.

Woods, J. (2011) The 9/11 effect: Towards a social science of the terrorist threat. *Social Science Journal,* 48: 213–33.

Worcester, R. (2001) The world will never be the same again: British hopes and fears after September 11th 2001. *International Journal of Public Opinion Research* www.mori.com.

Young, A. (2010) Images in the aftermath of trauma: Responding to September 11th. *Crime, Media, Culture,* 3(1): 30–48.

1

9/11

'Risk creep', fear and securitization

> Terrorism has now entered the daily lexicon of the average citizen
> (Griset and Mahan, 2008: 15)

Introduction

Offering a detailed chronological account of the events leading up to and following on from 9/11, Summers and Swann (2011: 440) posit: 'the true effect of the 2001 onslaught is less what it achieved than what it triggered'. This succinct summation taps into the veins of Taleb's (2010) thesis regarding the perils of excessive responses to Black Swan events that we raised in the introduction. Over the last decade 9/11 has incontrovertibly become *the* referent for debates about security in the Western world and this is evidenced in the wide range of responses to it. For Jenks (2003), 9/11 must be considered as a 'trangressive' event: one that cut across and blurred all boundaries in such a way that the taken for granted understandings associated with everyday life were thrown out of kilter. While Jenks accentuates the breaching of norms, the United States Secretary of State at the time, Colin Powell, sought to stress the creation of binaries post 9/11: 'in this global campaign against terrorism, no country has the luxury of remaining on the sidelines. There *are* no sidelines' (State Department, 2002: iii). While these two narratives of transgression and polarization seem to capture well the prevalent political and academic understandings of 9/11, we wish to emphasize that there are alternate ways of interpreting 9/11 in the same way that there were diverse possibilities that emerged from it in terms of countering terrorism. The question then is why, given a span of possible narratives used to make sense of this event (see Wibben, 2011), did those that connect together risk, fear and security come to prevail? One way of responding to this question would be to draw attention to the extant omnipresence of these factors in different facets of social life. For example, while Beck (2009) has bottomed out the role of negligent institutions in the rise of the risk society, Furedi (2002) draws our attention to the construction of fear within the political realm and in the mass media. In parallel fashion, Valverde (2011) asserts that almost every societal issue from the availability of food to the question of the 'nation-state' is now seen through the lens of security. Against this backcloth it is possible to discern the coming together of what Hallsworth and Lea (2011) call the 'security State' in the West. But how did we arrive at this seemingly fixed analytical point of entry and what role has criminology played in this journey?

Much of the academic debate within criminology that has surrounded the emergence of the security State has been built upon a rather limited appreciation of the concept of risk and the risk society (see O'Malley, 2010). This understanding variously draws upon the work of people such as Bauman, Beck, Foucault, Furedi and Giddens, often in a rather piecemeal and partial way (see Walklate and Mythen, 2008). Some time ago now, Sparks (1992) challenged the simplistic way in which criminologists were using terms such as risk, fear and danger, with Walklate (1997) arguing that the failure to appreciate the gendered nature of risk rendered the criminological preoccupation with risk and risk management problematic in the extreme (see also Hannah-Moffat and O'Malley, 2007). The preoccupation within criminology – and sub-disciplines such as victimology – with the 'crimes of everyday life', exposed in the seminal analysis of the culture of control offered by Garland (2001), has served to perpetuate this limited appreciation of risk. Such an appreciation has constrained not only the criminological capacity to make sense of 'micro' issues such as the fear of crime (Walklate and Mythen, 2008), it has also contributed to the reproduction of a circumscribed understanding of 'macro' issues such as the risks/crimes that are seen and those that remain shrouded. In respect of this latter issue, Hogg (2007) offers a pointed review of the (hidden) potential for criminology to make sense of what he refers to as 'political' crimes pre and post 9/11. His analysis foregrounds those critical criminological voices, evident from the 1960s to the present, in which such 'crimes' have been, and are, put on the agenda. But how does terrorism articulate with these developments?

In the years since 9/11, terrorist attacks aside, there have been many other events that could be cast as transgressive. Hurricane Katrina, the tsunami in Aceh and the Tohuku earthquake are all examples of major disasters that have provided further leverage for the view that the new millennium is one marked by risk, uncertainty and crisis. If we add to this list of events the prolonged wars in Iraq and Afghanistan, the enduring financial crisis that began in 2008, and the ongoing conflicts emerging from the Arab Spring, it is easy to see how contemporary life has become associated with indeterminacy and fragility. Of course, not all of the events recorded above are linked – either to each other or to 9/11. However they are presented here as a way of understanding the context in which social science in general, and criminology in particular, makes sense of, or fails to make sense of, the complex tapestry of contemporary life and the risks that are seen, as compared with those that are not seen, within that tapestry. While all of the incidents and processes described above have been captured in great detail in the Western news media, the dire human consequences of a failure to meet basic survival needs in many parts of the world seem not to feature in the risk register (see Mythen, 2014). As Sachs (2007: 2) points out: 'one billion people on the planet are too poor, too hungry, too disease-burdened, too bereft of the most basic infrastructure even to get on the ladder of development'.

In terms of 'advancing' knowledge about risk and security, criminological endeavours have historically prioritized the 'fear of crime'. This is not so surprising given the criminological preoccupation with tightly defined localized crimes as opposed to multi-causal global harms. Moreover, research has shown that the costs of the fear of crime, from the economic to the psychological, are substantial (see *inter alia*, Warr 2000, Dixon *et al.*, 2006). It is, of course, important not to lose sight of the fact that the transgressive events referred to above have also taken their toll in relation to fears. Yet here too the fears are culturally specific and geographically rooted. As Forst (2011: 274) reminds us, 'terrorism is a crime in the extreme, and fear plays a substantially more central role in terrorism than in conventional crime'. Interestingly, little attention has been paid to the fear of crime from this angle and the personal psychological consequences of terrorist attacks have received scant attention within criminology. Nonetheless, the links between terrorism as a crime, risk perception and fear are profound. Even more profound are the elementary questions that this relationship poses for criminology. What counts as crime, who is the criminal, who is the victim and how is victimization determined?

In the light of the hermeneutic challenges faced for criminology in understanding terrorism, the demand for a dialogic space for discussion is growing for those of a critical persuasion from different disciplinary agendas (international relations, security studies, cultural studies). The significance and influence of debates begun outwith criminology for criminology will be apparent in the chapters to follow. The broadening of definitional terms that has followed as a result of positive cross-disciplinary fertilization has meant that criminological uses of the concepts of risk, fear and security have at once come into question and widened. At the same time as critical criminologists have favoured fusion and experimentation with such influences, there has been a distinct re-entrenchment among mainstream criminologists keen to protect restricted, conventional notions of fear and risk considered amenable to the kinds of statistical calibration favoured by policy makers. Reflecting these shifting tides and intra-disciplinary developments, this chapter is concerned to document the rising spectre of risk within criminology and the limits to risk as a unit of analysis within that context. We wish to offer a starting point from which to retrospectively advance a critical evaluation of policy responses to 9/11 and a place from which to tease out the efficacy of the criminological response to those policy responses. In so doing this chapter will take as a focal concern the concepts of risk, fear and securitization. As we shall see, understandings of these concepts are slippery and intertwined. More-over, as discussed in Chapter 6, they have latterly become intimately connected with understandings of vulnerability and resilience. For now we wish to begin by offering an overview of the different theoretical perspectives on risk available to criminology. These different perspectives enable us to explore the different ways in which risk, fear and security have become linked with one another. Inasmuch as these considerations set out the ground for the chapters to come, it is first necessary to unpack the concept of risk and to distinguish the process of 'risk creep'.

The creep of risk

Bernstein's (1996) historically informed approach reminds us that the story of risk is simultaneously a story of control: a tale of efforts to conquer the forces of nature and to demarcate the present (modern) world from the past. One distinguishing feature between the present and the past is the drive to assert mastery over the unpredictable nature of human life. In sociological terms, the collapse of communism, the rise of religious fundamentalism, global warming, alongside events such as 9/11, are often cited as examples of control failure, symptomatic of a crisis of modernity. In this sense Berman's (1982) restatement of the Marxian assertion that 'all that is solid melts into the air' has even greater resonance today than when his book was first published. However, making sense of this apparent 'crisis' is fraught with problems. Returning to the issues of geography and voice discussed earlier, such sense making begs the questions of, a crisis for whom, when and under what conditions?

Both Furedi (2002) and Wilkinson (2010) strive to remind us that Western societies are healthy and safe places to live. In relative and absolute terms, across indicators such as mortality, health, longevity and crime rates it is arguably the safeness rather than the dangerousness of the modern habitat that is remarkable. Although pursuing very different paths, Wilkinson and Furedi are agreed that the notion of 'crisis' itself needs to be set within the constants of time and geography. Fashionable preoccupations with risk notwithstanding, it is important to remember that human life has always been risky. Humans have always been subject to ailments and epidemics, as the bubonic plague of the sixteenth century and the Spanish flu of the twentieth century serve to illustrate. Yet in previous epochs such hazards – then more commonly referred to as dangers than risks (Douglas, 1990) – were attributed to fate or the gods and taken to be endemic to the human condition. These kinds of risks and responses to them are still apparent in many parts of the world.

In academic circles, the publication of Ulrich Beck's book *Risk Society: Towards a New Modernity* – first published in German in 1986 and appearing in English in 1992 – signalled a sea change not only in terms of the salience of risk but also in terms of prevailing currents in the social sciences, and, by implication, criminological engagement with the topic. Prior to this, social science engagement with risk had traditionally been through a 'forensic' lens (Douglas, 1990). Such a forensic approach was reflective of a domain assumption within certain branches of criminology that risk is calculable and measurable: a view of risk that emanates from its conceptual origins in the world of insurance (Bernstein, 1996). It is an acceptance, as Short (1984: 713) observed some time ago, that separates causal theory and research from social policy. As a result, both become preoccupied with the symptoms of crime rather than with its cause(s). Thus within criminology risk has been used in a positivistic fashion to facilitate not only measurement (identifying the symptoms of crime) but also the development of risk assessment tools as a way of managing/controlling crime. Indeed this version of risk reveals criminology's deep embrace of the modernist project (Walklate, 1997).

Part of this modernist commitment has involved the coming into being of risk as a technology for regulation. Indeed, risk assessment and risk management have long been used to differentiate the risky and/or dangerous from the rest of 'us' in such a way that enables criminal justice professionals to contribute to the maintenance of social order and regulation (see O'Malley, 2010; Wilkinson, 2010). This is especially the case in areas around immigration, asylum, policing, detention, sentencing, probation and human rights. It is evident that risk, as it has been assessed and measured, has been, and still is, hugely important in informing and shaping policy; that is, in defining what it is that is knowable, actionable and doable in the face of known, measurable dangers. Mirroring what Innes (2001) dubs 'control creep' we can feasibly allude to risk's tentacles extending into almost all aspects of mainstream criminology as a process of 'risk creep'. Evidence of this can be discerned in debates around imprisonment (Murphy and Whitty, 2007), victimization (Davis *et al.*, 2007); policing (Ericson and Haggerty, 1997); crime control (Feeley and Simon, 1992); crime prevention, offender behaviour and victim protection (Newburn, 2009).

So, one of the key problems we encounter when we talk of and about risk is that it is used as a catch-all concept. As Beck (2009: 138) notes: 'the category of risk exhibits an expansive logic. It embraces everything'. The use of risk within criminology as something that is rational and calculable reflects an understanding of the concept as either uniform or unifying (O'Malley, 2004, 2006). This use of risk conflates risk as a measurable phenomenon with risk as it is diversely experienced (see Douglas, 1992; Lyng, 2005), wrongly conflates agency and structure (Walklate and Mythen, 2010) and masks the different theoretical trajectories that can be discerned within risk theorizing. In what follows we wish to unpack those different theoretical trajectories in order to better understand how the concepts of risk, fear and securitization have become interlinked within criminology, and the ways in which those linkages have fuelled criminal justice, and military and foreign policies post 9/11.

Theorizing risk: constructing fear and security

There is a vast literature on risk and making sense of it, in all its nuanced forms, can be rather daunting. Much of the work on risk can be situated along a continuum between two paradigms: realism and constructivism. Put simply, for realists, risks are real and measurable; for constructivists, risks are subjective and culturally constructed. Given that criminology as a discipline is populated by stakeholders with affinities that align with both of these paradigms, it is perhaps unsurprising that we can find elements of each of them within criminological understandings of risk. For example, the work of criminological psychologists, psychiatrists and forensic scientists, oriented to a realist view of risk, informs criminal justice professionals' risk assessment practices. The work of social scientists, oriented towards a constructivist view of risk, informs much theoretical analysis of the policies and institutional spaces occupied by those criminal justice professionals. The end result is a complex array of literature. For analytical purposes, in what follows we group this literature under two headings, though it should be noted that this is for ease of presentation only. The boundaries between and within the literature discussed under these headings are fuzzy, not distinct, and epistemological commitments to the paradigms of realism and constructionism are variable. These caveats notwithstanding, first we shall consider the different ways in which a constructivist approach to risk facilitates our understanding of risk and security at the level of the conceptual. Second we will consider the problems and possibilities associated with the realist underpinning of risk assessment practices. From here we will go on to elucidate the ways in which 'risk rationalities' (Rasborg 2012) have collectively shaped representations and understandings of terrorism.

As was suggested above, the presence of the constructivist paradigm on risk is largely felt within criminology as a result of the influence of the social sciences. This constructivist paradigm has fairly fluid characteristics though it is possible to identify two rather loose perspectives within it: weak constructivism and strong constructivism. As the influences within criminology of each of these perspectives is apparent so we shall say something about each in turn. There is some dispute on where exactly to locate the work of Beck, with most commentators suggesting that his work is best located between realism and constructivism (see Lupton, 2013; Mythen, 2014). Despite the realist inclinations that can be found in his early work, in the light of his more recent interventions we consider his take on risk to reflect a weak constructivism, albeit one that remains tinged by flashes of realism. Beck's impactful work (1992, 1995, 1999, 2009) has documented the sweeping effects of risk on everyday life and warned of the dangers of ignoring mounting global threats. This thesis is predicated on threats from 'natural hazards' (e.g. drought, earthquakes and flooding) and accidents (e.g. workplace injuries, fires), common in pre-industrial and industrial cultures to a growing collection of 'manufactured uncertainties', created by the impact of human activity. Beck's analysis anchors risk as a universal social feature that moves away from the commonality of need towards the foregrounding of the commonality of anxiety. Instead of being captured by the statement 'I am hungry', the risk society is defined by the maxim 'I am afraid' (Beck, 1992: 42). This shift has resulted in mounting pressure being placed on expert systems to deliver security and high levels of public trust in circumstances in which they have failed to do so (see also Giddens 1994, 1998). So the principal problems in contemporary risk societies do not stem from a dearth of goods, such as income, housing and health care, but arise out of a glut of bads, such as environmental pollution, crime and terrorism. Thus, for Beck, social institutions become preoccupied with avoiding bads – or at least being *perceived* to do so – in an attempt to retain public trust, control and legitimacy. This kind of logic has important ramifications, not only for the theory itself – in terms of how representative it is of actual human experience – but also for understanding how social cohesion is advanced and what safety might mean. It implies a universalism of experience: 'the dynamics of risk society are beyond status and class because global threats ultimately affect everybody, even those responsible for them' (Beck 2009: 22). Reduced to an adage, we are all in this together. So while Colin Powell insists there are no sidelines, Beck insists that there are no bystanders. This presumed democracy of risk, alongside the scale of mass media presentations of what is risky, renders risk both socially and politically explosive. It is something that none of us can escape from: 'global risks force us to confront the apparently excluded other, tearing down national barriers and mixing 'natives with foreigners' (Beck 2009: 15). Risk on this democratic scale raises two issues: how are apparently antiquated systems to control the volatile problems that the world risk society generates, and how do individuals stop themselves from becoming 'factories of fear' (*qua* Tillich 1952)? The answer to both dilemmas for Beck lies in subpolitics and the rise of the cosmopolitan citizen. The shift to cosmopolitanism in risk theorizing reflects a view of the world that considers the either/orism, sameness/difference debates as grand cul-de-sacs. Beck (2006) instead opts to advocate the liberatory potential of the both/and principle. Although such a framework seems, on the surface, to be transparently constructionist,

Beck wishes to convince us of the tangible destructive power of manufactured uncertainties such as genetic and nuclear technologies. In making a judgement about the impacts of manufactured uncertainties some degree of realism creeps in. To emphasize the necessity for political change, Beck is wont to assume that the worst-case scenarios of the risk society will become real unless we act urgently to prevent them. So far as positioning his work in relation to overarching paradigms, Beck has consciously resisted categorization, suggesting that realism and constructivism are but false dichotomies that hinder rather than progress our capacity to understand the social world (see Brown, 2013: 628).

Developing cosmopolitanism in a somewhat different direction Benhabib (2002) suggests the cosmopolitan position rather begs the question 'who are the "we"'? How do we coexist and accommodate difference? Hudson (2003, 2006) too has explored the possibilities and implications of such cosmopolitanism for criminology, pointing up the difficulties of taking account of the 'other' in the face of the brick wall of criminal justice systems rooted in politics and practices operating within a different conceptual framework. Thus, the recourse to the legal process that has characterized responses to terrorism (see Chapters 2 and 3), inevitably results in tensions between the modernism inherent within criminal justice policies and practices (and their associated commitment to the rational man of law) and the cosmopolitan demands for an appreciation of difference (a fundamental challenge to the rational man of law). These tensions raise a profound problem for liberal societies (*qua* Bell 1979): how much freedom to compromise for security? Thus risk and security become intimate bedfellows. To translate this into a Beckian framework, risk avoidance leads to security but only if the experts are listened to. In this way risk, security and justice are generated in a 'top-down' fashion. One does not exist without the other (see Zedner, 2009). Consequently, and inevitably, some voices are heard and others are silenced. This dilemma is equally discernable in the work of Bauman.

Using metaphor as his methodological tool (see Davis, 2013) Bauman takes the concept of 'reflexive modernization' developed by Beck *et al.* (1994) and uses this to contrast a previous age of solid modernity with a contemporary age of liquid modernity. In contrast to the relatively ascribed identity roles of solid modernity, in liquid modernity individuals are permanently disembedded. The notion of a 'whole life project' does not just become disrupted; rather, *qua* Marx and later Berman (1982), it melts into air. Living such a fragmented liquid life requires that the individual is flexible and adaptable, and must act, plan actions, and calculate the likely gains and losses of acting – or failing to act – under conditions of endemic uncertainty. We live, for Bauman (2000: 62), in a world in which 'no sailor can boast of having found a safe, let alone risk free, itinerary'. Young (2007: 3) suggests that this lack of mooring creates a 'precariousness of being' that is manifested in both social and individual processes. Bauman (2005: 82) argues:

> The security we fear . . . is no longer the kind of security Roosevelt or Beveridge had in mind. It is not the security of our place in society, of personal dignity, of honour of workmanship, self-respect, human understanding and humane treatment, but instead a security of the body and personal belongings. It is not security from those who refuse us jobs or deny our humanity when we are in a job . . . but security against trespassers on our property and strangers at the doorway, prowlers and beggars in the streets, sexual offenders at home and outside, poisoners of wells and hijackers of planes.

The fears and insecurities generated by this 'othering' have a distinct quality. They are, for Bauman, individualized rather than collectivized, fluid not static. Liquid fears, in Bauman's (2006) terms, have inherent plasticity and hermeneutic stretchiness. They are fears that can be harnessed by dominant social groups central to the process of risk definition.

In many respects risk, and the notion of a risk society, lie in the background but act as the frame for Bauman's work. Much more to the fore in his work is the impact that this feature of contemporary social and institutional life has on individuals and social relationships. Bauman's work reveals much to us about the nature of fear and uncertainty. In particular, how such uncertainty generates and sustains practices of 'othering' as we search for a secure mooring for our own lives. Accenting a stronger constructivist approach than found in the work of Beck, Bauman's influence is clearly discernable within contemporary criminological theoretical endeavour, particularly exemplified in the work of Jock Young.

As with weak constructivism, it is possible to discern in stronger forms of constructionism the influence of two accents within criminological work: that associated with the work of Foucault and generally termed 'the governmentality thesis' and that associated with the work of Furedi often referred to as the 'culture of fear thesis'. We shall say a little about each of these in turn. While Foucault did not write explicitly about risk, theorists inspired by his work (Foucault 1980, 1991) have reshaped his ideas to take account of it. Castel (1991), Dean (1999) and O'Malley (2004) have developed an understanding of the ways in which neoliberal institutions construct understandings of risk that facilitate the ordering of human behaviour. Central to the governmentality thesis is the notion of discourse. Through discourse, sets of ideas and knowledges become interlocked resulting in some ideas gaining credence and others receding. Aradau and von Munster (2008: 38) suggest: 'for a governmental approach, what counts is not whether terrorism can be controlled or not, but the *dispositif* that is being deployed to make action upon the contingent occurrence of terrorism thinkable and practicable'. This *dispositif*, in determining what is knowable and thinkable, ensures that power relations in society are reproduced not by force but by the interiorization of ideas and knowledges. Hence risk and security are socially constructed. Such knowledges produce human beings who are engaged in self-regulatory practices, since the discourses they are exposed to set the boundaries on what are considered to be acceptable and unacceptable behaviours. In this way, citizens are rendered 'prudential' (Rose, 1999).

Kemshall (2006: 65) argues 'prudentialism requires the citizen to adopt a calculating attitude towards most if not all of his/her decisions, whether these be decisions over healthy eating options or the installation of burglar alarms'. Such a prudential citizen conducts their affairs according to the principles of 'well being' and 'actuarial justice' (Feeley and Simon, 1992) and receives approval for doing so. These principles are rooted in the calculative assumptions associated with risk measurement and tend to encourage the attribution of blame. Butler (2002: 44) avers that, by determining 'who is an "immigrant", or an "asylum seeker", or a "criminal" or "mad" or a "terrorist" – discourses serve to sanction the political authority of their bearers and reinforce power and power relations'. In this way it is possible not only to govern through crime (Simon, 2007) but also to govern through terrorism (Mythen and Walklate, 2006). As we will empirically demonstrate in Chapter 4, in the aftermath of 9/11 young Pakistani Britons have been simultaneously the fearful and the feared, being aligned as they are by the media with 'home-grown' terrorism, while simultaneously recognizing that the State or the police may not be there to protect them from racist attacks (Sharp and Atherton, 2007). As some of the data discussed later in this book illustrates, individuals within this group may, in the interests of personal safety, constitute themselves as prudential citizens by adopting measures that distance them from common constructions of the 'terrorist other' (see Mythen et al., 2009; Walker, 2008). This vision of the prudential citizen, as expounded by the governmentality theorists, has had the effect of embedding a behavioural risk management response to a wide range of issues from health and social policy to crime. In focusing attention on what might be expected of a prudential citizen, it exposes, by implication, who and what is to be feared. So, as with weak constructivism, in stronger versions risk and fear are intimately connected, in this case through the desire to govern through manipulating and incorporating who and what it is to be feared.

Furedi's (2002, 2005, 2007) 'culture of fear' approach is arguably more heavily constructionist than that of neo-Foucauldians. He argues that the social preoccupation with risk, and particularly risk avoidance, is a symptom of the impact that the risk society's frightening array of bads have had. These bads have resulted in cultural and political paralysis. His work, overlapping in some respects, with that informed by the work of Foucault, puts to the fore the omnipresent language of risk in everyday life. So much so that his culture of fear thesis posits that risk is *the* filter through which people react to and make sense of their experience (Furedi, 2002: 5). This is manifested, according to

Furedi (1997: 173), 'through the celebration of suffering' in which 'society legitimises its fear of taking risks'. Somewhat in contrast with Beck's focus on global manufactured risks, Furedi believes that risks are predominantly cultural, promulgated and manipulated by politicians, the mass media, and those working in the welfare and security industries. The underlying motivation for this being that fearful populations are more easily governed and more likely to invest in a vast and growing range of security products and services – evidenced in the case of the United States post 9/11 by Forst (2011). Here again risk and fear become wedded, with fear becoming the medium through which risk is conceptualized and interpreted:

> Many of us seem to make sense of our experiences through the narrative of fear. Fear is not simply associated with high-profile catastrophic threats such as terrorist attacks, global warming, AIDS or a potential flu pandemic . . . there are also the quiet fears of everyday life.
>
> (Furedi, 2007: 1)

Hence, risk and security are produced and defined through the 'cultural scripts (ibid.: 5) of fear and anxiety'. Rather like Beck's interpretation of the risk society thesis, Furedi's strong constructivist take on risk is democratic in orientation. We are all subjected to the same media and political exhortations and the embrace of fear is difficult to resist or think outside of. However, as with Beck, there are dangers inherent in such a democratic presumption. First, the precedence given to risk avoidance not only distorts risk but also conflates our experience of risk as *only* being constituted as risk avoidance. Second, media emphasis on high risk events and behaviours with high impact consequences that many people will never experience, encourages people to become more inward looking and fearful. Thereby, what Furedi (1997: 170) dubs the 'fatalistic sociology of the precautionary principle' – something we will wrestle with shortly – disempowers critique and encourages people to do little more than try to avoid taking risks. Thus, 'sadly, shared meaning for most people is confined to fear of being a target rather than being inspired to stand up for a way of life' (Furedi, 2007: 98).

This rather fatalistic take on the human condition rests on the presumption of a 'neurotic citizen' (Isin, 2004), whereby individuals are induced to search for 'biographical solutions to systemic problems' (Bauman, 2006). As the rest of this book unfolds we shall see what shape and form these 'biographical solutions' take, particularly for some groups commonly associated with terrorism. Indeed, as we shall see from the material discussed, it is within the fuelling of neuroses that the precautionary principle, so favoured in policy, flourishes.

Interestingly, and of some relevance here, the mainstream 'fear of crime' debate within criminology has paid scant attention to the cultural construction of fear as elaborated by Furedi. Instead, fear of crime analysts have adapted an ever more complex approach to the measurement of the fear of crime, albeit one that draws on conventional understandings of crime. Such attempts to subject fear to calibration remain characteristic of work in this area, interventions from the periphery notwithstanding (see Lee, 2001; Walklate and Mythen, 2008). Longstanding and persistent attempts to quantitate fear in order to render it digestible in policy chunks are indicative of the realist embrace of risk in criminology and the importance of this embrace for policy and practice. As was suggested earlier, this has facilitated criminal justice practice in the maintenance of social order in very particular ways, and we shall turn to those practices shortly.

To summarize: the different ways in which social scientists think about risk, put simply, imply different things about the individual, institutions and the State. They also have different implications for how we might understand the nature of risk, fear and security, and the questions that those different understandings generate. From Beck's perspective, the events of 9/11 could be considered to be a 'classic' risk society problem since they carry with them all the hallmarks of manufactured risks. The attacks were indiscriminate in their impact, catastrophic in their consequences and impossible to insure against. Yet at the same time there are some incongruities here since, taken on a global scale, some countries and some citizens are evidently more in danger from such attacks than others. It rather depends on geography (Aas, 2012). In addition, while Beck's commitment to a notion of the cosmopolitan citizen opens up as well as closes down options for individuals, such actions are not always necessarily positive in their outcome. Public demonstrations against the relocation of known paedophiles in 'their' area are one illustration of this. A rise in what Beck refers to as 'risk consciousness' can and does add to confounding traditional modes of calculable risk assessment, as does the suicide bomber. Here fear becomes a product of individual risk positions (Taylor, 1996). Positions that include a range of factors in individuals' lives above and beyond crime itself – house prices, employment prospects, community cohesion – and in this way become much more closely connected with a sense of, or absence of, ontological security. It is this question of ontological security that is focal for Furedi.

For Furedi, risks are not simply 'out there'. Rather they are promoted by politicians, the media and experts. Such practices tap into the darker sides of the human psyche:

> The fact that more and more areas of life are seen as targets for terrorists – buildings, power stations, the economy and so on – has little to do with the increased capabilities of terrorists; rather it reflects the growth in competitive claims-making around fear and terror.
>
> (Furedi, 2007: 4)

All of this might well result in a neurotic citizen who has lost the capacity for rationality. Yet, neither risk, nor fear, nor security exist in hermetically sealed capsules. Fear and security are not naturally occurring, free-floating phenomena. Rather, they are constructed phenomena that are attached like a kite to human motions, actions and movements. The implication being that in order to properly understand risk, fear and security it is important to attend to the cultural networks through which these concepts are constructed and reinforced and can be applied to the emergence of fears about all sorts of crimes, from terrorism to identity theft. Developing this point, in more recent work, Furedi (2013) explores how risk and fear are manipulated to flow into the wider moral currents and agendas, such as the Jimmy Saville affair that came to light in Britain during 2012. This nod towards cultural specificity alerts us to the fact that, in contrast to a single 'culture of fear' we ought really to be talking about *cultures* of fear (Walklate and Mythen, 2008).

The governmentality approach to risk centres the discourses that dominant institutions produce and reproduce and through which individuals come to recognize and internalize what is risky, what there is to be feared and how to sustain their sense of security: 'In this way, fears about terrorism become linked to contemporary folk devils: immigrants, bogus asylum-seekers, religious zealots and dole scroungers' (Mythen and Walklate, 2008: 229).

Some have argued that this has resulted in crime becoming the master narrative in which terrorism is located (see Simon, 2007). However, what this approach rests on is the notion of a prudential citizen. A citizen whose compliant desire to avoid risk is capitalized on as a means of control. Thus, various government campaigns – notably in the United States, Britain and Australia – have engaged in concerted campaigns to 'responsibilize' (Garland, 2001) citizens for their own risk management in the face of emergency situations somewhat in preference to explicating institutional responses. In the spaces between what individuals are encouraged to do to protect themselves 'it is easy to slip into prejudices and assumptions about the enemy' (Oates, 2005: 7). The ties that bind this compliant, prudential citizen to ongoing dominant narratives become rather looser for the disembedded citizen found within Bauman's work.

What is most fearsome for Bauman (2006: 4) in the ebbs and flows of liquid modernity is 'the ubiquity of fears: they may leak out of any nook or cranny of our homes and our planet'. Risk, uncertainty, fear and insecurity become the dominant features social life with a major fear constituting being consigned to 'the wasted' (Bauman, 2005). Rather like Beck, Bauman considers this to be a democratic fear, even if it manifests itself more unevenly on the ground. This kind of social and economic precariousness takes its toll on everyone. While the 'winners' rise and soar, the 'losers' stumble and fall. Relative outcomes aside, all of this takes place in the context of universal uncertainty in the everyday presence of an unsettling canvas of 'butterfly effects' and unknowable futures. Hence rootlessness and insecurity predominate.

From a point of view, some of Bauman's ideas capture processes that women in particular have long been subjected to (Stanko, 1997; Campbell, 2005): the risks and uncertainties of knowing who can and who cannot be trusted against the backcloth of a generalized fear of sexual danger – the ubiquity of such fears lying as Morgan (1989) might say, in the steps that fall behind you. For Bauman, the liquid fears of the modern age include all of us, not just women.

So, each of the perspectives we have discussed pay differential attention to the concepts of risk, fear and security, link them in contrasting ways, and are suggestive of different understandings of the capacities and capabilities of human beings. They each also make different claims as to what is knowable and doable in the light of the different emphases they present. Yet, simultaneously, they all recognize, to varying degrees, the importance that risk has had in setting contemporary policy agendas and the different attention given to the various methods of measuring, evaluating and estimating risk. Given the preoccupation of much mainstream criminology and criminal justice professional concern with these practices, especially in the context of identifying and targeting terrorism, it is to a discussion of these methods that we shall now turn.

Realism, risk and criminal justice practice

As was suggested above, a feature of the presence of risk within criminology derives from those disciplines sharing in this space that have a more realist take on what risk is and how it can be measured. This position has led to a significant area of work informing criminal justice practice in the form of risk assessment. Approaches to risk assessment have come a long way since early endeavours to communicate 'objective' (crime) risks to a lay public presumed to be unknowledgeable and ill informed. Indeed, as Garland's (2001) thesis of responsibilization implies, it is 'simply assumed that individuals will embrace a calculative attitude to determining the risks that they face and adopt appropriate measures in the light of their probability of being victimized' (Haggerty, 2003: 196). Furthermore, O'Malley (2006: 49) has pointed out that 'crime prevention has succeeded in marrying risk with a more traditional social and behavioural form of criminology by translating the old causes of crime into risk factors'. Underpinning the identification of such risk factors is the presumption that not only is it possible to engage in risk sorting, differentiating the more risky people/behaviours from the less risky (Feeley and Simon 1992), it is also possible to assume that, as rational human beings, individuals will respond rationally when exposed to such sorting (Haggerty, 2003). Indeed, the exorable rise and presence of these practices has led some to argue that they have colonized debates about a range of social problems (see Tombs and Whyte, 2006), so much so that risk and risk assessment practices have become *the* way in which risk is ascertainable and reinforced.

Thus, it is possible to observe symmetry between the conceptual presence of risk in social science as the lens through which we understand the present world and the presence of risk assessment practices as the lens through which criminal justice professionals intervene in the present world. This symmetry asserts a worldview, the divergences within it notwithstanding, that has become the defining feature of how we think about what is doable and actionable. Moreover, embedded within this view, in terms of risk assessment practice in particular, is a shift in the question that informs this practice: from the 'what was' question to the 'what if' question. Our concern here is to document that shift.

Risk assessment tools – both clinical and actuarial – are used to inform risk profiling and the appropriate management of 'risky' populations, practices and places. This is as evident in informing responses to the threat from terrorism as it is in responding to other violent and/or sex offenders. Clinical risk assessment stems from the activities of medical and mental health practitioners and is an approach rooted in individual diagnostic techniques geared towards identifying individual personality factors and situational triggers for behaviour. These kinds of assessments are retrospective (not prospective) and have a poor record in prediction. Thus, clinical risk assessment can produce both false negative and false positive prediction: i.e. falsely predicting a behaviour (violence, for instance) will occur and it does not, or falsely predicting a behaviour will not occur and it does (Kemshall, 1996). On the other hand, actuarial risk assessment stems largely from the practices of the insurance industry. These practices are based upon statistical calculations of probability. Actuarial risk assessment offers statistically reliable information about groups of people or types of behaviour. Its aggregate powers of prediction in this sense are considerable. However, despite such strengths, actuarial risk assessment is not very useful for predicting the behaviour of individuals. It does not necessarily follow that what might be predicted for a group can be predicted for an individual. More recent advances in understanding and appreciating the efficacy of such risk assessment tools recommend the adoption of a combination of actuarial and clinical tools (Coid *et al.*, 2007) and also suggest there is some value in appreciating the different power of static and dynamic risk assessment methods (see Bonta, 1999). Such refinements apart, these tools are intended to facilitate the management of known offenders on the one hand as well as highlighting potential offenders and victims on the other. This is a practice that we will render concrete in Chapter 4 in the context of pre-emptive forms of regulation. As tools they are essentially concerned with prediction. However, logically they can never provide us with anything more than hypotheses concerning what *might* happen in the future. Returning to Taleb's Black Swans events can, and do, happen otherwise. Rooted in information based on past behaviour, they are fundamentally compromised since as Bernstein (1996: 334) reminds us: 'the past seldom obliges by revealing to us when wildness will break out in the future'. Despite this problem, decision making in the criminal justice system, especially decisions on the potential for recidivism, and decisions on the potential for future offending behaviour even if someone has not so far committed any offences, are frequently informed by a combination of clinical and actuarial risk assessment methods. They ask the question: based on what has happened, what might happen? Moving from the retrospective to the futuristic, since 9/11 the prescient question has arguably become what might happen in the worst case? Sunstein (2005) indexes this question to the growth of the 'precautionary principle' in the Western world. It is a principle that has emerged from the recognition of knowing that we do not know, infamously referred to by Rumsfeld (2002) as the 'unknown unknowns'.

In connecting the two parts of our discussion so far, we can observe some interesting linkages between the two approaches to risk with which we have been concerned in their respective 'discovery' of the 'unknown unknowns'. For instance, both Beck and Bauman develop the problem of unknown unknowns (although Beck prefers to employ the German word *nichtwissen*). Beck (2009: 115) has suggested that 'world risk society is a non-knowledge society in a very precise sense' in which non-knowledge needs to be seen as a product of more and better science. From here he proceeds to offer a typology of non-knowing. A typology that differentiates between different types of 'not knowing'; selective assumptions, wilful ignorance, reflected non-knowing, conscious inability to know, unconscious non-knowing and, finally, the inability to know (ibid.: 126). Of course, like all typologies, this serves as a heuristic device to facilitate an appreciation of the complexity of what is knowable under the conditions of 'reflexive modernization'. Indeed, from a point of view, Beck's desire to construct such a typology might in itself reflect a desire to render non-knowing knowable and can be coupled with what de Lint and Virta (2004) have referred to as the 'securitisation of everyday life': the routine practices through which the world is rendered 'knowable' for all practical purposes. Arguably these are the kinds of practices that emanate from the risk *dispositif* of the governmentality thesis and render us all fearful.

So both conceptually and practically it is evident that the presence of terrorism, and the 'suicide bomber' in particular, illustrates the limits of any predictive and/or pre-emptive strategies: we know that we do not know. Under these circumstances the precautionary principle fills the gap and affords the space in which a 'culture of suspicion' (Ericson, 2007) can flourish. Suspicion that in legal and policy terms can, and has been, constituted as 'actionable intelligence' (Amoore, 2007). Consequently, it could be argued that Bauman's (2006: 107) assertion that the paramount weapon of terrorism is fear – in which there are 'rich crops however inferior the quality of the seed' – is correct, since the precautionary principle blooms under these conditions. Indeed, Sunstein (2005: 65) wryly observes that: 'terrorists exploit probability neglect as do environmentalists and corporate executives': one of the unintended consequences of the 'precautionary principle'. Sunstein goes on to identify five mechanisms that make the precautionary principle work: the *availability heuristic* (making some risks especially likely to happen whether or not this is actually the case); *probability neglect* (encouraging people to focus on the 'worst case' even if this is highly unlikely); *loss aversion* (valuing the status quo); a belief in the *benevolence of nature*; and *systems neglect* (a refusal to acknowledge that interventions create risks of their own). Of all of these, probability neglect, as suggested above, is arguably the most prescient for the discussion here. Probability neglect, the drive to focus on the worst-case scenario, glosses a range of consequences of 'not-knowing' for risk, fear, the maintenance of (ontological) security, alongside identity formation and notions of citizenship. This creeping 'presence of the future' (Vedby-Rasmussen, 2004) and the rising presence of the 'what if' question in politically sensitive areas such as terrorism prevention and crime control, signals an important shift in institutional practices and policy making: the rising spectre of the worst-case scenario. So what might 'not knowing' imply for our understanding of policy responses to the 'unknown unknowns'? How have responses to the 'what if' question played themselves out? In the remainder of the book we will document the processes associated with the inexorable rise of the 'what if' questions along with the daunting and constraining (Western) presence of the risk rationalities documented here.

Conclusion: opening up some room for manoeuvre?

In this chapter we have explored the different perspectives available to criminology to make sense of risk, fear and security in the face of the rising concern with international terrorism. We have also traced the way in which risk as a concept has been used within criminology and moved politicians, policy makers and criminal justice professionals from a preoccupation with prediction based on 'what was' to modes of prediction based on 'what if'. These issues are further developed in Chapter 3. Put alongside the questions of geography and voice posed by Aas (2012) and Connell (2007), it is possible to suggest from this overview that it makes more sense to think of risk, fear and security as multi-textured. Moreover, they take on these qualities whether we are speaking as criminologists, experts in international relations, experts on security management or citizens. What is missing from much of the analysis that has taken place since 9/11 has been a full and deep appreciation of the multifaceted and multilayered nature of these terms both as debated *and as experienced*. Moreover, following in the spirit of Bell (1979), Fox-Piven (2010) further adds to our appreciation of these concepts. Her analysis, rather like Bell's, puts to the fore the economic context in which risk, fear and security need to be understood. She observes:

> Neoliberalism is of course still capitalism, but it is a new kind of capitalism, powered by a new logic. . . . In other words, neoliberalism means that politics and the State have become more important instruments in the age-old capitalist project of class domination . . . in sum, neoliberalism is a new *political* project to increase capitalist power and wealth.
>
> (Fox-Piven, 2010: 111, our emphasis)

While the extent to which this neoliberal project has informed institutional preoccupations globally is a matter for contestation and debate, it is certainly the case that it has taken a firm grip in most Western States. It is within this grip that we need to understand the rise of, and search for, the security State (Hallsworth and Lea, 2011). Our understanding of that search has started here with an appreciation of risk creep. However, as the new millennium has unfolded, and as we shall demonstrate, risk creep is coming to be superseded by resilience creep. Further, the disciplinary aspects of the neoliberal regime, implied by the analysis presented here, are likely to increase as austerity measures bite in those same Western States. Chapters 5 and 6 reveal more about how these practices have been articulated, the impact they have had, and on whom. However, what is also missing from the debates that have been presented here is a critical appreciation of the domain assumptions that have framed them. So while we have a wide range of conceptual armoury available to us to make sense of the current contradictions faced by neoliberal capitalism, that conceptual armoury in itself has proceeded with a range of assumptions about what might be 'new' about this 'new terrorism' moment, and what those assumptions take for granted about how this moment also serves to further the interests of powerful groups that steer the neoliberal capitalist project. In the next chapter we begin to unspool these assumptions and what they imply. In unravelling these issues, the search for a criminological voice, as we shall see, takes on particular dimensions.

References

Aas, K. (2012) The earth is one, but the world is not: Criminological theory and its geopolitical divisions. *Theoretical Criminology*, 16(1): 5–20.

Amoore, L. (2007) Vigilant visualities: The watchful politics of the war on terror. *Security Dialogue*, 38: 215–32.

Aradau, C. and Van Munster, R. (2008) Governing terrorism through risk: Taking precautions, (un)knowing the future. *European Journal of International Relations*, 13(1): 89–115.

Bauman, Z. (2000) *Liquid Modernity*. Cambridge: Polity Press.

Bauman, Z. (2005) *Liquid Life*. Cambridge: Polity Press.

Bauman, Z. (2006) *Liquid Fear*. Cambridge: Polity Press.

Beck, U. (1992) *Risk Society: Towards a new modernity*. London: Sage.

Beck, U. (1995) *Ecological Politics in an Age of Risk*. Cambridge: Polity Press.

Beck, U. (1999) *World Risk Society*. Cambridge: Polity Press.

Beck, U. (2006) *Cosmopolitan Vision*. Cambridge: Polity Press.

Beck, U. (2009) *World at Risk*. Cambridge: Polity Press.

Beck, U., Giddens, A. and Lash, S. (eds) (1994) *Reflexive Modernization: Politics, tradition and aesthetics in the modern social order*. London: Sage.

Bell, D. (1979) *The Cultural Contradictions of Capitalism*. London: Heinemann.

Benhabib, S. (2002) *The Claims of Culture*. Princeton: NJ: Princeton University Press.

Berman, M. (1982) *All that is Solid Melts into Air*. New York: Simon and Schuster.

Bernstein, P. (1996) *Against the Gods: The remarkable story of risk*. London: Wiley.

Bonta, J. (1999) Approaches to offender risk assessment: Static vs dynamic. *Research Summary*, 4(2): 1–2.

Brown, P. (2013) Risk and social theory: A new venture and some new avenues. *Health Risk and Society*, 15(8): 624–34.

Butler, J. (2002) *Postmodernism*. Oxford: Oxford University Press.

Campbell, A. (2005) Keeping the 'lady' safe: The regulation of femininity through crime prevention. *Critical Criminology*, 13: 119–40.

Castel, R. (1991) From dangerousness to risk. In G. Burchell, C. Gordon and P. Miller, (eds) *The Foucault Effect: Studies in governmentality*. London: Harvester Wheatsheaf, pp. 281–98.

Coid, J., Yang, M., Ullrich, S., Zhang, T., Roberts, A., Roberts, C. and Farrington, D. (2007) Protecting and understanding risk of re-offending: The Prisoner Cohort Study. *Research Summary*. London: Ministry of Justice.

Connell, R. (2007) The northern theory of globalization. *Sociological Theory*, 25(4): 368–85.

Davis, M. (ed.) (2013) *Liquid Sociology: Metaphor in Zygmunt Bauman's Analysis of Modernity*. Farnham: Ashgate.

Davis, P., Francis, P. and Greer, P. (2007) *Victims, Crime and Society*. London: Sage.

de Lint, W. and Virta, S. (2004) Security and Ambiguity: Towards a Radical Security Politics. *Theoretical Criminology*, 8(4): 465–89.

Dean, M. (1999) *Governmentality: Power and rule in modern society*. London: Sage.

Dixon, M., Reed, H., Rogers, B. and Stone, L. (2006) *CrimeShare: The unequal impact of crime*. London: IPPR.

Douglas, M. (1990) Risk as a forensic resource. *Daedalus*, 119(4): 1–16.

Douglas, M. (1992) *Risk and Blame: Essays in cultural theory*. London: Routledge.

Ericson, R.V. (2007) *Crime in an Insecure World*. Cambridge: Polity Press.

Ericson, R. and Haggerty, K. (1997) *Policing the Risk Society*. Oxford: Clarendon.

Feeley, M. and Simon, J. (1992) The new penology: Notes on the emerging strategy of corrections and its implications. *Criminology*, 30(4): 449–74.

Forst, B. (2011) Managing the fear of terrorism. In B. Forst, J. Greene and J. Lynch (eds) *Criminologists on Terrorism and Homeland Security*. Cambridge: Cambridge University Press, pp. 273–99.

Foucault, M. (1980) *Power/Knowledge*. Brighton: Harvester.

Foucault, M. (1991) Governmentality. In G. Burchell, C. Gordon and P. Miller (eds) *The Foucault Effect: Studies in governmentality*, London: Harvester Wheatsheaf: 87–104.

Fox-Piven, F. (2010) A response to Wacquant. *Theoretical Criminology*, 14(1): 111–16.

Furedi (1997/2002) *Culture of Fear: Risk taking and the morality of low expectation*. London: Continuum.

Furedi, F. (2005) Terrorism and the politics of fear. In C. Hale, K. Hayward, A. Wahidin and E. Wincup (eds) *Criminology*. Oxford: Oxford University Press: 343–62.

Furedi, F. (2007) *Invitation to Terror: The expanding empire of the unknown.* London: Continuum.

Furedi, F. (2013) *Moral Crusades in an Age of Mistrust.* London: Palgrave-Pivot.

Garland, D. (2001) *The Culture of Control: Crime and social order in contemporary society.* Oxford: Oxford University Press.

Giddens, A. (1994) *Beyond Left and Right: The future of radical politics.* Cambridge: Polity.

Giddens, A. (1998) Risk society: The context of British politics. In J. Franklin (ed.) *The Politics of Risk Society.* Cambridge: Polity Press.

Griset, P. and Mahan, S. (2008) *Terrorism in Perspective.* London: Sage.

Haggerty, K.D. (2003) From risk to precaution: The rationalities of personal crime prevention. In R. Ericson and A. Doyle (eds) *Risk and Morality.* Toronto: University of Toronto Press: 193–214.

Hallsworth, S. and Lea, J. (2011) Reconstructing Leviathan: Emerging contours of the security state. *Theoretical Criminology*, 15(2): 141–58.

Hannah-Moffat, K. and O'Malley, P. (eds) (2007) *Gendered Risks.* London: Routledge.

Hogg, R. (2007) Criminology, crime and politics before and after 9/11. *Australian and New Zealand Journal of Criminology*, 40(1): 83–105.

Hudson, B. (2003) *Justice in a Risk Society.* London: Sage.

Hudson, B. (2006) Beyond white man's justice: Race, gender and justice in late modernity. *Theoretical Criminology*, 10(1): 1362–4806.

Innes, M. (2001) Control creep. *Sociological Research Online* 6(3). www.socresonline.org.uk/6/3/innes.html

Isin, E. (2004) The neurotic citizen. *Citizenship Studies*, 8(3): 217–35.

Jenks, C. (2003) *Transgression.* London: Routledge.

Kemshall, H. (2006) *Reviewing Risk: A review of research on the assessment and management of risk and dangerousness: Implications for policy and practice in the Probation Service.* London: Home Office.

Lee, M. (2001) The genesis of fear of crime. *Theoretical Criminology*, 5(4): 467–86.

Lupton, D. (2013) *Key Ideas: Risk.* London: Routledge.

Lyng, S. (2005) *Edgework: The sociology of risk taking.* New York: Routledge.

Morgan, R. (1989) *The Demon Lover.* London: Mandarin.

Murphy, T. and Whitty, N. (2007) Risk and human rights in UK prison governance. *The British Journal of Criminology*, 47: 798–816.

Mythen, G. (2014) *The Risk Society: Crime, security and justice.* Basingstoke: Palgrave Macmillan.

Mythen, G. and Walklate, S. (2006) Criminology and terrorism: Which thesis? Risk society or governmentality? *British Journal of Criminology*, 46(3): 379–98.

Mythen, G. and Walklate, S. (2008) Terrorism, risk and international security: The perils of asking what if? *Security Dialogue*, Special Edition on 'Risk, Security and Technologies of the Political', 39, 2/3: 221–42.

Mythen, G., Walklate, S. and Khan, F. (2009) 'I'm a Muslim, but I'm not a terrorist': Risk, victimization and the negotiation of risky identities. *British Journal of Criminology*, 49(6): 736–54.

Newburn, T. (2009) *Criminology*. Devon: Willan.

Oates, S. (2005) Selling fear? The framing of terrorist threat in elections. In *Security, Terrorism and the UK*. ISP/NSC Briefing Paper 05/01.

O'Malley, P. (2004) *Risk and Uncertainty*. London: Glasshouse Press.

O'Malley, P. (2006) Criminology and risk. In G. Mythen and S. Walklate (eds) *Beyond the Risk Society*. London: McGraw-Hill, pp. 43–59.

O'Malley, P. (2010) *Crime and Risk*. London: Sage.

Rasborg, K. (2012) (World) risk society or new rationalities of risk? A critical discussion of Ulrich Beck's theory of reflexive modernity, *Thesis Eleven*, 108(1): 3–25.

Rose, N. (1999) *Powers of Freedom: Reframing political thought*. Cambridge: Cambridge University Press.

Rumsfeld, D. (2002) DoD News Briefing, 12 February, www.defense.gov/ Transcripts/Transcript.aspx?tTranscriptID=2636

Sachs, J. (2007) *Reith Lecture*. London: BBC.

Sharp, D. and Atherton, S. (2007) To serve and protect? The experiences of policing in the community of young people from black and other ethnic minority groups. *British Journal of Criminology*, 47(1): 746–63.

Short, J. (1984) The social fabric of risk: Towards the social transformation of risk analysis. *American Sociological Review*, 49: 711–25.

Simon, J. (2007) *Governing Through Crime*. Oxford: Oxford University Press.

Sparks, R. (1992) Reason and unreason in left realism: Some problems in the constitution of the fear of crime. In R. Matthews and J. Young (eds) *Issues in Realist Criminology*. London: Sage, pp. 119–35.

Stanko, E. (1997) Safety talk: Conceptualising women's risk assessment as a technology of the soul. *Theoretical Criminology*, 4(1): 479–99.

State Department (2002) Secretary Colin L. Powell: Statement upon the release of 'Patterns of Global Terrorism', Washington, DC, May 21.

Summers, A. and Swann, R. (2011) *The Eleventh Day: The ultimate account of 9/11*. London: Doubleday.

Sunstein, C.R. (2005) *Laws of Fear: Beyond the precautionary principle*. Cambridge: Cambridge University Press.

Taleb, N.N. (2010) *The Black Swan: The impact of the highly improbable*. London: Penguin.

Taylor, I. (1996) Fear of crime, urban fortunes and suburban social movements: Some reflections from Manchester. *Sociology*, 30(2): 317–37.

Tillich, P. (1952) *The Courage to Be*. Glasgow: Collins.

Valverde, M. (2011) Questions of security: A framework for research. *Theoretical Criminology*, 15(1): 3–22.

Vedby-Rasmussen, M. (2004) It sounds like a riddle: Security studies, the war on terror and risk. *Millennium: Journal of International Studies*, 30(2): 381–95.

Walker, C. (2008) Know thine enemy as thyself: Discerning friend from foe under the anti-terrorism laws. *Melbourne University Law Review*, 32(1): 275–301.

Walklate, S. (1997) Risk and criminal victimization: A modernist dilemma? *British Journal of Criminology*, 37(1): 35–45.

Walklate, S. and Mythen, G. (2008) How scared are we? *British Journal of Criminology*, 48(2): 209–25.

Walklate, S. and Mythen, G. (2010) Agency, reflexivity and risk: Which citizen? *British Journal of Sociology*, 61: 47–65.

Warr, M. (2000) Fear of crime in the United States: Avenues for research and policy. In *Criminal Justice 2000 Vol. 4: Measurement and Analysis of Crime and Justice*. Washington, DC: US Department of Justice.

Wibben, A.T.R. (2011) *Feminist Security Studies*. London: Routledge.

Wilkinson, I. (2010) *Risk, Vulnerability and Everyday Life*. London: Routledge.

Young, J. (2007) *The Vertigo of Late Modernity*. London: Sage.

Zedner, L. (2009) *Security*. London: Routledge.

2

CONSTRUCTING NEW TERRORISM

Discourse, representation and ideology

> You can't kill an idea.
>
> Anonymous soldier from US Marine Corps,
> cited in Anderson (2013: 108)

Introduction

In the preceding chapter we outlined the interconnections that have been established between risk, fear and security in the social science literature. We also briefly considered the implications of the turn to such concepts for criminology as a discipline. This is something we will return to later. We posited that an appreciation of the contingent and contested nature of concepts such as risk and security is a precursor to developing a critical approach to terrorism. Throughout the chapter we were concerned to demonstrate the extent to which 9/11 acted as a lever for various practical and policy agendas invariably developed in response to worst-case security imaginings. However, the events of 9/11 have not only served to reorient the conceptual agendas of the academy and the practical agendas of administrative criminologists and criminal justice professionals. The idea that 9/11 served as a break point in world security has been endorsed and promoted by various intelligence experts, politicians, novelists and media professionals (see Amis, 2008; Gardner, 2009; Kostakopoulou, 2009). An insistence on the remarkable nature of 9/11 has led to the common sense conclusion that such drastic actions by terrorists must be met with hitherto unprecedented counter-measures.

As we shall explicate, such an accent on the novel nature of 9/11 largely glosses over the historical ubiquity of terrorism in the West. Over the last half century a number of countries in Europe have faced the problem of political violence – from the attacks undertaken by the Baader-Meinhof group in Germany, to the ETA campaign for Basque independence in Spain and the armed struggle for the unification of Ireland directed by the Irish Republican Army (IRA). In response to these threats, various forms of legislation, surveillance and policing have been brought into force and revised national security policies rolled out. Nevertheless, such measures designed to fight terrorism have been eclipsed by the wave of securitization that has followed the 9/11 attacks. For us, this makes the response to terrorism in this case at least as – and arguably more – consequential than the defining incident itself. In many respects, the response to 9/11 has wreaked death and destruction on a scale that dwarfs the triggering incident (see Cornwell, 2011). The breadth and depth of the regime of securitization that emerged in the West in the first decade of the twenty-first century is historically without precedent. While the extent of counter-terrorism measures has varied from country to country, all Western capitalist nations have been pushed to assess the robustness of extant national security policies and to consider the implementation of new precautions and deterrents (see Borchgrevink, 2013; Patane, 2006; Safferling, 2006). In as much as divergences in policy making have became apparent across countries and regions, the establishment of a 'coalition of the willing', spearheaded by America, marked a significant departure in terms of the internationalization and militarization of counter-terrorism strategy. The war on terror – involving *inter alia* the military invasions of Afghanistan and Iraq, the detainment without charge of over 3,000 terrorist suspects considered 'enemy combatants' and the killing of an estimated 800 innocent civilians in attacks by weaponized drones – acts as something of a landmark in terms of the intensification of State violence against non-State actors. Notwithstanding the nuclear bombings of Hiroshima and Nagasaki, the 9/11 attacks have proven to be a defining moment in history, not so much in terms of the coming into being of the 'clash of civilisations' rashly predicted by Huntingdon (1996), but more as a permission point for extraordinary security and military policies. It is in *this* sense, that taken-for-granted assumptions about safety, risk and security have been unsettled, uprooted and reconfigured (see Edmunds, 2011; Sciullo, 2012; Vedby-Rasmussen, 2004).

While we will focus more fully on transformations in security *practices* in Chapters 4 and 5, in this chapter it is our objective to interrogate the *ideational assumptions* that underpin the widely held claim that 9/11 signalled the onset of a new form of terrorism. We begin by narrating the assumed features of new terrorism before going on to assess some of the claims advanced by securocrats and politicians about the effects of new terrorism. Noting both continuities and transformations in the use of political violence – of which terrorism is just one form – we question the premises that underpin the discourse of 'new terrorism' and elucidate the ideological security work performed by the State, academics and the media in building a narrative of threat that elides historical tensions, deals in absolutes and obscures evident complexities. These are the very contradictions of terrorism that resonate with the blueprint suggested by Bell (1979).

New terrorism: a radical rupture?

Although the idea of 'new terrorism' gained popular credence after 9/11, it is important to recognize that assertions regarding the emergence of a fundamentally distinct and novel form of terrorism arose somewhat earlier in security and intelligence circles. Poynting and Whyte (2012: 5) note that the genealogy of the new terrorism thesis can be traced back to the counter-insurgency policies used in Latin America in the late 1980s which were endorsed by academics embedded in the military establishment. Nevertheless, an article written by Walter Laqueur (1996) acts as something of a standard bearer for new – or, as he originally described it, 'postmodern' – terrorism. In view of the status given to this intervention in the wider literature, we shall outline his argument in a little more detail.

The crux of Laqueur's (1996; 2000; 2003) argument is that the motivations, strategies and weapons deployed by terrorist groups have altered markedly over the course of recent history, such that the nature and impact of political violence in the modern world is dramatically different from that experienced in previous epochs. According to Laqueur (1996: 26) – writing some five years before the 9/11 attacks – 'current definitions of terrorism fail to capture the magnitude of the problem worldwide', meaning that a reconfigured conceptual paradigm is required. While Laqueur's ideas had initial backing among intelligence experts and media commentators, there can be no doubt that the take-up of the new terrorism thesis was significantly enhanced after 9/11. In retrospect, Laqueur's thesis appears as a ready-made post-hoc rationalization for the unexpected events of 9/11 and the apparent inability of the State to secure the security of its citizens: 'the new terrorism is different in character, aiming not at clearly defined political demands but at the destruction of society and elimination of large sections of the population' (Laqueur, 2000: 81). The ideational pull of the concept of 'new' terrorism has proved strong for those in the political spotlight and assumptions regarding the novel magnitude of the threat being faced have been routinely reproduced in the rhetoric of the 'war on terror':

> Facing clear evidence of peril, we cannot wait for the final proof – the smoking gun – that could come in the form of a mushroom cloud.
>
> (Bush, 2002)

> September the eleventh was not an isolated event, but a tragic prologue . . . a new and deadly virus has emerged. The virus is terrorism whose intent to inflict destruction is unconstrained by human feeling and whose capacity to inflict it is enlarged by technology.
>
> (Blair, 2003)

In subsequent chapters we will illuminate the extent to which the political framing of new terrorism has been crucial in attempts to mobilize public support for both international military incursions and domestic counter-terrorism measures. What is more, post 9/11, the apocalyptic type of terrorism described by Blair and Bush above has been specifically associated with Islamist fundamentalist networks, such as Al Qaeda, Al Shabaab, Jemaah Islamiyah and Lashkar-e-Taiba. Although different accents have been placed on specific facets of new terrorism, if we look at the literature in the round, we can identify six connected areas of transformation that have been used to underscore the historical uniqueness of new terrorism. These relate to organizational structure, magnitude, targets, geography, weaponry and technology. For the purposes of analytical clarity, we will delineate the contours of each of these areas in turn.

First, proponents of the new terrorism thesis argue that the organizational composition of terrorist groups has evolved from a hierarchical to a horizontal structure. While traditional terrorist groups such as the IRA and ETA have – or previously had – relatively autocratic leadership, members who shared united goals and were drilled to accept top-down instruction, new terrorist groups accommodate a spectrum of viewpoints, possess multiple objectives and have a flat rather than a vertical structure (see 9/11 Commission Report, 2004; Morgan, 2004). Al-Qaeda, for example, has been described as an ideational fulcrum that radicalizes and inspires individuals and small networks rather than a tightly structured and hierarchically controlled organization (see Burke, 2005; Zedner, 2009: 128). Such groups are said to be dependent on philosophical, political or religious commitment to the cause and function through a cellular or networked structure that is not dependent on face-to-face contact or systematic mechanisms of command and control (see Maras, 2013a: 52; Neumann, 2009: 7).

Second, security analysts and academics have reasoned that the magnitude of the attacks undertaken by new terrorist groups is comparatively large with the killing of 2,977 people on 9/11 a case in point. In order to highlight the enormity of the problem, the former British Prime Minister Tony Blair went as far as comparing the threat of new terrorism with that presented by Nazism in the mid-twentieth century (see Waugh, 2004: 5). Security analysts such as Hoffman (1999) argue that there are several reasons for this shift towards 'high-lethality' attacks, including advances in strategic tactics and more sophisticated techniques of deploying violence.

Third, it has been commonly argued that the type of targets selected by terrorists has altered. Although civilian casualties were frequently the result of attacks by traditional organizations such as the IRA and ETA, their strategic objectives were largely geared towards damaging infrastructure, disrupting capital accumulation and deterring tourism. What Laqueur (2000: 4) somewhat euphemistically calls 'nuisance terrorism' can be contrasted with the clinical attacks executed by new terrorist groups seeking to maximize on numbers of human casualties (Barnaby, 2003; Morgan, 2004). Thus, Laqueur (1996: 32) posits that 'the new terrorism is different in character, aiming not at clearly defined political demands but at the destruction of society and the elimination of large sections of the population'.

Fourth, and related to organizational structure and magnitude, proponents of the new terrorism thesis argue that the geographical range of terrorist organizations has increased. In as much as recruitment for traditional terrorist groups has largely operated on a local scale, new terrorist organizations enlist followers across the globe (see Burke, 2005; Ould Mohamedou, 2007). While established groups such as ETA and the PLO are engaged in national and regional liberation wars, new terrorist groups seek to launch international attacks. Cross-boundary religious beliefs and motivations are an archetypal trait of postmodern terrorism, affording new terrorist groups the possibility of undertaking cross-continental assaults on a historically unprecedented scale (see Neumann, 2009: 7). For instance, violent attacks attributed to followers of Al-Qaeda have occurred in Casablanca, Algiers, Istanbul, Bali and Madrid (see Riedel, 2008: 10). It is presently estimated that there are in excess of 5,000 Al-Qaeda sympathizers capable and prepared to use violence to further their aims, based in over 60 countries around the globe (see Skinns *et al.*, 2011: 3). This expansive territorial scope serves to increase uncertainty about future sites of attack with the possibility of becoming a victim of a terrorist attack likely to impact on people's perceptions of the threat level.

Fifth, those adhering to the new terrorism thesis aver that the range and the type of weaponry used in attacks has mutated. The availability and accessibility of more powerful weaponry means the possibility for wreaking large-scale human damage exists. Following on from the deployment of commercial planes as weapons in the 9/11 attacks, frantic and hasty assessments were made about the vulnerability of nuclear facilities and petro-chemical plants (see Peters, 2004: 4). Over a decade on from 9/11, concerns continue to be expressed within security and intelligence circles about the deployment of chemical, biological, radiological and nuclear (CBRN) weapons by extremist groups. Whittaker (2012: 39) reasons that, the wherewithal to acquire a nuclear bomb may be way beyond the majority of terrorist groups, gathering the materials required to make a radiological dispersion device or obtaining and cultivating biological and chemical agents is certainly not. Indeed, the British intelligence agency MI5 has gone as far as to say that a dirty bomb attack is inevitable (see Hopkins and Goldenburg, 2003). An attack on the Tokyo subway in 1995 by the Aum Shinrikyo cult attests to this fact. Members of the group dispersed the nerve gas Sarin from a plastic bottle punctured by the pointed tip of an umbrella killing ten people and injuring over 5,000 (see Barnaby, 2003: 125). Subsequent to this there have been further less successful attempts to deploy chemical and biological substances to cause harm, including ricin, bubonic plague bacteria and hydrogen cyanide (see Gurr and Cole, 2002). The wider availability of such materials remains a source of concern for some, as does the possibility that terrorists may acquire deadly materials from States with anti-Western agendas (see Hoffman, 1999).

The sixth area of transformation involves the deployment of media technologies to facilitate promotional campaigns, execute day-to-day operations and plan new types of attack (Riedel, 2008: 4). New terrorist organizations make strategic use of websites, social networks and bulletin boards to disseminate their values and to attract new members (see Cheneworth, 2010: 99). As Peters (2004: 4) puts it: 'postmodern terrorism is telegenic: it is aware that wars and terrorism must use the media in all its forms to shape the subjectivities of the viewing public'. The density and prevalence of media networks is also said to have increased the capacity for transnational networking between terrorist groups with similar enemies (see Kegley and Blanton,

2010: 205). Further, a number of cases have been reported in which terrorist groups have sought to destabilize nation States and private companies through the use of cyber attacks, including a large-scale attack on US banks that targeted JP Morgan Chase, Bank of America and U.S. Bank (see Goldman, 2012). Such 'info-terrorism' or 'cyber-warfare' has become a growing concern for many States vulnerable to terrorist attacks and there has been a steep rise in attacks on government departments and businesses in recent times (Klimburg, 2011; Miekle, 2011). Given the huge reliance within Western nations upon computer-driven electronic systems – from cash machines to prison security sensors and hospital equipment – widespread disruption of computer networks by cyber-terrorism could cause serious human harm (see Ayers, 2009; Mansfield-Devine, 2011). Aside from cyber attacks, both hacking and identity theft from members of the public through phishing is a growing source of income for terrorist groups (see Burn-Murdoch, 2013).

So, at a superficial level, there is no shortage of examples that can be used to illustrate the apparent distinctiveness of the modern terrorist threat. The persuasiveness of the new terrorism thesis can be evidenced by the concurrence between politicians, media professionals and academics regarding its existence. Yet, as popular as the new terrorism thesis is, and as plausible as it may seem on the surface, it is important that criminologists scrutinize the claims being made and interrogate the material permissions that acceptance of this thesis enables. As Poynting and Whyte (2012: 5) observe, 'the new terrorism thesis sets up an understanding of an enemy that is both more apocalyptic and dangerous, and at the same time less amenable to traditional forms of control'. It also implicitly buys into presumptions about legitimate and illegitimate violence/warfare, which in and of itself is problematic especially if the focus on 'newness' remains located within presumptions of tactical difference as opposed to historical continuities. Pursuing this observation, in the remainder of the chapter we wish to focus on the concrete evidence of transformations in political violence, the continuities that are elided in the new terrorism thesis and the ways in which the new terrorist threat has been institutionally mobilized in policy and practice. As we will indicate, for us these omissions and distortions are sufficient to indicate that criminologists should actively challenge the new terrorism thesis rather than passively accept and perpetuate it.

Evaluating the new terrorism thesis: oversights, gaps and caveats

The new terrorism thesis has proven to be attractive on account of its conceptual tidiness and the way in which it acts as a coda for describing some of the contours of change in the use of political violence. However, many of the component parts of the new terrorism thesis are contestable and place an undue emphasis on transformations rather than continuities. As we shall see in Chapters 3 and 4, the impacts of a general political consensus about the existence and effects of new terrorism have produced draconian policies resulting in death, destruction and entirely indefensible human rights abuses. Before turning to consider some of the unsettling practices of State violence and coercion permitted by the discourse of new terrorism, it is first worth pausing to interrogate some of the claims made by its advocates. While there is some substance in the claim that some of the tactics, technologies and strategies used by terrorist groups have evolved over time, the principal claims of the new terrorism thesis have been challenged (see McGhee, 2008: 5; Field, 2009). The attachment of the adjective 'new' is not only relational but also value laden in that it assumes a historical break rather than a gradual continuum of change in forms of political violence. Nevertheless, as we shall see, several of the features associated exclusively with new terrorist groups are equally attributable to groups that have used political violence in earlier times. In the interests of clarity, we will broach each of the six key elements of the new terrorism thesis discussed above and subject each of them to scrutiny in turn.

First, there is some credence in the assertion that the command structure of terrorist groups has evolved over time and that certain groups have developed cross-continental networks of followers. In many respects this is an expectable consequence of a multimedia world characterized by free flows of information and access to a plurality of political, religious and cultural values and positions. It is quite logical that the underlying process of globalization – marked by increased geographical mobility of information, people and products – should facilitate changes in the composition of groups using political violence, in the same way that it has affected the structure of other institutional formations. Furthermore, we can observe continuities rather than a definitive break between the organizational shape of new and old terrorist groups. For instance, the IRA – often cited as an example of a traditional national terrorist group – deployed a cell structure in its operations and also attracted financial donations from sympathizers in numerous countries around the world. Thus, we can perhaps say that terrorist organizations have modified the activities and objectives in line with patterns of social change rather than state categorically that these have been radically reconfigured. Despite extensive media coverage of Al-Qaeda's aspiration to establish a Muslim caliphate, it needs to be remembered that many groups using political violence in the world today are interested primarily in altering local rather than global circumstances. There has also been a pronounced tendency to wrongly suggest that the threat to the West posed by Islamic extremist became real on 9/11 when the lineage is much longer than this. Indeed, Osama bin Laden declared holy war on America over a decade prior to 9/11 and had already sanctioned attacks in the 1990s in Saudi Arabia, Kenya and Tanzania (see Holloway, 2008: 3).

Second, although the attacks on the United States in 2001 led to a large loss of human life, widespread fears expressed about the emergence of a series of high magnitude attacks on a similar scale have proven to be overstated. This is not to complacently assume that major terrorist attacks will not arise in the future, clearly they will. Yet the scale and frequency of terrorist attacks against Western nations in modern society may not turn out to be dramatically dissimilar from that of previous ages. Reinforcing this point, data presented by academics in the *Global Terrorism Database* suggests that the United States has actually witnessed fewer terrorist attacks in recent times when compared with previous decades (see Rogers, 2013). Clearly there are methodological complexities to consider when compiling data about terrorist attacks. For instance, definitional decisions about what counts as terrorism may inflate or reduce the data collated on the number and scale of attacks. One only has to consider the number of atrocities attributed to 'terrorist insurgents' in Iraq to get an idea of how modes of categorization may shape the construction and representation of the threat. Yet the point remains in respect of the disequilibrium between the fears expressed post 9/11 and the materiality of attacks.

The third facet of the new terrorism thesis relates to the targets selected by terrorists. Inasmuch as 9/11 may have alerted the world to the capacity of terrorist groups to launch ambitious attacks on symbolic sites, in many respects the specific targets attacked were predictable. Given their emblematic economic and political status, the Twin Towers and the Pentagon have long been considered high-value targets for groups seeking to attack the United States of America. This point aside, the shock and horror that emerged in response to 9/11 led to widespread concern in media, political and intelligence circles about future targets (see Peters, 2004: 4). Nevertheless, the deliberate targeting of areas of civilians is far from new. It is a strategy that has a long history. Many 'old' terrorist organizations sought to target areas of public use and consumption, as the IRA bombs exploded in Birmingham, Manchester and Warrington attest. The fourth aspect of the new terrorism thesis relates to the claims made about the changing geography of political violence much vaunted in State security discourses over the last two decades. As Tony Blair (2004) put it: 'we have got to be totally vigilant in the face of the threat because all major countries around the world face the same threat'. These kinds of sweeping and context-less assertions are infrequently accompanied by anything as trifling as evidence. It is certainly true that some terrorist networks, such as Al-Qaeda, have followers who are potentially willing and able to use political violence in many nations. But the idea that all nations are equally at threat from a primed and militarized enemy is fallacious. The patterns of attack launched by individuals committing to the philosophy of Al-Qaeda are not particularly unpredictable and are driven by long-standing grievances against particular States and power blocs. In this sense, we should not be surprised by further attacks conducted by Islamic extremists in England or America, but it would be surprising if such attacks occurred in Iceland or Andorra. Again this returns us to the significance of geography pointed up by Aas (2012) in the introduction to this book.

Fifth, the assumptions made about the preferred weaponry of contemporary terrorist groups are somewhat unstable with considerable variance existing between the strategies used by different groups. The artillery commonly used by old terrorist groups – IEDs, nail bombs and mortars – remain very much in use today and are still the weapons of choice for some groups. Clearly, factors such as access and financial capacity will determine choices about the particular weapons that terrorists utilize. In the new terrorism thesis the focus of attention is very much directed towards the *potential* rather than the actual use of CBRN weapons. In our view, the possibility that terrorist groups may seek to use CBRN weapons against their enemies has been overplayed and the likelihood is that smaller-scale operations using bombs and guns will continue to prevail. Again, in many ways, we should not be surprised that individuals and groups seeking to cause harm and provoke fear would want to use CBRN materials that may be at their disposal. The impact of such attacks is highly dramatic. They attract intense media coverage, undermine national security pledges of the State, and have the capacity to intensify anxiety among members of the public. We might also cast back to historical examples that question the novelty of using CBRN as weapons of attack. Modes of biological warfare, for example, have been practised for several centuries. The inestimable capacity of terrorist groups to acquire CBRN weapons can lead to speculation and risk rumours. The fears expressed by George Bush about Iraq's weapons 'capability' stands as a case in point, most notably the fantastical claim that Saddam Hussein had:

> a massive stockpile of biological weapons that has never been accounted for, and is capable of killing millions . . . we know that the regime has produced thousands of tons of chemical agents, including Mustard gas, Sarin nerve gas, and VX nerve gas.
>
> (Bush, 2002)

As we shall see in Chapter 3, the intent of new terrorist groups to cause mass destruction and their technological capability to commit 'high-lethality' attacks has persuaded some to believe that new terrorism constitutes an existential threat that necessitates that exceptional security measures be taken. In constructing the terrorist risk as beyond the parameters of expectable security threats, traditional checks and balances on the impact of legal measures on civil and human rights have fallen away (Kostakopoulou, 2009: 177).

Finally, in respect of the sixth area of transformation, the use of new media technologies to maintain allegiances and as a vehicle for malevolent activity, we might point out these factors are hardly peculiar to new terrorist groups. The inexorable rise of social media and other internet-based activities has become a source of social connection and potential for a continuum of criminal activities – from cyber bullying, the sexual grooming of children to more 'routine' fraud. Clearly terroristic activity is at the extreme end of the spectrum but the way in which terrorist groups have used the internet – both to attract followers or for illegal financial activity – is not unique to these groups nor remarkable in and of itself. Indeed, large-scale cyber attacks are often sanctioned by State actors, rather than terrorists sat in shadowy rooms. This arena of transformation produces challenges across a wide spectrum of human behaviour – both criminal and legal – and is another dimension along which the 'new' terrorism thesis has been overplayed. So, where do these criticisms leave us in relation to explaining the popularity of the new terrorism thesis? Why has the discourse of new terrorism taken such a hold? Whose interests does it serve? What exactly is it that critical criminologists should be resisting?

The political economy of the terrorism industry

Despite staking out a sceptical position, we would not like to suggest that the discourse of new terrorism is part of an organized conspiracy through which power elites consciously mask reality in order to pursue their own economic and political objectives. While this kind of argument is simplistic, it is clear that the prevalent view regarding the novelty of the terrorist threat has important knock-on consequences on policy making and is an ideational precursor for enabling both military incursions and the introduction of new domestic counter-terrorism laws.

The narrative of new terrorism is thus the underlying mood music that sets the rhythms and motions that a range of agencies – including private security companies, charities and local government – are encouraged to dance to. There are thus important institutional consequences that flow from acceptance of the new terrorism thesis. For instance, there is evidence to suggest that the discourse of new terrorism affects not only public perceptions, but also the design of funding calls, the manufacture of combative technologies and urban design – some of which we will go on to discuss in Chapter 6. Post 9/11 huge flows of capital have been initiated on the basis that a new paradigm in political violence required requisite investment to be effectively countered and defeated. Further, we can identify an ideational concurrence between specific centres of expertise specializing in terrorism research and the dominant political view on the nature and potential of terrorism. It is perhaps no coincidence that several well-known academics who have been pivotal in stating the case for a shift towards new terrorism – among them Paul Wilkinson, Walter Laqueur and Bruce Hofmann – have all been employed by institutions centrally involved in major State funded projects in the UK and the USA, including the Centre for the Study of Terrorism and Political Violence, the Center for Strategic and International Studies and the RAND Corporation. Such institutions are themselves powerful players in the broader process of securitization and have the capacity to lobby and influence State securocrats, the media, policy makers and private security contractors. It is important then to be aware of the networked nature of securitization and the material consequences of accepting and promoting a particular view of the nature of political violence in contemporary society. Clearly, once established, new threats present opportunities for political piggy-backing and engender sizeable economic opportunities in terms of generating new business.

So, the new terrorism thesis is one that has largely been accepted and promoted by institutions and agencies at the front line of combating terrorism. This is particularly the case for those charged with predicting future plots and intervening to prevent their materialization, such as the Central Intelligence Agency and the National Security Agency in the United States and MI5 and GCHQ in Britain. Moreover, there is evidence that lead security and intelligence agencies in Britain and America have operationalized their tactics and strategy on the basis of this fundamental shift in the nature of terrorism. What is noticeable is the consistent narrative shared by academics advocating the new terrorism thesis and intelligence services personnel: 'international terrorism from groups such as Al Qaeda presents a threat on a scale not previously encountered . . . networks seek to carry out terrorist attacks around the world, aiming to carry out high impact attacks causing civilian casualties' (MI5, 2013). Similarly, in the United States, the US Federal Bureau of Investigation (FBI), for example, makes reference to a 'new trend in terrorism . . . of less frequent but more destructive attacks' (see Copeland, 2001: 7). As a consequence of fears about terrorism, a range of preparedness programmes to be enforced in the event of a critical terrorist incident have been put in place in the UK, including mock drills staged in urban areas to simulate conditions in the aftermath of a WMD attack, alongside major policy initiatives implemented which are designed to prevent individuals being attracted to violent extremism. In the United States, the National Guard established Rapid Assessment and Initial Detection (RAID) teams primed to respond in the event of a WMD attack. The first tranche of these teams were set up in 1999 at a cost of $52 million, with another $38 million being designated in 2000 to set up five more. As we shall discuss in Chapter 6, in addition to central government security and intelligence agencies, the range of meso and local level responding agencies in the event of a critical incident has been extended and deepened. In austere times there are tangible economic persuaders for actors and organizations to endorse a paradigm shift in tackling political violence that focuses attention in particular ways from risk to resilience as we will discuss in Chapters 5 and 6. In such a climate it is doubtful that proposed projects that dispute or challenge the dominant way of conceiving the terrorist threat are likely to secure funding from major sources that have promoted the discourse of new terrorism. Therein, a decidedly narrow way of viewing the terrorist threat – one that extracts such a threat from historical and contemporary cultural, economic and political conditions – is perpetuated.

By way of qualification, we should note that there are many dissenting voices in the academy that have challenged the idea of new terrorism, both at a political and a policy level (Blakeley, 2009; Jackson *et al.*, 2010). Further, we need to recognize that the view regarding the status of the terrorist threat – and the appropriate manner of combating it – differs between and within countries and continents. Arguably, it is within Anglophone countries such as the UK, America, Canada and Australia that the narrative of new terrorism has been most vociferously articulated and most readily accepted in the mass media and politics. Yet there are different interpretations of the terrorist threat in circulation and rival views on which measures will be effective in the long run in reducing episodes of political violence (see Bauman and Lyon, 2013; Mythen, 2012).

Conclusion: so what is 'new' about 'new terrorism'?

Having made a critical assessment of the evidence, it would appear that there are similarities as well as changes in the motivations and practices of terrorist organizations (Whittaker, 2012: 34). The range of grievances expressed by modern terrorist groups today are not dissimilar to those that have driven such groups to turn to political violence in the past. Religious dispute, ethnic and tribal tensions, economic exploitation, cultural imperialism and injustice remain prevalent reasons for resorting to violence (see Riedel, 2008). In subjecting the discourse of new terrorism to analysis there are, of course, many reasons to be concerned about future threats. With transportation routes widened by globalization and the fragmentation of States possessing nuclear weaponry, the likelihood of an attack using chemical, biological or radiological weapons – or acquiring the substances and chemicals necessary to construct a dirty bomb – has doubtless increased. In this sense, Beck's risk society thesis has social resonance, as do Bauman's observations about the precariousness of the contemporary age. Yet, while it is important to be prepared for such an attack eventuating, we have argued here that the idea of new terrorism – and the language associated with it – has been exaggerated and over-extended. A clear case of a culture of fear, *qua* Furedi? The establishment of a culture of fear around terrorism – albeit fragmented rather than all embracing –

is important not just in terms of psycho-social effects, but also in terms of what it allows in at a policy level. We would agree with Gill (2006: 42) that since 9/11, 'we have witnessed a classic example of "securitisation" in which the terrorist threat has been presented as existential, thus requiring emergency measures outside the normal bounds of procedure'.

As we shall see in subsequent chapters, acceptance of the primary elements of the new terrorism thesis and its embodiment in military and security policy has produced highly deleterious consequences. With the luxury of hindsight, the events of 9/11 do not appear to have been the harbinger of a sequence of grisly and catastrophic attacks. Although individuals inspired by Islamic fundamentalism have committed serious attacks since this time – for instance in London and Madrid – these have largely born the hallmarks of old rather than new terrorism, involving mortar and nail bombs, not CBR weapons. With this in mind, Field (2009) advises that it is best to conceive of transitions in the use of political violence as a process of evolution rather than one of revolution. In many respects, rather than a root and branch shift from one form of terrorism to another, there are continuities as well as departures from the past in the way in which contemporary terrorist groups operate (see Whittaker, 2012: 33). Arguably, the new terrorist moniker encourages a uniform view of political violence and one that tends to imagine Islamic fundamentalist groups as the exemplar of such violence. It should be pointed out that modes of attack used by terrorists were in transition way before 9/11. Further, several attacks that have component parts of the new terrorism thesis were not conducted by Islamist extremists but lone actors or isolated groups, for example the Oklahoma City attacks and the Aum Shinrikyo cult assault on the Tokyo subway system (see Barnaby, 2003: 125; Maras, 2013b: 90). Within the realm of groups and actors that display elements of the new terrorist profile, vastly divergent objectives are articulated. Shoko Asahara, the leader of the Aum Shinrikyo cult, stated that it was the mission of his group to spark a wave of destruction that would lead to Armageddon, while Timothy McVeigh hoped that his bomb attack on the Federal Office building in Oklahoma would instigate a national rebellion against the State in America.

An appreciation of the tensions between 'new terrorism' as an ideational referent and an empirical reality is important for several reasons. Conceptually, it is important that our theoretical frameworks for making sense of contemporary times capture these times meaningfully. Practically, it is important that counter-measures introduced to reduce the threat of terrorism are based on firm evidence rather than rhetoric. In the next chapter we will go on to excavate the power relationships that have underpinned recent State responses to terrorism and the consequences that this has had. As an entrée, we are minded to raise the connections between ideology, representation and power accented by Foucault (1977: 224):

> The formation of knowledge and the increase of power regularly reinforce one another in a circular process . . . it is a double process then: an epistemological 'thaw' through a refinement of power relations; a multiplication of the effects of power through the formation and accumulation of new forms of knowledge.

References

9/11 Commission Report (2004) *Final Report of the National Commission on Terrorist Attacks Upon the United States*. Washington, DC: National Commission on Terrorist Attacks.

Aas, K. (2012) The earth is one, but the world is not: Criminological theory and its geopolitical divisions. *Theoretical Criminology*, 16(1): 5–20.

Amis, M. (2008) *The Second Plane: September 11, terror and boredom*. London: Vintage.

Anderson, B. (2013) Afghanistan: The soldiers' stories. *Esquire*. February Edition, 108–15.

Ayers, C. (2009) The worst is yet to come. *Futurist*, 49: 7–9.

Barnaby, F. (2003) *How to Build a Nuclear Bomb and Other Weapons of Mass Destruction*. London: Granta.

Bauman, Z. and Lyon, D. (2013) *Liquid Surveillance: A conversation*. London: Polity.

Bell, D. (1979) *The Cultural Contradictions of Capitalism*. London: Heinemann.

Blair, T. (2003) Speech to Congress. Washington, 17 July.

Blair, T. (2004) Speech to Sedgefield Constituency. Durham, 5 March.

Blakeley, R. (2009) *State Terrorism and Neoliberalism: The north in the south*. London: Routledge.

Borchgrevink, A. (2013) *A Norwegian Tragedy*. Cambridge: Polity.

Burke, J. (2005) *Al-Qaeda: The true story of radical Islam*. London: IB Taurus.

Burn-Murdoch, J. (2013) UK was world's most phished country in 2012. *The Guardian*, 7 February: 11.

Bush, G. (2002) *Speech on Iraq*. Cincinnati, 7 October.

Cheneworth, E. (2010) Democratic pieces: Democratization and the origins of terrorism. In R. Reuveny (ed.) *Coping With Terrorism: Escalation, counterstrategies and response*. Albany: SUNY Press.

Copeland, T. (2001) Is the new terrorism really new? An analysis of the new paradigm for terrorism. *Journal of Conflict Studies*, 21(2): 1–16.

Cornwell, R. (2011) War on terror set to surpass costs of Second World War. *The Independent*. 30 June.

Edmunds, J. (2011) The new barbarians: Governmentality, securitization and Islam in Western Europe. *Contemporary Islam*, 6: 67–84.

Field, A. (2009) The new terrorism: Revolution or evolution? *Political Studies Review*, 7: 195–207.

Foucault, M. (1977) *Discipline and Punish: The birth of the prison*. London: Penguin.

Gardner, D. (2009) *Risk: The science and politics of fear*. London: Virgin.

Gill, P. (2006) Not just joining the dots but crossing the borders and bridging the voids: Constructing security networks after 11 September 2001. *Policing and Society*, 16(1): 27–49.

Goldman, D. (2012) Major banks hit with biggest cyberattacks in history. *CNN News*, September 28. Available at: http://money.cnn.com/2012/09/27/technology/bankcyberattacks/index.html?hpt=hp_t3 (accessed 13 March 2014).

Gurr, N. and Cole, B. (2002) *The New Face of Terrorism: Threats from weapons of mass destruction*. New York: IB Taurus.

Hoffmann, B. (1999) Introduction. In I. Lesser, B. Hoffman, D. Ronfeldt, M. Zanini and B. Jenkins (eds) *Countering the New Terrorism*. California: RAND, pp. 7–38.

Holloway, D. (2008) *9/11 and the War on Terror*. Edinburgh: Edinburgh University Press.

Hopkins, N. and Goldenburg, S. (2003) MI5 says dirty bomb attack is inevitable. *The Guardian*, 18 June: 4.

Huntingdon, S. (1996) *The Clash of Civilisations and the Remaking of World Order*. New York: Simon & Schuster.

Jackson, R., Murphy, E. and Poynting, S. (2010) *Contemporary State Terrorism: Theory and practice*. London: Routledge.

Kegley, C. and Blanton, S. (2010) *World Politics*. Boston, MA: Wadsworth.

Kibbe, J. (2012) Conducting shadow wars. *Journal of National Security Law and Policy*, 5: 373–92.

Klimburg, A. (2011) Mobilising cyber power. *Survival: Global Politics and Strategy* 53(1): 41–60.

Kostakopoulou, D. (2009) How to do things with security post 9/11. In P. Noxolo and J. Huysmans (eds) *Community, Citizenship and the War on Terror*. Basingstoke: Palgrave Macmillan.

Laqueur, W. (1996) Postmodern terrorism: New rules for an old game. *Foreign Affairs*, September Edition. Available at: www.foreignaffairs.com/articles/52432/walter-laqueur/postmodern-terrorism-new-rules-for-an-old-game (accessed 16 April 2014).

Laqueur, W. (2000) *The New Terrorism: Fanaticism and the arms of mass destruction*. Oxford: Oxford University Press.

Laqueur, W. (2003) *No End to War: Terrorism in the 21st century*. New York: Continuum.

McGhee, D. (2008) *The End of Multiculturalism? Terrorism, integration and human rights*. Buckingham: Open University Press.

Mansfield-Devine, S. (2011) Hacktivism: Assessing the damage. *Network Security*, 8: 5–13.

Maras, H. (2013a) *Counterterrorism*. New York: Jones and Burlington.

Maras, H. (2013b) *The CRC Press Terrorism*. London: CRC Press Reader.

Meikle, J. (2011) Cyber-attacks on UK at disturbing levels, warns GCHQ chief. *The Guardian*, 31 October. Available at: www.guardian.co.uk/technology/2011/oct/31/cyber-attacks-uk-disturbing-gchq (accessed 10 March 2013).

MI5 (2013) Available at: www.mi5.gov.uk/output/terrorism.html (accessed 13 December 2013).

Morgan, M. (2004) The origins of new terrorism. *Parameters*, Spring Edition, 29–43.

Mythen, G. (2012) Who speaks for us? Counter-terrorism, collective attribution and the problem of voice, *Critical Studies on Terrorism*, 5(3): 1–16.

Neumann, P. (2009) *Old and New Terrorism*. Cambridge: Polity Press.

Patane, V. (2006) Recent Italian efforts to respond to terrorism at the legislative level. *Journal of International Criminal Justice*, 4: 1166–80.

Peters, M. (2004) *Postmodern Terror in a Globalized World*. Glasgow: University of Glasgow.

Ould Mohamedou, M. (2007) *Understanding Al Qaeda: The transformation of war*. London: Pluto Press.

Poynting, S. and Whyte, D. (eds) (2012) *Counter-Terrorism and State Violence*. London: Routledge.

Riedel, B. (2008) *The search for Al Qaeda: Its leadership, ideology and future*. Washington, DC: Brookings.

Rogers, S. (2013) Four decades of US terror attacks listed and detailed. *The Guardian*, 17 April: 8.

Safferling, C. (2006) Terror and law: German responses to 9/11. *Journal of International Criminal Justice*, 4: 1152–65.

Sciullo, N. (2012) On the language of counter terrorism and the legal geography of terror. *Willamette Law Review*, 48: 317–41.

Skinns, L., Scott, M. and Cox, T. (2011) *Risk*. Cambridge: Cambridge University Press.

Vedby-Rasmussen, M. (2004) It sounds like a riddle: Security studies, the war on terror and risk. *Millennium: Journal of International Studies*, 30(2): 381–95.

Waugh, P. (2004) Blair: Britain must never be afraid to fight terrorists. *The Independent*, 13 March: 1.

Whittaker, D. (ed.) (2012) *The Terrorism Reader*. London: Routledge.

Zedner, L. (2009) *Security*. London: Sage.

3

THE WAR ON TERROR

Power, violence and hegemony

> Zero deaths apply only to the Western military. The bombs they
> drop kill a lot of people who are to blame for living underneath.
> But these casualties are Afghans, Palestinians . . . they don't belong
> to modernity.
>
> (Badiou, 2012: 9)

Introduction

In Chapter 2 we both traced the components of the new terrorism
thesis and examined the reasons for its rapid uptake in security, media,
political and academic circles. Although 9/11 is commonly assumed
to signal the beginnings of a 'new era of terrorism' (Martin, 2004: 2),
we have argued that the claims made by proponents of the new
terrorism thesis are partial and mix fact with fiction. Further, the
tendency to represent and understand 9/11 as an epochal event masks
the reality that 'the pre-9/11 and post-9/11 worlds were continuous,
not discontinuous' (Holloway, 2008: 1). Building on these principles,
in this chapter, we wish to encourage an understanding of major
terrorist attacks such as 9/11 and 7/7 not simply as isolated occurrences
emerging spontaneously within particular geographical settings, but as
ruptures occurring in response to a sequence of antecedent events within
a world marked by economic and political flux and historically
entrenched faith conflicts.

We begin the chapter by providing a short history of the war on
terror, charting key moments in the evolution of a turbulent process

that has lasted well over a decade. In the second section we examine a range of objections that have been raised against the war on terror, ranging from the conceptual to the moral; the ethical to the humanitarian. Pursuing and developing these objections, we go on in section three to elucidate the contradictions present in the policies pursued through the war on terror and to problematize both the material and ideational objectives of this project. Having reflected on what the war on terror 'moment' tells us about dominant conceptions of risk and security, we conclude by asking what criminologists might do to expose the evident contradictions in State counter-terrorism policy. We will be arguing throughout that supra-national economic problems and geopolitical power struggles cannot be divorced from both specific acts of terrorism and strategic policy decisions about appropriate ways of countering terrorism. Using military and foreign policy developed by the United States and British governments post 9/11 as a touchstone for discussion, we will examine the extent to which such measures have been legitimate, proportionate and effective in enhancing security. Scrutinizing the underlying rationale for the 'war on terror' (WOT), we question the extent to which military interventions have been supported by credible evidence and ask whether such forays have been primarily driven by establishing lasting peace or more deep-seated economic and hegemonic aspirations of powerful Western nation States.

Terrorism, risk and harm: a peculiar metric?

It is beyond dispute that there is a tangible risk of terrorist attacks being undertaken in Western nations by either organized Islamic extremist networks or individuals inspired by the ideologies and worldviews of such groups. This risk is arguably particularly pronounced in countries with colonial histories in Asia, the Middle East and Africa and/or those nations that have centrally been involved in the WOT. What *is* subject to question is the magnitude and the extent of this threat. Of course, accurately estimating the level of risk in the case of terrorism is a fraught endeavour, given the uncertainties involved. In such activity, the problems of uncertainty and *nichtwissen* identified by Beck (2009) and Bauman (2006) are rife. Combining the discussion in Chapter 1 on the efficacy of risk assessment methods with the interrogation in Chapter 2 of the 'new' terrorism thesis, it is evident that different actors, agents and institutions will use different bases and sets of information on which to make their assessments (see Fischhoff and Kadvany, 2011: 141). The question remains then as to what makes a reliable quantifying mechanism: the number of attacks that have occurred in the recent past; the number of individuals committed to Jihadi philosophy; the number of active cells in a country; the type of weaponry possessed by active terrorist groups; or the 'chatter' picked up by members of the intelligence services? The diversity of these possible metrics and the sheer uncertainties involved in calibrating them means that contradictory views will inevitably emerge, even within relatively closed circles. Such divergent assessments of the same problem underscore the contests and conflicts that surface around 'manufactured uncertainties' such as terrorism (Beck, 2009). For Bauman (2006: 99), it is our failure to be able to quantify threats that exhibit a 'non-calculable probability', resulting in vexing issues for both institutions and individuals. In the UK for instance, while the British Prime Minister, David Cameron (2011) describes terrorism as 'the biggest threat that we face today', the government's Independent Reviewer of Terrorism Legislation David Anderson QC (2011: 27) notes that the annual average number of deaths in Britain over the last century from terrorist attacks is just five, making it 'an insignificant cause of mortality in the United Kingdom'. Anderson (2011: 27) goes on to point out that more people are killed in the UK each year by bee and wasp stings than from terrorist attacks. The echoes of Furedi's (2002) culture of fear chime loudly here. It would seem that anxieties about the terrorist threat are somewhat out of kilter with the harm it causes, at least if we take the base level metric of human lives lost as the basis for our judgement.

Against the backcloth set out in Chapter 1 of knowing that we do not know, while the scale and the frequency of future attacks is difficult to predict, what we can say with certainty is that the risk of a terrorist attack has been politically prioritized. If we look at government responses to a range of risks in society it is evident that a hierarchy of harms exists. In short, some risks clearly count more than others. Given that at least eighty people are killed each year in the course of working duties in the British construction industry (see Tombs and Whyte, 2008) we might want to know why terrorism rather than construction work is classified a 'highest priority risk' in the National Security Strategy Report (2010: 23). Of course, there are especial reasons why terrorist attacks are unpalatable to the general public. Such attacks can be indiscriminate, they appear without warning and produce grisly consequences. Indeed, the two axes that are defined as significant in heightening risk perceptions by researchers in the psychometric tradition – 'dread' and the 'unknown' – are frequently attributed to terrorist attacks (see Slovic, 2000). Yet, above and beyond this, there is a deal of constructive and representational work that goes on – in politics, the media, academia – which raises public awareness of the terrorist threat. As Durodie (2004: 15) reasons: 'terrorist attacks take on a different role dependent upon what they represent to particular societies at particular times, rather than solely on the basis of objective indicators, such as real costs and lives lost'. While we expect to publicly mourn the victims of terrorist attacks or commemorate the lives of soldiers that fall in battle, construction workers that die at labour depart the world silently and without fanfare.

From a point of view, changing modes of response to the terrorist threat are bound up with a broader power shift away from national government towards global governance, reflecting particular assumptions regarding the nature and meaning of globalization (see Connell, 2007). As such, notions of both 'terrorism' and 'war' have been reconfigured in recent years. This process of transformation has led some social theorists to claim that the quest for public safety can no longer be adequately understood as a local or indeed a national enterprise: 'national security is, in the borderless age of risks, no longer national security' (Beck, 2002: 14). This is doubtless true. The current conflicts occurring across the Middle East – from Egypt to Syria – demonstrate that the contours of political violence have become much hazier, often involving different factions with competing claims to territory, region and nation. In conflict situations, it is now not uncommon to hear both sides – if they can be so determined – applying the label 'terrorist' to one another. In Beck's (2002: 8) view, there has been an 'individualization of war', whereby conflicts are not simply waged between States, but also by individuals and groups against each other and against the State. Such 'post-national' wars have multitudinous effects and challenge established methods of calculating risk and encouraging the reconstitution of security practices. Before we engage with these broader complexities, it is first necessary to define the central post-national conflict of the present century that is our primary focus here: the war on terror.

Defining the war on terror: contours and spikes

The war on terror (WOT) – also sometimes referred to as the Global War on Terrorism (GWOT), and, in the British context, the 'war against terrorism' (WAT) – is a phrase coined by the former American President George W. Bush. It refers to a concatenation of security processes and military practices set in train after the terrorist attacks on the United States in 2001. In direct response to 9/11, George W. Bush declared that the attacks constituted an act of war, thereby setting the framework for the militaristic response to follow (see van Brunschot and Kennedy, 2008: 89; Pilger, 2012). Bush first publicly used the phrase 'war on terror' in an address to a joint session of Congress on 20 September 2001: 'our war on terror begins with Al-Qaeda, but it does not end there. It will not end until every terrorist group of global reach has been found, stopped and defeated' (Bush, 2001). From this moment forth, the 'war on terror' became a widely used idiom in politics, security and intelligence circles, academia and in the media. In many respects, the WOT has served as a linguistic shorthand that encompasses an amorphous range of activities. Setting clear boundaries between ally and foe, the unashamedly bullish discourse of the WOT constructs a range of descriptors to determine the enemy, such as 'rogue states' and 'outlaw regimes' (see Whittaker, 2012: 332). Viewed through this monocular, not only countries but entire regions have been accorded risky status. Within the discourse of the WOT there is an amalgamation of problematic States that are collectively considered as an 'axis of evil' – variously including Iraq, Iran and North Korea (see Martin, 2013: 103). Such malevolent States and actors are directly contrasted with an honourable and righteous 'coalition of the willing' in order to create clear boundary lines between a righteous 'us' and a malicious 'them' (Lilleker, 2006: 108). The political manufacture of consent by George Bush and Tony Blair, expressed succinctly in the maxim: 'you are either with us or you are with the terrorists' (Bush, 2001) constructed the enemy as both beyond reason and dispossessed of moral values, and simultaneously affirmed the need to simply eradicate malevolent actors discounting any possibility of negotiation or dialogue (see Pilger, 2012: 88). As such, the language of the WOT is intended to ideologically coerce and to manufacture public consent for international military forays: 'the new axis of evil (ever expanding or reconstituted according to expediency) has a similar function to the old enemy in disciplining populations internally as well as mobilizing war footings for adventures abroad' (Poynting and Whyte, 2012: 8). As Keppel (2009) has argued, the WOT discourse can be understood as an attempt to create a persuasive grand narrative to justify US foreign policy to the public after 9/11. However, such intentions cannot be said to have produced positive outcomes, either at an ideational or a material level. Furthermore, as we shall illuminate, use of the term 'war' in the context of terrorism linguistically permits exceptional and otherwise unacceptable forms of intervention and violence by the State (see Sciullo, 2012).

In material terms, the war on terror is constituted by incursions and interventions made against organizations and regimes identified as terroristic in Asia, Africa and the Middle East. Although the United States and the United Kingdom have been at the forefront of the WOT, other countries – including Australia, Canada, Denmark, France, Italy, the Netherlands, Pakistan, New Zealand and Norway – have also been involved. The beginnings of the WOT lie in the legal authorization for the use of military force passed in America on 14 September 2001. This act sanctioned the use of military violence to punish those responsible for the 9/11 attacks and the use of such force against other nations and organizations deemed to aid or abet terrorists. Interestingly, fourteen of the 9/11 hijackers were Saudis, one from the United Arab Emirates and two were born in Egypt (Riedel, 2008: 5). Chiming with Beck's observations regarding post-national conflicts, no military action was taken by the United States against any of these nations. Although the most controversial aspects of the WOT have been *Operation Enduring Freedom* (the Afghanistan war) and *Operation Iraq Freedom* (the invasion and occupation of Iraq), a host of other global policies have been launched. For example, *Operation Active Endeavour*, a NATO naval operation in the Mediterranean designed to interrupt the movement of terrorists, and repeated drone attacks in Federally Administered Tribal Areas in Pakistan (see Maras, 2013: 134). In addition to these wide-ranging policies and practices, the WOT has also been put into practice by large-scale attempts to arrest and detain suspected terrorists – most notoriously in the US military base at Guantanamo Bay – and the kidnap and torture of suspected terrorists through extraordinary rendition (see Poynting, 2010).

It is important to recognize that the assumptions inscribed within the new terrorism thesis run concurrently with the philosophy of the WOT. Underpinning the WOT is the ingrained assumption that the terrorist threat in the twenty-first century is not only threatening and dangerous, but potentially apocalyptic. These facets are well captured in the following statement made by George W. Bush (2002):

> In 1995, after several years of deceit by the Iraqi regime, the head of Iraq's military industries defected. It was then that the regime was forced to admit that it had produced more than 30,000 liters of anthrax and other deadly biological agents. The inspectors, however, concluded that Iraq had likely produced two to four times that amount. This is a massive stockpile of biological weapons that has never been accounted for, and capable of killing millions.

Notwithstanding the veracity of such claims, as we shall see in Chapter 5, the construction of dystopic futures and the attempt to tap directly into public anxieties proved to be a common feature of the discourse of the WOT and paved the way for Bush and Blair to respond by actively constructing what Bourke (2006: 28) refers to as a 'new paradigm of resistance'. Rather transposing a more traditional understanding of resistance, this new paradigm effectively dispenses with previous forms of regulation and negotiation and instead presents State violence and direct coercion as the only effective means of combating terrorism. The assumption that new terrorist groups have both the capability and the intent to, in Laqueur's words, 'bombard the earth' (2000: 264) has acted as a ready-made rationale for the use of exceptional measures. In effect, military force is not only just, it is a necessity. Having claimed that their request to the Taliban to turn over Al-Qaeda operatives linked to the 9/11 attacks being harboured in Afghanistan had been refused, the US and UK governments maintained that there was a need to act pre-emptively as a mode of 'self defence' against future attacks (Maras, 2013: 123). As Tony Blair (2005) later put it in the aftermath of the 7/7 attacks in London: 'let no-one be in any doubt, the rules of the game are changing'. As we shall see in Chapter 4, the logic of pre-emption not only looms large in such rhetoric, it also filters through into specific practices of securitization.

At this juncture it is important to note that the use of pre-emptive force against terrorists by the United States pre-dates 9/11. In 1998 in response to the bombing of US embassies in Kenya and Tanzania the government launched missile strikes in Sudan and Afghanistan. This action was presented as self-defence under article 51 of the UN charter. Those supportive of pre-emptive war such as Tony Blair (2001) maintain that it is a necessary and legitimate response to a threat of huge magnitude: 'whatever the dangers of the action we take, the dangers of inaction are far, far greater'. In the context of the WOT it is argued that the threat of devastation by weapons of mass destruction, the global nature of the threat, the mobility of terrorists, and the willingness of rogue States to support, arm and secrete terrorists, all make pre-emptive action necessary. In so far as punitive strikes can be described as reprisals against terrorist attacks that have materialized, pre-emptive strikes are deployed to destabilize and deter terrorists from conducting future attacks (see Martin, 2013: 221). The preference for pre-emption is perhaps most famously captured in the so-called 'one percent doctrine' advocated by the former US vice President Dick Cheney: 'if there was even a one percent chance of terrorists getting a weapon of mass destruction – and there has been a small probability of such an occurrence for some time – the United States must act now as if it were a certainty' (Cheney, cited in Suskind, 2006: 2). The ramifications of the WOT are troubling, with the US government having reserved the right to attack pre-emptively and unilaterally (see Loader and Walker, 2007: 85).

Issues of pre-emption aside for the moment, the WOT drew explicit attention to the activities of figureheads, such as Osama bin Laden, the former Iraqi leader Saddam Hussein and Abu Musab al-Zarqawi, the proclaimed leader of Al-Qaeda in Iraq. All have since been executed. Hussein in 2006 at the behest of the incoming Iraqi government that displaced him, bin Laden in Tora Bora in 2011 by American military operatives and al-Zarqawi in 2006 in an air raid by the US air force on a village north of Baghdad. However, it was the invasion of Afghanistan – now, very much the elephant in the room in terms of American and British foreign policy – that was the first major incursion made in the war on terror. Initially led by American and British troops, this incursion operated locally with the support of the Afghan Northern Alliance. Despite failing to meet either the military or the political objectives set in Afghanistan, the American and British governments followed up the October 2001 invasion of Afghanistan with the military invasion of Iraq in March 2003. President Bush and Prime Minister Blair justified this invasion on the basis of two claims. First, Saddam Hussein had secretly developed weapons of mass destruction (WMD) that could be readily assembled and deployed against Western nations. Second, that Hussein had cultivated links with anti-Western terrorist networks, including Al-Qaeda. In hindsight, both of these claims turned out to be fallacious, with the UN's own inspectors identifying no evidence of WMDs prior to or after the 2003 invasion and military occupation of Iraq (see Martin, 2013: 103). In the case of Iraq, the ousting of Saddam Hussein in 2003 created a sizeable power vacuum that signalled the onset of a phase of bloody conflict between groups making competing claims for power. Although the US government formerly returned the sovereignty of the State to an interim government headed by Prime Minister Ayad Allawi in the summer of 2004, the violence between warring Sunni and Shia factions has been unceasing and relentless. Since US troops formally pulled out of Iraq in 2011 violence in Iraq has intensified, exposing glaring questions about the mandate for the initial invasion and strategic planning pre-occupation. At the time of writing it is estimated that almost 200,000 people have been confirmed killed as a direct result of the invasion and occupation of Iraq. Over 130,000 of these are not soldiers, nor insurgents, but non-combatant civilians (Iraq Body Count, 2014). Although President Barack Obama sanctioned the scaling down of ground military operations by American forces, he has nonetheless presided over the use of force by stealth by the American State, most notably through weaponized drone attacks operationalized by the military and the CIA. The use and scale of drone attacks to target suspected terrorists increased significantly from 2008 onwards, particularly in Pakistan and Afghanistan, but also in other countries including Libya and Yemen. This is an issue to which we will return later in the chapter.

The ideology of the WOT: objections, contradictions and resistance

As Jackson (2005) posits, the war on terror is not only a material struggle between warring forces, it is also an ideational project. It involves physical practices – such as military force, intelligence operations and mass surveillance – but it also seeks to produce an ideational effect through spreading a set of values, beliefs and morals about security in the modern world. As we shall see, the attempts to win hearts and minds in regions of conflict such as Iraq, Afghanistan and Pakistan have been derailed by the sheer scale of death that has ensued since the instigation of the WOT. Unsurprisingly, many objections have been made against the WOT over the last decade. It is estimated that 36 million people took to the streets to protest against the invasion of Iraq, with large-scale demonstrations taking place in Canada, Australia, Britain and Germany (see Callincos, 2005: 2). Aside from growing discomfort about military involvement among sections of the general public and the dire human consequences that have ensued as a consequence of the WOT, legal objections have been raised about its legitimacy. Iraq was invaded and occupied by the USA and the UK without the authorization of the United Nations Security Council, an act that was declared unlawful by the UN Secretary General Kofi Annan. Lawyers, philosophers and military strategists alike have argued that for a war to be legitimate and just, those instigating force must both demonstrate the right to go to war (*jus ad bellum*) and exhibit the right conduct in war (*jus in bello*) (see McGarry *et al.*, 2012). In the case of Iraq, *jus ad bellum* was not proven to the satisfaction of international law, meaning that the occupation was not legally legitimate. Revelations regarding the conduct of British and American troops – in Abu Graib and Guantanamo Bay – brought to the fore further concerns about *jus ad bellum*. Such is the strength of feeling, many human rights lawyers and peace campaigners have called for both George W. Bush and Tony Blair to be indicted for war crimes (see BBC News Online, 2012). Thus, once again, divergent views regarding the use of violence and the contested nature of social labelling come to the fore. In as much as Western democratically elected governments may declare terrorist attacks illegal, those defined as terroristic use the same just war rationale that such States deploy as a basis for their actions. Pre-emptive strikes by Western nations are themselves deemed by such groups to be illegitimate and to constitute war crimes. Although the rationale used is similar, the positions of State and non State groups is underpinned by completely contrasting views about what constitutes legitimate violence, who is able to justly deploy it, against whom and under what conditions. Given the diametrically opposed nature of such perspectives, it is not difficult to see how a cycle of violence is established that is very difficult to break. Indeed, some would argue that, despite the huge human costs, it may ultimately serve the hegemonic interests of Western nations to be involved in prolonged conflicts. Poynting and Whyte (2012: 8) reason 'wars without end' offer scope for both enhancing social control in terms of targeting groups, activities and practices deemed to be hostile or undesirable, and possess a disciplinary function in terms of coercing weaker nations to comply with the demands of dominant States.

Alongside trenchant critiques of the underlying geopolitical motivations for launching the war on terror, several academics and cultural commentators have raised conceptual and linguistic objections. In this vein, Addicott (2008) posits that the 'war on terror' is neither an accurate descriptor nor a phrase that makes sense given that terrorism is not an enemy but rather a method used by a perceived enemy. True as this may be, we can see the potential benefits of elasticity for States involved in waging the war on terror. Moreover, van Brunschot and Kennedy (2008: 89) note:

> [T]he absence of a flesh and blood enemy with which this type of conflict could be waged meant that the focus was on a method rather than on an entity, although Al-Qaeda and rogue states came to personify the terrorist method.

This tendency to associate terrorism with the methods used by Islamic Fundamentalist groups rather than to recognize the spectrum of actors that seek to use violence has been inscribed in domestic and international policy making. As the following passage in the 9/11 Commission report indicates: 'the enemy is not just "terrorism" some generic evil . . . the catastrophic threat at this moment in history is more specific. It is the threat posed by Islamist terrorism – especially the Al-Qaeda network, its affiliates and its ideology' (2004: 362 cited in Maras, 2013: 134). The dangers of simply equating terrorism with Islamic fundamentalism resound loudly in countries such as Norway and the UK that have suffered attacks by racist right-wing extremists.

In Chapter 2 we contended that the discourse of new terrorism has acted as an ideological prop for the war on terror. Echoing the tendency towards binaries and the negation of ambiguities, the WOT has involved the ideational creation and maintenance of an 'absolute enemy' that is at once ubiquitous and universal (Evans, 2011: 73). This enables the WOT to span across a range of territories and conflicts. While there may be some similarities in modes of attack, the objectives of groups using political violence differs markedly. As it challenges the cohesion of an homogenous enemy stereotype this fact is often overlooked. Groups with very different histories, aspirations and objectives – from the Uighurs demanding independence from China to Chechan separatists – have been merged and constructed as part of a generalized international terrorist threat. As such, the discrete claims and objectives of groups using violence against the State and civilian populations become clumsily rolled into a singular terrorist enemy. This is both blinkered and disingenuous. Local and regional claims to territory, identity and self-determination become conflated and lumped together with global ambitions. Furthermore, acts of violence and suppression conducted by States with poor human rights records are legitimated through recourse to the fight against a common global enemy. As Fairclough (2003: 9) notes, the power of dominant ideologies is not so much in what they represent, but in what they exclude, such as unequal power relations and histories of domination and exploitation. Rose (2000) points out that coexistent modes of risk management operate to separate out the safe from the risky, those that work on the premise of inclusion and those that seek to work on pathologies through tactics of exclusion. Building on this observation, and speaking in the context of East–West relations, Said (1978) argued that those sharing beliefs and values that are determined as being outside dominant Western frameworks are routinely classified as 'other'. Such a separation is, of course, exacerbated in times of conflict and crisis when the lines between a decorous, righteous 'us' and a disruptive, transgressive 'them' is set in stone (Joffe, 1999: 23). As we will discuss in Chapter 5, the videos recorded by the young British men that were responsible for the 7/7 attacks in London make frequent reference to the inaction of the West in defending Palestine against Israeli attacks and the illegal invasion of Iraq and the occupation of Afghanistan. These driving motivations are more than inconvenient for adherents to the new terrorism thesis, as they undo the basis of the original classification. As one of the attackers, Mohammed Sidique Khan, stated in a video recorded prior to the 7/7 attacks:

> Your democratically elected governments continuously perpetrate atrocities against my people all over the world. And your support of them makes you directly responsible, just as I am directly responsible for protecting and avenging my Muslim brothers and sisters. Until we feel security, you will be our targets. And until you stop the bombing, gassing, imprisonment and torture of my people we will not stop this fight. We are at war and I am a soldier. Now you too will taste the reality of this situation.

What is clear in this passage is that the man who would go on to kill both himself and others rejected the label of terrorist. In his own self-image Sidique Khan is a 'soldier' who is at 'war' in much the same way as Allied troops are engaged in the 'war on terror'. Indeed, in his reality it is the British State that is terroristic in its 'bombing, gassing, imprisonment and torture' of Muslims. This example lights up the subjectivity involved in constructing who or what is at risk and risky. In the testimony of Sidique Khan, the issue at stake is not only who is the aggressor, but also who is the transgressor. For him, the answer is the British State, for the British State the answer is radical extremists such as Khan. The tendency of politicians and security officials to simply dismiss the actions of individuals such as Khan as either mindless actions or the result of religious indoctrination results in a failure to engage with the expressed values and opinions regarding British domestic and foreign policy of young men such as Sidique Khan (see Gill, 2009: 155). In effect, the use of emotive pejorative terms, such as describing terrorists as 'evil' and 'monstrous' effectively forecloses debate about the motivational explanations of those conducting terrorist attacks.

Disregarding whether the acts of those inspired by Al-Qaeda can possibly be considered as just responses to the violence sanctioned by the British State in Muslim countries, it has to be conceded that there are a cluster of political reasons why extremist groups such as Al-Qaeda might want to attack countries such as the US, including: 'unflinching support for Israel's occupation of Palestinian territories, the continued assistance to authoritarian Arab regimes, and the expanded US military presence in the Middle East' (Ould Mohamedou, 2007: 10). Despite Al-Qaeda's unceasing claims to be fighting against 'western economic imperialism', neoliberal commentators have presented the 9/11 attacks predominantly as a senseless act of malice disconnected from any political intent (see Riedel, 2008: 5; Lilleker, 2006: 200). As Beck (2009: 12) reasons, the generalization of terror threat has not only raised public anxieties but also led to dilemmas of definition: 'it is increasingly difficult to make a clear and binding distinction between hysteria and deliberate fear-mongering, on the one hand, and appropriate fear and precaution, on the other'. As we shall see in Chapter 4, the 'threat imagination' of world risk society is not only accentuated, it begins to act as a motor for intervention. The dominating prevalence of discourses of terrorism – and, moreover, security practices – form part of a broader arc of disciplinary control through which citizens are encouraged to adhere to governmental objectives and bring themselves to order:

> One could argue that . . . various governments – certainly in the US and in Britain – have attempted to . . . incite and seduce the public by manipulating the emotional responses to September 11 in order to direct conduct. The narrative of war was used to construct the very idea of a 'war on terror' and to unify public opinion behind the various strategies designed to wage this war.
>
> (Burkitt, 2005: 685)

We cannot assume, of course, that members of the public passively accept the ideologies embedded in the discourse of the WOT. Nevertheless, the political ramping up of the terrorist threat has coincided with public perceptions of a sizeable and growing risk. Opinion polls conducted in the UK in 2011 show that over 75 per cent thought that terrorist attacks in Europe would increase in the next three years, with only 8 per cent estimating that they would decrease (see Anderson, 2011: 27).

In our view, the intertwined discourses of 'new terrorism' and the 'war on terror' provide a doctored representation of the present that is often pitched out with historical and/or geopolitical context. Peters (2004: 7) suggests that 'the representation of political violence as *terrorism* – its narrativization and its embodiment as a discourse – reifies it, cutting it off from other forms of violent behaviour and often disguising or preventing examination of claims to political legitimacy'. Such a myopic approach fails to pay attention to the explanations for action given by those engaging in political violence. It erases the importance of acknowledging and investigating the inherently political nature of terrorism, whether it is utilized by State or by non-State actors (see Poynting and Whyte, 2012: 3). Yet the tendency to remove politics from understandings of *non-State* violence is not a novel phenomenon. It should be remembered that a range of methods of violence has been developed by the British State in the course of empire building over centuries. While Islamist terrorist groups directly state that their actions are a response to the violence of Western nation states, such explanations cannot be let in to the uniform discourse of the WOT, which seeks to vanquish ambiguity and denies historical antecedents. This failure to recognize the role of the past in shaping contemporary political violence is noted by Whittaker (2012) who discusses the tendency to a-historicize terrorist attacks and the frequent failure to recognize 'precipitants', i.e. salient events and processes that precede attacks and act as drivers for violent action. To this end, the imperialist ventures of the past impact both in terms of intra-nation conflicts and in terms of anti-Western sentiment in parts of Africa and the Middle East. Interventions made long ago – such as the 1917 Balfour declaration and the separation of Palestine in 1922 – have produced reverberations that continue to the present day. The observations made by Fromkin (1989: 565) in the 1980s are no less relevant today:

> The settlement of 1922, therefore, does not belong entirely to the past; it is at the very heart of current wars, conflicts, and politics in the Middle East, for the questions that Kitchener, Lloyd George, and Churchill opened up are even now being contested by force of arms, year after year, in the ruined streets of Beirut, along the banks of the slow-moving Tigris-Euphrates and by the waters of the Biblical Jordan.

Despite erasing unpleasant colonial histories, the ideological nature of security discourses surrounding State violence and the use of military force is not lost on those involved in modern governance. Given both public unpopularity and the failure to meet prescribed objectives during military missions in Iraq and Afghanistan, the term 'war on terror' is now less frequently used by politicians and policy makers, though it remains prevalent in the media. In both the United States and the United Kingdom strategic attempts were made to mute the war on terror and to adopt alternative phraseology. In March 2009 the United States government under Barack Obama altered the name of military operations from the 'Global War on Terror' to the more anodyne moniker 'Overseas Contingency Operation' (OCO), with the

President requesting that Pentagon staff refrain from using the former term. Somewhat earlier in April 2007 Tony Blair's successor, Gordon Brown, publicly abandoned the use of the phrase 'war on terror', similarly advising cabinet ministers to cease using the nomenclature (see Reynolds, 2007).

Geopolitics, power and State terrorism: risk hypocrisies

While media, academic and political interest has been concentrated on the actions and possible plans of groups such as Al-Qaeda, as our earlier discussion suggests, it is important to acknowledge that States themselves frequently resort to the use of force to achieve their objectives (see Jackson *et al.*, 2009; Mason, 2012). It should be remembered that terrors are practised, witnessed and felt in and through both the 'asymmetrical' wars of the present and the 'regular' wars of the past. Stohl (2012: 45) reminds us that, if we are to consider terrorism as an act in which intentional violence is used that produces fear in the victim and/or community then it is reasonable to suggest that States can be, and indeed frequently are, terroristic. Further, as Whittaker (2012: 335) points out, 'most states engaged in terrorism choose to do so. They take into account the price they will be required to pay for their activity, in exchange for the benefits gained by the attainment of their policy goals'. Insofar as the State reserves the legal right to use violence in warfare, well over 100 million people perished in warfare over the course of the twentieth century (see Green and Ward, 2004: 1; Eagleton, 2000: 15). Further, while the First and Second World Wars led to huge losses of soldiers in battle, the civilian death toll from 'regular' war has risen markedly in more recent conflicts. In the first decade of the twentieth century 90 per cent of war casualties were soldiers. In the ninety-three wars between 1990 and 1995, the same percentage was civilian casualties (see Society Matters, 2004). In effect, advances in technology and new modes of warfare have shifted the risk from soldiers to civilians. During the course of the war in Iraq, 179 British troops died, compared to an estimated 130,000 civilians.

Aside from wars begun on dubious mandates, Carrabine *et al.* (2009: 435) remind us that, 'state officials can legitimately kill, injure, intimidate and torture people'. History demonstrates that States are capable of impressing terror on populations through a range of violent practices, including genocide, warfare, assassinations, threats by paramilitaries and so-called death squads (Martin, 2013: 85). The killing of over 100,000 Kurdish Iraqi citizens by Saddam Hussein in the Al-Anfal campaign and the 30,000 left-wing activists 'disappeared' by successive right-wing States in Argentina serve as examples of acts of terrorism that are neither morally legitimate nor legitimated under international law (see Boyle, 2013: 93). As Wilson (2013: 33) points out, State terrorism is no aberrational lapse in the modern State, but rather one of its modes of operation. Nevertheless, there remains a discernible tendency in the media and in academia to draw attention to State political violence wielded by non Western States rather than to focus on those enacted somewhat closer to home. Recent European history is rich with examples of counter-terrorism policies and strategies of violence that have been bloody and barbaric – from Spain's dirty war to the paramilitary executions undertaken in Northern Ireland (see Ciocchini and Khoury, 2012; Stohl, 2012). Thus, many of the practices and techniques of violence used by terrorist groups are also deployed by the State under the guise of counter-insurgency or counter-terrorism measures. It is beyond doubt that the violence enacted by the State has killed and injured more people than have terrorist groups (Poynting and Whyte, 2012: 1). We have referred elsewhere to situations where the State reproduces the very behaviours it claims to be fighting against in the name of security as 'risk hypocrisies' (Mythen and Walklate, 2012). To explore this concept in the context of the WOT we wish to illumine four controversial practices: detention without charge, extraordinary rendition, torture and the use of weaponized drones.

While the British and American governments reproached Saddam Hussein for detaining Kurdish citizens without charge or trial, since 9/11 an alarming number of citizens have been, and remain, detained without charge at the behest of the UK and the US State. In the US, a spike in this practice occurred directly after 9/11 with the US government rounding up and arbitrarily detaining over 1,000 people whose profiles and details the government refused to make publicly available (see Chomsky, 2003). Under the extensive powers enabled by the PATRIOT Act, the US State subsequently arrested and incarcerated hundreds of people – largely of Middle Eastern descent – in notorious 'fishing expeditions', without levelling formal charges, allowing the possibility of application for bail or offering the prospect of a trial (see Welch, 2006). Since 9/11 around 775 prisoners – rights stripped and identities reduced to the status of 'enemy combatant' – have been held under repressive conditions without charges at the infamous military prison situated at Guantanamo Bay. Some of those that remain detained at the Camp have now been imprisoned for over a decade. In the UK, aside from those detained in Iraq to whom we will return to shortly, over fifty suspected terrorists were held indefinitely without charges being heard at Belmarsh prison, prior to this practice being declared illegal in 2004.

In addition to infinite detention, the shadowy practice of 'extraordinary rendition' has been publicly exposed. So far as formal explanations go, extraordinary rendition is described as a strategy of gleaning information from terrorist suspects using a variety of methods of interrogation (see Gough *et al.*, 2011: 4). In practice, it involves the kidnap, detention and movement of terrorist suspects to countries where the threshold for the use of violence by the State is low (Gill, 2006: 24). Once in situ, suspects are subjected to a mix of intense questioning and 'enhanced interrogation techniques' – read torture – by intelligence agents. Despite denials by the British State, it has since been established that aircraft used explicitly by the CIA in extraordinary renditions have flown in and out of UK territory over 200 times since the 9/11 attacks (see Norton-Taylor, 2010). Aside from the objectionable moral bankruptcy of extraordinary rendition, in such cases the credibility of intelligence leading to intervention is critical. The logic behind the practice of extraordinary rendition is that torture can be rendered legally permissible and used in attempts to gain information from suspects in countries with diminished protection of human rights. Over and above this, many of the people held at Guantanamo Bay have claimed that various forms of torture were a regular part of imprisonment, including beating, whipping, water boarding, sleep deprivation, sexual humiliation and forced exposure to pornography. US military documents made public in the recent Wikileaks disclosure of 400,000 military field reports reveal systematic abuse of prisoners by US and UK troops. What is shocking is both the range of methods of serious abuse and torture and the sheer number of cases that were simply stamped 'no further investigation required' (see Iraq Warlogs, 2010: 2). In the case of UK forces, allegations have emerged about the use of torture against prisoners held in a military interrogation centre near Basra. Over 200 former inmates brought high court proceedings alleging that Joint Forces Interrogation Team systematically subjected them to food and sleep deprivation, sensory deprivation and threats of execution. The ex-prisoners claim they were sexually humiliated by female soldiers, beaten, forced to kneel in stress positions for up to 30 hours and subjected to electric shocks (Cobain, 2010). In the well-publicized case of Binyamin Mohamed, the appeal court released CIA intelligence that showed that MI5 were aware that he had been subjected to inhumane and degrading treatment (see Taylor-Norton, 2010). The appeal court also rejected the subsequent demand by the government and security services that any evidence of the State's knowledge about the treatment of Guantanamo Bay inmates must be suppressed in a civil case. The recent decision to award UK citizens previously incarcerated in Guantanamo Bay compensation packages to prevent the case going to court amid claims of maltreatment seems at odds with the British State's denial that its agents and soldiers had no knowledge of torture being used. This decision does little to assuage the concerns of those that believe that torture was practised and sanctioned by the UK military and secret services. In each of these cases we find the very actions and behaviours attached to terrorists and defined as amoral by Western States being enacted by Western nation States and/or their representatives.

The risk hypocrisies that emerge around indefinite imprisonment, extraordinary rendition and torture are also present in the increasing use of armed drones. Drones are aerial vehicles guided by computers or by remote control by military personnel. Although drones have been used extensively for surveillance, it is their use for dispatching bombs that has proven to be controversial. As drones are unmanned, a ground controller must sanction the release of weapons. Drones have been used in military combat for some time by the United States and have been deployed as a military tool to implement so called 'surgical strikes' designed to target specific individuals or groups. They have been used by the US government in many countries including Somalia, Yemen, Pakistan and Afghanistan and there have been a number of high profile terrorists killed by drone attacks, including Baitullah Mehsud and Wali ur Rehman (see Awan, 2013). For advocates, the appeal of drones is not only their apparently precise dispatch of missiles, but also the fact that they eliminate the possibility of military casualties on the part of the aggressor. In effect death and injury is sought at no risk to the party exacting violence. Yet a series of legal complaints have been raised about the deployment of drones. Aside from the legality of entering the airspace of other countries and dropping bombs on their territory, the biggest controversy has been around the number of civilian casualties that are caused as a consequence of drone attacks. A joint report by the Stanford International Human Rights and Conflict Resolution Clinic and the Global Justice Clinic (2012) estimates that between 2,541 and 3,450 people have been killed in drone attacks with 844 of these being innocent civilians. Further, UN Human Rights Special Rapporteur Ben Emmerson recently reported that at least 2,200 people have been killed in Pakistan alone by drone strikes in the last decade. More disturbingly, Emmerson estimates that around 600 of these were not combatants but ordinary citizens. It is clear that Barack Obama has sought to mobilize the use of drones as a less costly military alternative to ground troops, with a threefold increase in the use of drones recorded between 2008 and 2011 (see Kibbe, 2012). Public pressure has mounted on President Obama to explain the continued use of drones and in May 2013 he signed a document that outlined guidelines for the use of force against terrorists and stated the need for 'near-certainty' that civilians would not be killed or wounded before drone strikes are sanctioned (see Saul, 2013). The extensive loss of life as a direct result of such attacks is not only unacceptable, it also produces negative psychological side effects for populations that are forced to live in fear of future attacks. So far as international relations are concerned, weaponized drone attacks are thus likely to exacerbate rather than reduce hostilities against the West (see Awan, 2013).

So, although Western capitalist States proclaim the right to retain a monopoly on the use of violence this does not mean that their actions should be exempt from scrutiny or challenge. Indeed, quite the opposite. It is beyond refute that many aspects of the war on/against terrorism both domestically and internationally flout basic human rights and contravene established legal statutes (see Beck, 2012: 48). The processes and practices of indefinite detention, extraordinary rendition and torture are clear examples of the capability of Western capitalist States to diminish human rights, enact violence, deliberately inflict pain and suffering, and to instil fear in populations. As Miller and Sabir (2012: 13) suggest: 'the adoption of counter-insurgency doctrine and practice in counter-terrorism by the British state results in a series of measures and practices that bear more than a passing resemblance to "terrorism" as officially defined by the UK government'. As Bauman (2006: 107) observes, attempting to fight terror with war appears to be something of 'a contradiction in terms'. However, the discourse of 'new terrorism' and the 'war on terror' has permitted the State to pursue a weighty military agenda internationally while simultaneously deflecting attention away from exceptional law and order measures, and systematic State violence; arguably the root causes of political violence. At a wider level, the ideology underpinning the WOT has demonized Muslims, attempted to legitimize torture by magnifying deviance and had 'the ideological effect of further normalizing the perception of its Muslim targets as the enemy of everything that free societies embody' (Evans, 2011: 73). There is a palpable need to factor the role of Western governments more firmly in to discussions about the production and escalation of terrorism (see Jackson *et al.*, 2009). This requires first recognizing that States such as Britain and America are both capable of committing violence that is terroristic and, second, acknowledging that they are capable of deploying (counter) terrorism as a political tool to secure governance and reinforce control. As the State becomes inured to moving 'beyond the law' (Gill, 2009: 154), claims made regarding the protection of 'liberty' and 'security' are thrown into sharp relief. At a time in which the tendency towards spin and political manipulation of information is pronounced, it is more important than ever that abuses of power are revealed and that forms of State denial are themselves refuted (see Cohen, 2001; Welch, 2006). Following Hillyard (2009), we will go on to argue in Chapter 5 that there is more than enough evidence to suggest that the UK and the US governments can reasonably be described as 'exceptional states'. The expansion of law, the increased use of informal measures of control, mass surveillance and the willingness to act either outside or against law all attest to this. Turning Hillyard's (2009) phrase about face, Agamben (2005) refers to 'states of exception' to describe the creeping presence of practices that derogate from the normal rules of law. These appear in many guises, from times at which legal regulations are suspended to extra-legal measures in which the State deviates from proscribed procedures to de facto states of exception where the State does not seek to suspend or replace extant laws but instead acts in direct contravention to them. In the chapter that follows we will be providing concrete examples of 'exceptional states' producing 'states of exception'.

Conclusion: whose war, whose terror?

We have argued that a palette of contestable knowledge claims underpin the discourse of 'new terrorism' and the permission it grants both for the militaristic 'war on terror' and the suspension of normal rights and liberties. Despite the contradictions inherent in the new terrorism thesis, the propensity among intelligence experts and securocrats to imagine 'a kind of sea monster intent on leaving tsunami-like destruction in its wake' (Ericson, 2008: 60) has encouraged politicians in power bound spaces to implement extreme and draconian countermeasures. It needs to be acknowledged that the hyperbolic tenor of the WOT transcended the discursive and has produced monumental material consequences. As Jackson (2005: 9) observes: 'language and practice . . . are inextricably linked: they mutually reinforce each other'. In highlighting the coming together of ideas and actions, our analysis of the modes of violence utilized by the State leads us to question whether counter-terrorism measures are exclusively designed to combat terrorism or whether other social control and coercive agendas are being smuggled into policy, such as the hegemonic aspiration to spread Western liberal values across the globe (see Loader and Walker, 2007: 85).

The war on terror fails to engage with the root causes of terrorism conducted by Islamist extremist groups, including economic and cultural imperialism, military violence by Western nations in Muslim countries, endemic poverty and weak structures of national governance. Within such a context, the use of pejorative absolute terms such as 'evil' effectively forecloses debate about the root causes of terrorism. Casting terrorists as beyond reason, the discourse of the war on terror dissolves any possibility of establishing dialogue with non-State groups using violence. By limiting the focus of terrorism on non-State rather than State actors, Western nation States routinely become positioned as victims rather than aggressors (see Poynting and Whyte, 2012: 1). It is estimated that almost 260,000 people have lost their lives as a direct consequence of the international war on terror – more than perished in the Second World War (see Cornwell, 2011). With this statistic in mind, the claim that the war on terror would make the world a safer place looks as fantastical as it is fallacious. Indeed, it is quite likely that the wars in Iraq and Afghanistan have rendered Western nations more rather than less vulnerable to terrorist attacks (see Hartley, 2009: 17; Thiel, 2009). As Young (2009: 151) provocatively puts it:

> The truth is that there is little to objectively distinguish between normal warfare and terrorism except for the level of power and legitimacy which State agents have over their less powerful opponents: the worry is that it is the imaginary difference that is used to justify 'normal' violence.

It is vital that the British State recognizes the cultural, religious and political values that drive the actions of those willing to resort to terrorist attacks. Groups such as Al-Qaeda have made clear their objections to 'western economic imperialism'. Regardless of their veracity, these are rarely aired in political or media circles, nevermind debated (see Lilleker, 2006: 200). Unless there is serious engagement with the historical role of the West in creating the conditions of anger and resentment that fuel terrorism, both domestically and internationally, it is unlikely that the current cycle of violence will be broken. In defining and approaching 'terrorism' as a protean enemy, the British and US government have failed to grasp the discrete histories of particular conflicts between State and non-State actors. The hopelessly general, haphazard and haplessly executed war on terror is an indication of the State's failure to acknowledge diverse power struggles and to tackle the underlying drivers of political violence. In reducing terrorism to a singular object to be defeated by force, the grievances of non-State groups using violence – including colonial exploitation, economic imperialism, religious bias and geopolitical exclusion – are concealed.

This creation of the 'enemy', uniformly understood and unifying in its intent, bears a remarkable similarity with the uniform and unifying use of risk and understandings of 'riskiness' found within academic discourses generally and criminology in particular. Yet, given the questions that the events of the twenty-first century pose for criminology as a discipline, it is arguably uniquely placed to give voice to the contradictions that 'new terrorism' and the 'war on terror' contain. These contradictions are not lost on Chomsky (2003: 7): 'we cannot address terrorism of the weak against the powerful without also confronting the unmentionable but far more extreme terrorism of the powerful against the weak'. Taking heed of Chomsky's caveat, it is important that criminology seeks to engage with the political economy of states of exception and the way in which they may be driven by complex motives that extend beyond the search for 'security'. If we begin to think of human security in the round, the annual number of casualties from terrorist attacks is firmly put in perspective when set against the harm and destruction caused by malnutrition and starvation (see Jackson, 2005: 92). The huge disparity in spending on national security as against foreign aid by 'advanced affluent' nations tells its own tale about which regions count. As Sachs (2007: 2) asked in the fourth of his Reith Lectures: 'how can we choose, as we do in the United States, to have a budget request this year of $623 billion for the military – more than the rest of the world combined – and just $4.5 billion for all assistance to Africa and think this is prudent?' Given the capacity to draw across cognate disciplines, criminology and criminologists have the capacity to contest and redefine security. The casting aside of normal moral constraints to the use of violence, the underlying rationales that permit exceptional measures and the use of excessive force and torture by the State since 9/11 indicate that the redrawing of security should be assigned priority status.

References

Addicott, J. (2008) *War on Terror/War on Metaphor*. Israel: International Policy Institute for Counter-Terrorism.

Agamben, G. (2005) *State of Exception*. Chicago, IL: University of Chicago Press.

Anderson, D. (2011) *Report of the Independent Reviewer on the Operation of the Terrorism Act 2000 and Part 1 of the Terrorist Act 2006*. London: HMSO.

Awan, I. (2013) US drone attacks are further radicalising Pakistan. *The Guardian*, June, 2: 9.

Badiou, A. (2012) *In Praise of Love*. London: Serpents Tail.

Bauman, Z. (2006) *Liquid Fear*. Cambridge: Polity Press.

BBC News Online (2012) Desmond Tutu calls for Blair and Bush to be tried over Iraq. 2 September. Available at: www.bbc.co.uk/news/uk-19454562 (accessed 14 January 2014).

Beck, U. (2002) On World Risk Society. *Logos*, 1(4): 1–18.

Beck, U. (2009) *World at Risk*. Cambridge: Polity Press.

Beck, U. (2012) *Twenty Observations on a World in Turmoil*. Cambridge: Polity.

Blair, T. (2001) *Speech at Labour Party Conference*. Blackpool, 2 October.

Blair, T. (2005) *Speech to Parliament*. London, 5 August.

Bourke, J. (2006) *Fear: A cultural history*. London: Virago.

Boyle, J. (2013) The case of Saddam Hussein's terror against the Kurds and the international response. In G. Duncan (ed.) (2013) *State Terrorism and Human Rights*. London: Routledge, pp. 73–102.

Burkitt, I. (2005) Powerful emotions: Power, government and opposition in the war on terror. *Sociology*, 39(4): 679–95.

Bush, G. (2002) *Speech on Iraq*. Cincinnati, 7 October.

Bush, G. (2001) *Speech to Joint Session of Congress*. Washington, 20 September.

Callincos, A. (2005) Anti-war protests do make a difference. *Socialist Worker*, 1943: 2–3.

Carrabine, E., Cox, P., Lee, M., Plummer, K. and South, N. (2009) *Criminology: A sociological introduction*. London: Routledge.

Chomsky, N. (2003) *Power and Terror: Post 9/11 talks and interviews*. New York: Seven Stories.

Ciocchini, P. and Khoury, S. (2012) The war on terror and Spanish state violence against Basque political dissent. In S. Poynting and D. Whyte (eds) *Counter-terrorism and State Political Violence*. London: Routledge, pp. 178–98.

Cobain, I. (2010) Iraqi prisoners abused at UK's Abu Ghraib. *The Guardian*, 6 November: 4.

Cohen, S. (2001) *States of Denial: Knowing about atrocities and suffering*. Cambridge: Polity Press.

Connell, R. (2007) The northern theory of globalization. *Sociological Theory*, 25(4): 368–85.

Cornwell, H. (2011) War on terror set to surpass costs of Second World War. *The Independent*, 30 June: 6.

Durodie, B. (2004) The limitations of risk management: Dealing with disasters and building social resilience. *Argang*, 8(1): 14–21.

Eagleton, T. (2000) *The Gatekeeper*. London: Vintage.

Ericson, R. (2008) The state of preemption: Managing terrorism through counter law. In L. Amoore and M. de Goede (eds) *Risk and the War on Terror*. London: Routledge, pp. 57–76.

Evans, J. (2011) Politics, stereotypes and terrorism: The politics of fear in liberal democracies. *International Journal of Interdisciplinary Social Sciences*, 6(5): 71–8.

Fairclough, N. (2003) *Analysing Discourse: Textual analysis for social research*. London: Routledge.

Fischhoff, B. and Kadvany, J. (2011) *Risk: A very short introduction*. Oxford: Oxford University Press.

Fromkin, D. (1989) *A Peace to End All Peace: The fall of the Ottoman Empire and the creation of the modern Middle East*. New York: Henry Holt.

Furedi, F. (2002) *Culture of Fear: Risk taking and the morality of low expectation*. London: Continuum.

Gill, P. (2006) Not just joining the dots but crossing the borders and bridging the voids: Constructing security networks after 11 September 2001. *Policing and Society*, 16(1): 27–49.

Gough, R., McCraken, S. and Tyrie, A. (2011) *Account Rendered*. London: Bitebook.

Green, P. and Ward, T. (2004) *State Crime: Governments, violence and corruption*. London: Pluto Press.

Hartley, K. (2009) Defence R&D data issues, *Defence and Peace Economics*, 17(3): 169–75.

Hillyard, P. (2009) The exceptional state. In R. Coleman, J. Sim, S. Tombs and D. Whyte (eds) *State, Power, Crime*. London: Sage, pp. 129–45.

Holloway, D. (2008) *9/11 and the War on Terror*. Edinburgh: Edinburgh University Press.

Iraq Body Count (2014) Available at: www.iraqbodycount.org (accessed 7 January 2014).

Iraq Warlogs (2010) *The Guardian*, Special Supplement. 23 October.

Jackson, R. (2005) *Writing the War on Terrorism*. Manchester: Manchester University Press.

Jackson, R., Murphy, E. and Poynting, S. (2009) *Contemporary State Terrorism: Theory and practice*. London: Routledge.

Joffe, H. (1999) *Risk and the Other*. Cambridge: Cambridge University Press.

Keppel, G. (2009) *Beyond Terror and Martyrdom: The future of the Middle East*. Boston, MA: Harvard University.

Kibbe, J. (2012) Conducting shadow wars. *Journal of National Security Law and Policy*, 5: 373–92.

Laqueur, W. (2000) *The New Terrorism: Fanaticism and the arms of mass destruction*. Oxford: Oxford University Press.

Lilleker, D. (2006) *Key Concepts in Political Communication*. London: Sage.

Loader, I. and Walker, N. (2007) *Civilizing Security*. Cambridge: Cambridge University Press.

McGarry, R., Mythen, G. and Walklate, S. (2012) The soldier, human rights and the military covenant: A permissible state of exception? *International Journal of Human Rights*, 16(8): 1183–95.

Maras, H. (2013) *Counterterrorism*. New York: Jones and Burlington.

Martin, G. (2004) *The New Era of Terrorism: Selected readings*. London: Sage.

Martin, G. (2013) *Essentials of Terrorism*. New York: Sage.

Mason, V. (2012) No permission to shoot in Gaza. In S. Poynting and D. Whyte (eds) *Counter-terrorism and State Political Violence*. London: Routledge, pp. 116–39.

Miller, D. and Sabir, R. (2012) Counter-terrorism as counterinsurgency in the UK war on terror. In S. Poynting and D. Whyte (eds) *Counter-terrorism and State Political Violence*. London: Routledge, pp. 12–32.

Mythen, G. and Walklate, S. (2012) Global terrorism, risk and the state. In S. Hall and S. Winlow (eds) *New Directions in Criminological Theory*. Cullompton: Willan, pp. 317–32.

National Security Strategy Report (2010) *A Strong Britain in an Age of Uncertainty*. London: HMSO.

Norton-Taylor, A. (2010) Guantánamo payout deal is climax of years of denials of UK role in rendition. *The Guardian*, 16 November.

Ould Mohamedou, M. (2007) *Understanding Al Qaeda: The transformation of war*. London: Pluto Press.

Peters, M. (2004) *Postmodern Terror in a Globalized World*. Glasgow: University of Glasgow Press.

Pilger, J. (2012) The great game. In S. Poynting and D. Whyte (eds) *Counter-terrorism and State Political Violence*. London: Routledge, pp. 85–96.

Poynting, S. (2010) Render unto Caesar. *Criminal Justice Matters*, 82: 14–15.

Poynting, S. and Whyte, D. (2012) Introduction: Counter terrorism and the state. In S. Poynting and D. Whyte (eds) *Counter-terrorism and State Political Violence*. London: Routledge, pp. 1–11.

Reynolds, P. (2007) Declining use of war on terror. *BBC News Online*. 17 April. Available at: http://news.bbc.co.uk/1/hi/uk_politics/6562709.stm (accessed 10 January 2014).

Riedel, B. (2008) *The Search for Al Qaeda: Its leadership, ideology and future*. Washington, DC: Brookings.

Rose, N. (2000) Government and control. *British Journal of Criminology*, 40: 321–39.

Sachs, J. (2007) Economic Solidarity for a Crowded Planet, *Reith Lecture 4*. BBC: London.

Said, E. (1978) *Orientalism*. New York: Pantheon.

Saul, H. (2013) Pakistan claim 400 civilians killed by drone strikes and asks US to release death toll figures. *The Independent*. 19 October.

Sciullo, N. (2012) On the language of counter terrorism and the legal geography of terror. *Willamette Law Review*, 48: 317–41.

Slovic, P. (2000) *Perception of Risk*. London: Earthscan.

Society Matters (2004) Volume 6. Open University: Buckingham.

Stanford International Human Rights and Conflict Resolution Clinic/Global Justice Clinic (2012) *Living Under Drones: Death, injury and trauma to civilians from US drone practices*. New York University/Stanford University.

Stohl, M. (2012) Can States be Terrorists? In R. Jackson and S. Sinclair (eds) *Contemporary Debates on Terrorism*. London: Routledge.

Suskind, R. (2006) *The One Percent Doctrine*. New York: Simon & Schuster.

Taylor-Norton, R. (2010) Just how big is the terrorist threat? *The Guardian*, 17 September. Available at: www.theguardian.com/commentisfree/2010/sep/17/terrorism-speech-head-security (accessed 15 April 2014).

Thiel, D. (2009) *Policing Terrorism: A review of the evidence*. London: The Police Foundation.

Tombs, S. and Whyte, D. (2008) *Safety Crimes*. Cullompton: Willan.

van Brunschot, E. and Kennedy, L. (2008) *Risk, Balance and Security*. London: Sage.

Welch, M. (2006) Seeking a safer society: America's anxiety in the war on terror. *Security Journal*, 19: 93–109.

Whittaker, D. (ed.) (2012) *The Terrorism Reader*. London: Routledge.

Wilson, T. (2013) State terrorism: A historical overview. In G. Duncan (ed.) *State Terrorism and Human Rights*. London: Routledge, pp. 14–32.

Young, J. (2009) *The Vertigo of Late Modernity*. London: Sage.

4

COUNTERING TERRORISM?

Risk, pre-emption and partial securities

> We live in times where the injunction is to render the future actionable, where all high impact, low probability events are imagined and acted upon as certainties.
>
> (Amoore, 2013: 157)

Introduction

As discussed in Chapter 3, in response to attacks in New York, Washington and London, the British and the American State jointly espoused and adopted an activist international approach to terrorism, pursuing aggressive militaristic policies against and within countries thought to harbour terrorist groups. As we shall see in this chapter, pre-emptive policies have also been favoured in terms of the internal management of national security. Further, the discourse of 'new terrorism' has similarly underpinned changes in domestic crime and security policy driving the implementation of a range of counter-measures. We will argue here that a clear shift in the logic of risk assessment can be discerned among politicians, security practitioners and criminal justice professionals, involving a move away from retrospective estimations of harm to an outlook based on futurity that prioritizes worst-case scenarios (see Amoore, 2013; Amoore and de

Goede, 2008; Aradau and van Munster, 2008; Mythen and Walklate, 2008). Thus, having focused largely on the internationalization of the terrorist threat in previous chapters, in this chapter we wish to examine some of the impacts and effects of domestic counter-terrorism policies, specifically those based on the logic of anticipatory risk. In order to provide a concentrated account of the impacts of lingering 'what if' questions, we will direct our attentions to examples and cases from the United Kingdom. First, we will seek to highlight the joins between measures designed to combat the global war on terror and domestic law and order policies. In this discussion we argue that the attempt to 'govern through terrorism' can be traced in the execution of anti-democratic legislation affecting domestic policing, detention and surveillance. Second, we contend that, in addition to underpinning the war on terror, the discourse of new terrorism connects with a broader politics of risk that is disproportionately directing social policies and potentially hiking up security fears among members of the public. Embedded within these connections is a preoccupation with pre-emptive policies and practices. As we shall see, the turn to pre-emption not only has ramifications for counter-terrorism practices, it also raises questions about the wider balance in society between liberty and security. This, of course, is the dilemma posed by Bell (1979) over thirty years ago.

In order to broach how the connections identified above manifest themselves, we will draw upon particular examples that bring to the surface some of the contradictions that emerge when the State seeks to use modern law to control future crimes. To concretize these contradictions, we draw on evidence from empirical work we have been involved in that has focused on the effects of counter-terrorism legislation on specific groups defined as risky. In our discussion of this evidence we emphasize the threats to free speech and civil liberties experienced by those unfairly rendered suspect. Extending our analysis from the direct effects of legislation to the broader social consequences of risk labelling, we finish by discussing the ways in which pre-emptive counter-terrorism measures both endanger justice at a macro level and inhibit security at the micro level.

Risk and regulation: the creeping presence of the future

The logic of risk has had an inexorable rise in both academic criminology and criminal justice practices (see Ericson and Haggerty, 1997; Mythen and Walklate, 2008; O'Malley, 2010). Following on from the discussion begun in Chapter 1, it is arguably in the realm of counter-terrorism that the anticipatory aspects of risk have been most visibly stretched. In the context of counter-terrorism, the specified goal of pre-emptive policies is to decrease the level of risk by disrupting and apprehending those seeking to use violence before harms material-ize. Pre-emption thus refers to the institutional tendency to intervene in cases where risk of harm is inexact or unspecified, on the proviso that waiting for things to happen presents a grave threat to public safety (see Maras, 2013: 127). Zedner (2007: 259) puts it this way: 'pre-emption stands temporally prior to prevention of proximate harms: it seeks to intervene when the risk of harm is no more than an unspecified threat or propensity as yet uncertain and beyond view'. Under the logic of pre-emptive risk early action is necessary in order to protect the rights of the many, even if this should result in reducing the civil liberties of a minority of people. This logic of trading off lost individual liber-ties in favour of greater collective security has been commonly inscribed in policy, as indicated in the UK National Security Strategy (2012: 23): 'to protect the security and freedom of many, the State sometimes has to encroach on the liberties of a few: those who threaten us'.

Notwithstanding problems around how the few are distinguished, it is not just the State that provides cues about risk and steers on security. As Beck (2009: 39) notes, the 'staging and expectation of catastrophe' is a defining characteristic of media culture in the modern world, especi-ally where security is concerned. Alongside the threat levels defined by intelligence agencies, the media serves as a cultural apparatus for imagining the future: from news stories about failed plots to infotain-ment programmes and documentaries speculating about the kind of weaponry that may be used in future attacks. Further to these creative activities, the political pronouncements of politicians are vital in the social construction of the terrorist threat. Interestingly, these pro-nouncements have been decidedly inconsistent over the last decade:

characterized by a contradictory mix of frank disclosure, denial, leaks to the media and speculation about upcoming dangers (see Mythen and Walklate, 2006a). This rather jumbled approach across State agencies has led to the production of a fair amount of confusion and a blurring of the boundaries between the real and the imaginary. In such conditions of 'hyper-riskality', in which the imagined risk becomes more 'real' than the material threat, the possibility of injustices occurring is considerable (see Mythen and Walklate, 2010).

In tracing the recent history of security vistas, the 9/11 Commission's reference to a lack of foresight in imagining the kinds of attacks that may transpire in the future was significant in motoring a shifting calculus of risk. What was considered to be a failure of imagination has led to a shift in the management of security away from retrospective estimations of harm towards futuristic prediction. As Hudson and Ugelvik (2012: 9) observe: 'unlike the normal logic of risk management, precautionary logic does not entail actuarial calculations of the likelihood of the disastrous event occurring, its mere possibility is sufficient to bring forth preventive actions'. It is these preventive actions that we will turn to shortly. Since 9/11 what Vedby-Rasmussen (2004) refers to as the 'presence of the future' can be glimpsed across a range of political, academic and cultural representations of the threat. A plethora of worst-case possibilities have been verbally and visually imagined, including air strikes against nuclear facilities, the detonation of radiological dispersal devices in urban areas and malicious contamination of public water supplies (see de Goede, 2008: 156). As noted in Chapter 3, the language of the leaders of nations that have spearheaded the war on terror has constantly drawn attention to the catastrophic future that may ensue if the threat is not tackled robustly in the present.

The pre-emptive turn in the regulation of security is thus underpinned by the *representational* practices of pre-mediation: politics, policy – and, by implication, some arms of the academy – and the media. National counter-terrorism legislation, coercive foreign policy and military incursions are all ideationally underpinned by pre-imagined harms of the future. There are many perils to be alert to in this regard, particularly when fears about worst-case scenarios rather than evidence of them begin to inform policy making. What are the limits and boundaries to our imaginaries? How far should securocrats travel in trying to envisage and predict the future? What if the sea monsters described by Ericson (2008) turn out to be but sea urchins? Clearly, we should make some kind of differentiation and acknowledge that horizon-scanning activities will always have their place in security management. Hypothetical scenarios are doubtless useful tools in training police and emergency services to be prepared to respond to unusual attacks. Nevertheless, in our view, risk imaginings are not a sensible basis for modifying counter-terrorism law. If ideational projections of worst-case scenarios filter into material forms of regulation we can expect the securitization of more or less anything and everything (Salter, 2008: 251).

What is interesting in the case of pre-emptive modes of risk management is the coalescence between the conceptual interpretations of changing security practices among theoreticians and the explanations of politicians involved in policy making at the sharp end. So much did the ideological terrain shift in terms of what was acceptable in regulating the (imagined dystopic) future, that Tony Blair's defence regarding the invasion of Iraq at the Chilcott Inquiry was based around the conviction that we live in dangerous times that require the application of a 'new calculus of risk'. Curiously, the idea of a changing calculus of risk had previously been debated in academic circles, albeit in more critical terms (see Beck, 1995; Mythen and Walklate, 2006b). Although the degree of hyperbole around terrorism has lessened since the departures of Blair and Bush, the logic of anticipatory risk remains pivotal in counter-terrorism strategy. In addition to embarking on international military exploits, in the first decade of the twenty-first century the governance of British security was reconstituted through several rafts of legislation, including the Terrorism Act (2000), the Anti-Terrorism, Crime and Security Act (2001), the Prevention of Terrorism Act (2005), the Terrorism Act (2006) and the Counter-Terrorism Act (2008). Although it might be argued that all laws are intended to deter would-be offenders and reduce future risks, it is the preventive angle of regulation that has been most explicitly developed in recent legislation. The introduction of new offences such as glorification of terrorism, acts preparatory to terrorism, and giving and receiving terrorist training signify attempts to intervene early in the cycle before would-be terrorists launch attacks. Such precautionary powers have been welcomed by senior police officers and intelligence agents persuaded that pre-emptive measures are necessary to enhance public safety (see Parker, 2013). This is constitutive of a sizeable shift in the management of security and, as we shall evidence, one that hampers and ostracizes citizens who find themselves classified as risky.

As the quote cited earlier from the UK National Security Strategy highlights, while neoliberal States have prided themselves on the commitment to secure the safety of all citizens, such pledges have become contingent and conditional rather than absolute. What is rendered explicit in such statements is a process of de-responsibilization by which the State distances itself from guaranteeing fundamental human rights and gravitates toward policies that sanction reductions in rights for some as a necessary sacrifice to protect the safety of others. Such justifications for exceptional measures often involve attempts at ideological incorporation that appeal to 'in' groups and strive to convince the majority that measures will only affect a dangerous minority to which they do not belong and should be mindful of. As such, the State is involved in an hegemonic effort to create a clear divide between a safe 'us' and a dangerous 'them' whose rights, by definition, cannot be compared with 'ours'. In this sense, access to security and the principle of justice are being recast as partial and contingent not absolute and non-derogable. How is this state of partial securities put to work?

Practising pre-emption: unpicking domestic security strategies in Britain

In as much as policies of prevention and pre-emption have had a growing presence in several areas of crime control over the last two decades – notably antisocial behaviour, street robbery and sexual offences against minors – it is in the realm of counter-terrorism that they have featured most frequently. Given our broader objectives, it is not possible to analyse either the drivers or the effects of the wide range of counter-terrorism legislation introduced in the United Kingdom in the twenty-first century. What we do wish to do is to illuminate specific aspects of pre-emptive legislation that have become statute and to consider their impacts on the values and behaviour of groups subjected to them.

The reams of counter-terrorism legislation introduced in Britain between 2000 and 2008 have been historically unprecedented and the subject of heated debate (see Kibbe, 2012; Miller and Sabir, 2012). Amid the furore, it has been laws based on the principle of pre-emption that have proven to be the most controversial (see McCulloch and Pickering, 2009; Zedner, 2009). Arguably the most contentious pre-emptive measures have been stop and search powers permitted under Section 44 of the Terrorism Act (2000), the crime of glorification of terrorism established under the Terrorism Act (2006) and the extension of the period of detention without charge also brought in under the Terrorism Act (2006). As we shall see, the legitimacy of each of these measures has been legally contested. Before we specifically discuss Section 44, it should be noted that stop and search powers have a long and controversial history that predates their enshrinement in counter-terrorism law. Stop searches were first introduced under the Police and Criminal Evidence Act (1984) in direct response to a series of disturbances in British cities. Building on these initial powers, Section 60 of the subsequent Criminal Justice and Public Order Act (1994) allowed a police officer to stop and search a person 'in anticipation of violence' provided that the search takes place in an area that has been pre-authorized by the police as dangerous or in which violence has or appears likely to occur. Aside from questions of effectiveness, widespread complaints have been raised over many years about the inordinate use of these forms of intervention on black and minority ethnic individuals. The debate continues among criminologists concerning the extent to which such interventions are proportional or not – that is proportional with the ethnic composition of the wider population or proportional with those who are available to be subject to such interventions (see Parmar, 2011; Waddington *et al.*, 2004). The statistics on the rate of stop and search under Section 60 shows that black people are, on average, around 11 times more likely to be stop searched than whites (Runnymede Trust, 2010). Section 44 of the Terrorism Act (2000) went a step further than the existing Section 60 powers, permitting police officers to search individuals without recourse to 'reasonable suspicion' that an offence either has been committed or is being planned. Under Section 44, permission was granted to stop and search any person in designated zones without requiring grounds for so doing. In an attempt to cast a wide net, sizeable areas such as Greater London were classified as areas in which people could be stopped and searched without suspicion. In as much as no formal directive was issued to target specific ethnic populations, various sets of statistics on Section 44 show that the powers were inordinately deployed against black and Asian people, particularly those from Pakistani and Bangladeshi communities (see Kundnani, 2009; Pantazis and Pemberton, 2009). The policy of ramping up the use of stop and search in the years directly after the 7/7 bombings does not appear to have resulted in successful apprehension of individuals involved in terrorism. Home Office statistics show, for instance, that over 100,000 people were stopped and searched under Section 44 counter-terrorism powers in 2009–10 without a single arrest resultantly being made for terrorism related offences (Cobain, 2010).

It is apparent that the overuse of Section 44 powers has resulted in a form of racial profiling that has criminalized entire communities. Aside from the prejudicial way in which Section 44 has been operationalized by the police, the powers have transpired to be problematic at a legal level. Way beyond the formal goal of countering terrorism, political protestors, photographers, journalists and tourists have all been illegitimately stop searched under the powers. Interestingly, it was ultimately a case brought to the European Court of Human Rights by Kevin Gillan and Pennie Quinton – a journalist and a peace activist respectively – that led to the powers being declared illegal. Both had been subject to stop searches under Section 44 while travelling to a demonstration against an arms trade fair. The court ruled that article 8 of the European Convention on Human Rights had been broken and that the powers were insufficiently circumscribed providing inadequate legal safeguards against abuse. Following on from the judgement by the European Court in 2010, a Counter-Terrorism Review commissioned by the Home Office reported that Section 44 should be repealed and in 2011 the British government announced that stop and search powers would be reviewed. In 2012, Section 44 was replaced by the Protection of Freedoms Act, which permits a senior police officer to designate an area for stop and search without suspicion only if it can be reasonably surmised that an act of terrorism is likely to occur. This act is unnervingly similar to a policy recently adopted in Denmark, as we shall discuss in Chapter 5.

In addition to the emotional impact on innocent individuals subjected to stop searches, relations between black and minority ethnic (BME) communities and the police have become strained (see Spalek and Lambert, 2008). As intimated above, such complaints are not new. They have a legacy that pre-dates 9/11. However, as Diprose *et al.* (2008: 274) point out, while the ambition of pre-emptive strategies is to enhance security and control, they may actually serve to increase tensions, accentuating rather than attenuating the risk of violence. While debates about the iatrogenic effects of counter-terrorism legislation rumble on, we should be aware that the processes of risk regulation that British Muslims have been subjected to are not unique and have historical precursors. Stuart Hall and colleagues (1978) produced a detailed account of the ways in which the State was using exceptional processes and procedures in an attempt to maintain social control in a time of crisis. The crisis they analysed was that of street mugging, largely denoted as a crime committed by 'Blacks' in the British media. Hillyard's (2009) work detailing the treatment of Irish Catholics in the late 1960s and early 1970s draws similar conclusions regarding the deleterious effects of stereotypical assumptions and policing of populations. So too does McGovern (2010) in his comparative study of Irish Catholics and British Muslims. What this work reminds us is that the introduction of draconian legislation, utilization of repressive and illegitimate forms of social control, and the tendency to wield brutal force indiscriminately are not unique attributes of the contemporary State.

Returning to more contemporary examples of pre-emptive legislation, in addition to stop and search powers, the Terrorism Act of 2000 allowed the forty-eight-hour detention limit to be raised to seven days with the permission of the courts. This period was doubled to fourteen days in 2003 and then doubled to a maximum of twenty-eight days under Section 25 of the Terrorism Act 2006, again subject to approval from judicial authorities. Following on from the 7/7 attacks, the UK government led by Tony Blair lobbied to raise the maximum permissible time for detention without charge to ninety days. It is important to recognize that Britain stands out as anomalous in the length of its pre-charge detention period in comparison with other countries threatened by terrorism. The maximum permissible period of detention without charge in the United States is two days, in Spain it is seventy-two hours and in Italy twenty-four hours. In effect, detention without charge null and voids the ancient right of *habeas corpus* and shifts the assumption of presumption of innocence until proved guilty to presumption of guilt unless innocence can be proven (see Zedner, 2009). The emergence and consolidation of what Hudson and Ugelvik (2012: 8) describe as a 'preventive state' lays waste to the presumption of innocence in favour of pre-emptive intervention. At a sweep, defending against the imagined catastrophic future permits the removal of basic rights and freedoms in the present. Given that the threshold for levelling terrorism related charges has been reduced with the introduction of offences such as glorification of terrorism, it is difficult to appreciate why such long periods were placed on the statute, despite being infrequently used. One commonly used justification in recent years has been the 'ticking bomb scenario' beloved in popular media in which a terrorist suspect is thought to possess information that could prevent a large-scale attack from occurring. Although it remains debatable whether lengthier periods of detention would actually enable interrogators to extract useful information, this scenario has served as a powerful metaphor dredged up to defend various 'states of exception' ranging from secret surveillance to torture. History shows that exceptional measures justified as permissible as a temporary response to security crises tend to become permanent over time. In other words, what began as the exception soon becomes the norm (see McCulloch and Pickering, 2009). The policies and practices described above are emblematic of a broader drift toward pre-emption in policing and surveillance. Nevertheless, it is important to appreciate that this process of securitization is partial and has diverse consequences. To this end, we would argue that, as well as a state (condition) of partial security existing, we can also discern a State (institution) of partial securities which permits the rights of 'risky' communities to be suspended or removed, while 'safe' communities retain standard privileges.

Prevention of terror or terrors of pre-emption?

Research undertaken by academics since 9/11 indicates that Muslims have been subjected to a range of hostilities including Islamophobic abuse (Allen, 2010), media stereotyping (Abbas, 2011: 130) and racist attacks (Frost, 2008). While ethnic minorities in the UK have historically suffered the consequences of institutional racism, since 9/11 Muslim minority groups have been widely constructed as risky in media and political discourse. Following the 2005 bombings in London, this process of stigmatization – often articulated through fears about 'home-grown' terrorism – intensified. A range of studies have demonstrated that since the 9/11 attacks, Muslims have been the target group identified in counter-terrorism in terms of legal measures, surveillance, policing and security policy (see Pantazis and Pemberton, 2009; Poynting and Mason, 2006). Yet it is clear that aspects of discrimination have involved misguided assumptions about race as well as faith. As Spalek (2008: 25) points out, post 9/11 it was not only British Muslims that were attacked, harassed and victimized but also Hindus and Sikhs, whose attackers had presumed them to be Muslims on account of their skin colour and/or appearance. The suspicion experienced by Muslims in the public sphere has been vectored through a range of coercive interventions, including air stewards removing passengers from planes, security guards forcibly escorting young men from shopping centres and non-Muslims refusing to occupy train carriages with Muslims. Coupled with the security interventions sanctioned by the State, and the victimization and harassment experienced by Muslims in the public sphere, this has led to an environment of anxiety and distrust (Bauman, 2006: 123). Contradictorily, at the same time as facing tangible forces of stigmatization and exclusion, British Muslims have been exhorted to help in the fight against terrorism by proactively surveying their own communities and confronting those possessing extremist ideas. But how is this surveillance enforced practically at a policy level?

The UK's overarching counter-terrorism strategy named CONTEST comprises four interconnected strands of activity: Pursue, Prevent, Protect and Prepare. The first two of these strands are very much configured around the principle of pre-emption. While elements of the Pursue strategy have been documented, in light of the contradiction highlighted above, the Prevent initiative is worthy of further analysis. The Prevent strand of CONTEST constitutes the UK government's response to radicalization. The Prevent strategy (2011) is constituted by five goals. The first is to challenge violent extremism by utilizing moderate voices to combat destructive ideology. The second is to disrupt extremism and to challenge any organizations or individuals who seek to promote it. The third goal is to support individuals that are deemed susceptible to extremism. The fourth objective is to increase local communities' resilience to extremists and the fifth is to tackle the grievances felt by local communities. Since its inception in 2007–08 it is fair to say that Prevent has been extremely controversial (see Heath-Kelly, 2012; Kundnani, 2009; Thomas, 2012). Although the present iteration of the Prevent strategy formally seeks to tackle all kinds of extremism, including that of the far right, in practice it has been areas with large Muslim populations that have been party to initiatives under Prevent. The aspiration underpinning Prevent is to challenge the ideas that underpin extremism and make terrorism attractive to some. By exhorting Muslims in particular to proclaim violence as illegitimate and to align with core British values, the objective of Prevent is to discourage religious extremism and prevent radicalization from occurring while promoting moderate forms of Islam. Pitched as an attempt to win the 'hearts and minds' of Muslim Minority Communities, the Prevent strategy has been widely maligned with many objections being raised against both the policy and its practices (see Miller and Sabir, 2012: 21). In effect, Prevent has sought to co-opt individuals within and outwith Muslim communities to both survey those communities and to attempt to affect behavioural change in those that may be attracted to radical Islam (see Kundnani, 2009). In the first instance, it has been argued that individual Muslims have been targeted indiscriminately with the consequence that hundreds of thousands of innocent civilians have been wrongly suspected and surveyed (see Miller and Sabir, 2012: 13). Second, processes of data gathering set in train under Prevent clearly infringed civil liberties with youth workers, teachers and religious leaders being asked to gather and share personal data about young people, including their friendship groups, sexual preferences and religious commitments (see Dodd, 2010). Third, the focus of Prevent was unerringly on Muslim communities rather than other non-Muslim communities where far right extremism has been largely allowed to flourish unimpeded by intervention (see McGhee, 2010: 36). Fourth, the particular types of pre-emptive intervention have been criticized with young children being classified as risky often on account of the histories of other family members or peers (see Kundnani, 2009). The creep of risk looms large in Prevent with individuals being designated not so much as risky, but as at risk of being risky (see Heath-Kelly, 2012). PREVENT

On a more positive note, some of these problems produced by the first iterations of the Prevent policy have since been acknowledged, with the coalition government reworking the policy it inherited from Labour: 'the *Prevent* programme we inherited from the last Government was flawed. It confused the delivery of Government policy to promote integration with Government policy to prevent terrorism' (Prevent Strategy, 2011: 8). Further, a Communities and Local Government select committee stated that the Prevent programme had 'stigmatized and alienated' British Muslims (Dodd, 2010). Nevertheless, the new version of Prevent has itself been subject to further criticism with the surveillant angles seemingly increased and the community cohesion aspects receding (see Awan, 2013; Thomas, 2013). What is more, as we shall see, much of the damage caused by ill thought through policies such as Prevent has already happened. Arguably, Prevent is somewhat typical of rather schizophrenic policy making by the State, which, on the one hand targets Muslims as threats to national security, while on the other asking for their assistance in the ideational battle against extremism. Spalek (2008: 181) observes that the type of surveillant citizenship demanded of British Muslims under policies such as Prevent places them in a challenging and uncomfortable position:

Muslims' responsibilities as active citizens have increasingly been framed by anti-terrorist measures that encourage internal community surveillance so that the responsible Muslim citizen is expected to inform the authorities about the activities, suspicious or perceived to be suspicious, of their fellow community members, and actively help deal with any potential extremism.

Here we see that the tentacles of responsibilization have ramifications for both the community and the self, throwing out contradictory and mixed messages about the security and protection of minority groups in contemporary society.

Managing an enforced risk identity: performing security

In support of this point, and to reinforce some of the problems regarding specific aspects of counter-terrorism legislation described earlier, we wish to present some of the findings of a qualitative study conducted with young Muslims aged 18–25 in the North West of England (see Mythen, 2012a; Mythen, 2012b; Mythen *et al.*, 2013). The study was designed to investigate the impacts and effects of dominant security discourses and changing counter-terrorism practices on the values, behaviour and perspectives of participants. By giving voice here to the perspectives of some of our participants, we hope to give precedence to the experiential aspects of securitization that are often overlooked in the clamour to build new theories and concepts. For the purposes of illustration we touch briefly here on three prevalent processes discussed across focus groups and subsequent in-depth interviews: risk subjectification, checking and hushing.

In many respects, risk subjectification describes the core process of stigmatization through which Muslims are constructed as dangerous. This process is diffuse, permeating many social spheres including the media, politics, education, policing and welfare. Through the process of risk subjectification Muslims become multiply defined as a 'suspect population' with recourse to racial, religious and/or ethnic traits, rather than on the basis of dubious or questionable behaviour. Through the process of risk subjectification respectful and law-abiding people become defined as dangerous by virtue of sharing some or other of the characteristics of the 'typical' terrorist:

> *Qasim*:   That's what they're doing, profiling anyone who fits the Muslim stereotype and persecuting them. So if you're Asian-looking, you've had it.

A layer beneath this, participants in our study made reference to the impacts of specific aspects of policy, such as Section 44 stop and search and the glorification of terrorism. Insofar as the surveillant gaze was experienced ubiquitously in the public sphere, direct stop and search interventions by the police were frequently cited as an unjust and tiresome hindrance for male participants:

> *Ameen*:   Can I just give a personal experience, yeah? Going into college I was stopped and searched. That was for no reason whatsoever other than that I'm a Muslim. It makes you . . . uhm . . . obviously I've nothing to hide, I've nothing to fear. I answered all the questions they asked me because there was no reason for me not to. But it does kind of make you feel a little bit, you know . . . even though I'm not scared of the police, every time you see them now you think: 'shit'. You just try and put your head down and walk on because you know that they're looking at you. And nine times out of ten they are looking. When they stop you they look through your bag and ask what you've got. People are walking by and watching it and then you're standing at the bus stop with that person or getting on the train with them.
>
> *Abid*:   I got stopped in Manchester once. It was around that whole 9/11 thing. My brother got stopped three times in one day. In one day. Just for random stop and search. In the end he completely lost the plot with the coppers and they threatened to put him in a cell so he had to calm down. Three times in one day!

Ameen's personal recollections indicate the complexities for the self generated by such interventions and the troubling process of having to deal with guilt, which is both implicitly and explicitly imposed. Further demonstrating frustration about the collective attribution of risk towards Muslims, the following exchange between Taj and Yasmin indicates the connectivity between processes of stigmatization, uncertainties regarding the boundaries of counter-terrorism legislation and processes of self-censorship:

> *Taj*: There are radical elements in all religions, so why persecute us all? Most – nearly all – Muslims stand against the use of violence, but that's not to say we don't understand the reasons why. They've succeeded in shutting us up; people are too scared of the consequences that might happen. All it takes is saying the wrong thing in front of the wrong person, where it's taken as encouraging terrorism, then who knows what might happen and that's the thing that scares me, not just what might happen to me but those I care about.
>
> *Yasmin*: You're right; you have to be so careful now . . . anything can be understood as glorifying terrorism. Remember what happened to the guy demonstrating against the blasphemous cartoon, he said the wrong thing and then he's in prison for supposedly encouraging other people to commit violence. So now there is two types of free speech, one for Muslims and one for everyone else.

This interchange between Taj and Yasmin is indicative of a process of hushing through which Muslim voices and opinions are tempered or silenced out of anxieties about falling foul of the law. As Hina and Anita go on to explain, fear of being criminalized for expressing a political viewpoint can hinder free speech:

> *Hina*: You do have to be careful now about what and where you say things in case you get arrested. Although I don't think it's right to do anything that encourages people

> to injure someone else, you have to be able to protest against things you don't agree with.
>
> *Anita*: You've got to be careful, just in case. You never know who's listening to you, in case they misinterpret what you're saying. It's not right, but that's the way things are now.

As these discussions indicate, one of the central problems created by the introduction of pre-emptive counter-terrorism offences such as 'glorification of terrorism' and 'indirect encouragement' is that they are loosely defined and open to broad interpretation. This definitional imprecision has rendered such laws difficult to apply with certainty in the courts (see Zedner, 2009: 132). Aside from complications of jurisprudence, one of the outcomes of oblique counter-terrorism laws has been uncertainty about what is a legitimate political perspective and what might constitute an incitement to terrorism and result in committing a criminal offence. The indeterminacy associated with not being certain about the boundaries of free expression meant that many of the young people we spoke to had made the decision to err on the side of caution and to keep their political views private. In addition to problems arising out of stop and search and glorification of terrorism, some participants such as Zaf expressed alarm about the impact of pre-emptive forms of regulation on Muslims in general:

> *Zaf*: As far as policy goes, it's supposed to be pre-emptive. Basically means they can pretend they've got information to do what they want. So at home they can lock you up for three months and in the Middle East you can have pre-emptive strikes because there are imaginary weapons of mass destruction. Muslims just can't win. It's a complete attack on so many levels; you may as well give in. Pre-emptive means that they don't have to prove that you are guilty. So it's guilty until proven innocent for Muslims. Now if you think of it like that, it shows that we don't even have the same rights as anyone else. Everyone else is innocent until proven guilty.

In each of the focus groups we ran, examples were given by participants about an intensified level of scrutiny in the public sphere and the feeling of being surveyed for signs of dangerousness. This chimes with Zedner's (2009: 149) observation: 'the exceptional security measures once thought necessary only in zones of highest risk (like airports and borders) have spilled over into ordinary life and ordinary places'. The frustrations of being classified as threatening and having to negotiate a tainted identity had produced for many participants various dramaturgical displays of safeness, including specific sartorial choices, avoiding carrying particular risky objects such as rucksacks and keeping a trimmed rather than a long beard (see Mythen *et al.*, 2013). The pervasiveness of the process of risk subjectification results in Muslims having to negotiate and manage enforced risk identities and the associated mental and physical challenges associated with this. In our studies participants described various forms of self-surveillance that they undertook in order to transmit safeness. These actions are resonant with Foucault's observations regarding the conduct of conduct induced by disciplinary discourses:

> Conduct is the activity of conducting (conduire) of conduction (la conduction) if you like, but it is equally the way in which one conducts oneself (se conduit), lets oneself be conducted (se laisse conduire), is conducted (set conduit) and finally, in which one behaves (se comporter) as an effect of a form of conduct (une conduite) as the action of conducting or of conduction (conduction).
>
> (Foucault: 2009: 193)

As a result of the process of risk subjectification and in direct response to the risky status that had been projected onto them, some participants had adopted practices of 'checking' and 'hushing' to demonstrate their 'safeness' and/or to reduce the possibility of experiencing racially motivated victimization. We define 'checking' behaviours as those where self-inspection leads to the conscious performance of self-restraint. Checking behaviours materialized in assorted forms, including the selective use of dialect, alterations to physical and sartorial displays and the curbing of outward behaviour in the public sphere. These practices of self-censorship extend well beyond what might be considered routine practices of reflexivity common to patterns of identity building in modern life and are troubling for at least two reasons. First, checking responses are coerced and restrictive in that they are born out of concern about victimization, criminalization and retribution. Second, hushing practices infer that, for some young Muslims, freedom of speech is being impeded. The conversation between Rehana and Shams succinctly encapsulates some of the personal dilemmas and frustrations generated by checking and hushing:

> *Rehana*: It makes me feel like I have to watch what I say and work harder to show I'm not like that. I resent that.
> *Shams*: But why should we have to prove we're alright?

It is this requirement to present an outwardly safe identity that reveals the coercive social pressures that a pervasive climate of suspicion has engendered. The risk society inhabited by the young British Muslims of Pakistani origin that we spoke to seemed a different world from that inhabited by white non-Muslims. It is disconcerting that, in formally democratic liberal nations, individuals from minority groups are inhibited to articulate legitimate political perspectives and feel obliged to censor their opinions. Regrettably, practices of checking and hushing are manifestations of a latent view that both freedom of speech and protection from persecution were not principles that participants either experienced in practice, or felt they could rely on. So, a paradoxical situation has occurred for many young Muslims in the UK, where they simultaneously find themselves defined as risky while personally feeling *at risk*. Despite their relative safeness – in terms of probability of offending – prevailing political discourses and security practices that fix them as dangerous serve to increase their vulnerability to assault, abuse and unwarranted questioning. As a consequence of being located in this ambiguous position – at once defined as 'risky' while simultaneously feeling at risk – 'checking' and 'hushing' behaviours can be interpreted as attempts to face off the tag of dangerousness and to achieve relative safety in the light of not inconsiderable threats to personal security. It is perhaps the very elasticity of applications of risk and security by the State that enables counter-terrorism powers to be inadequately circumscribed. As we have argued, legal interventions designed to bolster security can lead to reductions in human rights for some groups.

The tangible short-term consequence of pre-emptive securitization around terrorism in Britain at least has been an undoubted deterioration in the relationship between Muslim communities and the police. Mutual cooperation between minority communities and the police can only be founded on relationships of trust (Spalek and Lambert, 2008). Besides eroding relations between Muslim minority groups and the police in the short term, the anger and resentment produced by 'early interventions' and 'target hardening measures' have fuelled feelings of injustice and social marginalization. In this sense the implementation of pre-emptive counter-terrorism measures may have more severe long-term ramifications, 'impeding effective intelligence and contributing to a general drift towards, rather than away from, support for violent Islamism' (Thiel, 2009: 2).

Conclusion: a State of partial security?

In this chapter we have focused on the way in which a climate of suspicion generated about and around Muslims coupled to the implementation of exceptional pre-emptive policies invokes acts of self-surveillance on behalf of those rendered risky to deflect stigma and reduce the probability of victimization. Thus, rather than the narrow notion of security advanced by the State – commonly boiled down to prevention of crime or countering terrorist attacks – we would advance a more expansive notion of security. In the findings presented here, it becomes clear that the 'security' sought by the State is partial rather than absolute, conditional rather than granted. Security for some often comes at the expense of the security of 'others'. We have thus argued here that a double-edged *State of partial security* exists in contemporary Britain. For those possessing profiles that are considered safe, security is granted. For 'others' who are ascribed risky identities, safety and protection cannot be guaranteed. To this end, the neoliberal promise of universal security appears now to be laid on sands that have shifted. The eminence of this partial approach to security produces some rather knotty issues that require unpicking.

First – and in the light of fatal errors in policing and intelligence – we would want to ask about the evidential basis for determining just who it is that threatens us and just how sure we need to be before forceful interventions take place. In this regard, it is important to note that the application of methods of pre-emption and pre-crime may formally be designed to aid prevention, but they do not automatically lead to it. As McCulloch and Pickering (2010: 33) note: 'prevention is an outcome while pre-crime and pre-emption are strategies. Pre-empting threats through pre-crime laws translates into prevention only if the laws are effective'. The regrettable cases of Forest Gate and Stockwell illustrate well the perils of legally sanctioned but ill-informed pre-emptive interventions (see Coleman and McCahill, 2011: 138; Smith, 2012). Second, the operationalization of security policies that envisage a generic and ethnically explicit 'other' have raised concerns about the erosion of civil liberties for minority groups labelled as risky (Mlodinow, 2009: 191). Essentially, securitizing practices that operate differentially determine who 'has the right to have rights' (McGhee, 2010: 93). Third, the dragnet policing of suspect(ed) communities has alienated and angered many people that the police and intelligence services hope to rely on to provide information about extremist behaviour, hence a 'failed and friendless' Prevent policy (see Thomas, 2010). Fourth, when, by the State's own definition, the 'us' – those that uphold their social rights and responsibilities and behave lawfully – are wrongly classified as suspect on the basis of racial and ethnic characteristics and erroneously categorized as 'them' – we need to ask what 'security' and 'justice' actually mean in the modern age.

It is probable that the pre-emptive turn in security management – around terrorism but also in other areas of crime control – will lead to the further expansion of the surveillant assemblage and a widening of the public spaces in which security operates. Although premediations are performative entities, they can be wielded to justify and sanction undemocratic coercive practices. In many respects such forms of regulation can be conceived as acts of sovereign power by the State in that they function 'by authorizing acts that have the force of law even when they do not adhere to the rule of law' (Amoore, 2013: 13). At present, the political offering of a safe future good life is replaced by a vision of dystopic insecurity. Consequently, it is imperative that criminologists seek to deconstruct both the logic of pre-imaginings of harm and their substantive outcomes. As States have sought to bolster national security post 9/11 the personal rights of suspected groups have been eroded (Zedner, 2007). If the pursuit of security comes at the expense of human rights, then not only is the quality of that security compromised, but the very principles of democracy are undermined. To ensure that social justice is upheld, it is imperative that pre-imaginings of harm and the emergent security regimes taking shape through the 'What if?' prism are scrutinized evidentially and contested politically. The palette of pre-imaginings of harm around terrorism not only denote attempts to persuade the public about the legitimacy of State coercion, but also act as forms of dramaturgy that simulate the resolution of the future in the present. The contemporary definitional struggle over terrorism is thus not only about the immediacy of the here and now, but also over how the future is imagined, by whom and with which ideological objectives.

In conclusion, it is important that we monitor the diffusion and transference of exceptional measures, counter terrorism legislation and State violence. The military force actioned in the war on terror and the panoply of exceptional counter-terrorism measures implemented have palpable ramifications for the criminal justice system. With tongue only just in cheek, Steinert (2003: 271) remarks: 'we will soon see "pre-emptive strikes" against crime and hear justifications of "collateral damage" as "regrettable but unavoidable"'. Thus, academically, there is then a need to broaden out understandings of violence within criminology and to further probe the ways in which the State uses, justifies and perpetuates violence (see Pantazis and Pemberton, 2009; Tombs and Whyte, 2008). At a legal level, what has occurred in the last decade is the appearance of laws that break laws – or, in Ericson's terms 'counter-laws' (2008). This tendency – most pronounced in the USA and Britain – of bypassing or violating existing law by introducing new laws works on the twisted principle that 'legal order must be broken to save the social order' (Hebenton and Seddon, 2009: 346). What Ericson describes as 'laws against law' not only undermine existing statutes but serve as an emblem of a cynical and anti-democratic tendency. In effect, repressive counter-laws effectively act as holding mechanisms until they are declared illegal when new temporary measures are put in place, themselves later to be declared illegal. As with the fallout from the war on terror, the breakdown in trust between Muslim minority groups (MMGs), the State and the police has arguably heightened rather than reduced the risk of terrorist attacks in the near future (see Thomas, 2012).

In the chapter that follows we move our gaze away from the British domestic agenda and consider the ways in which the construction of those deemed to be risky transcends national boundaries. Exploring comparatively the ways in which riskiness has been constructed affords us the opportunity to return reflecting upon the parallels or lack of them, between social science thinking in general, and criminological thinking in particular, with the policies that have driven such constructions. This is particularly evident when we examine the presumptions that underpin some of the thinking that lies behind targeting those deemed to be risky: the routes into radicalization.

References

Abbas, T. (2011) *Islamic Radicalism and Multicultural Politics*. London: Routledge.

Allen, C. (2010) *Islamophobia*. London: Ashgate.

Amoore, L. (2013) *The Politics of Possibility: Risk and security beyond probability*. Durham: Duke University Press.

Amoore, L. and de Goede, M. eds. (2008) *Risk and the War on Terror*. London: Routledge.

Aradau, C. and Van Munster, R. (2008) Governing terrorism through risk: Taking precautions, (un)knowing the future. *European Journal of International Relations*, 13(1): 89–115.

Awan, I. (2013) Let's prevent extremism by engaging communities not by isolating them. *Public Spirit*. December Edition. Available at: www.public spirit.org.uk/the-importance-of-local-context-for-preventing-extremism (accessed 23 January 2014).

Bauman, Z. (2006) *Liquid Fear*. Cambridge: Polity Press.

Beck, U. (1995) *Ecological Politics in an Age of Risk*. Cambridge: Polity Press.

Beck, U. (2009) *World at Risk*. Cambridge: Polity Press.

Bell, D. (1979) *The Cultural Contradictions of Capitalism*. London: Heinemann.

Cobain, I. (2010) London bombings: The day the anti-terrorism rules changed. *The Guardian*. 7 July: 2.

Coleman, R. and McCahill, M. (2011) *Surveillance and Crime*. London: Sage.

de Goede, M. (2008) Beyond risk: Pre-mediation and the post 9/11 security imagination. *Security Dialogue*, 39(2): 155–76.

Diprose, R., Stephenson, N., Mills, C., Race, K. and Hawkins, G. (2008) Governing the future: The paradigm of prudence in political technologies of risk management. *Security Dialogue*, 39(2): 267–88.

Dodd, V. (2010) MPs demand investigation into Muslim spy allegations against Prevent. *The Guardian*, 30 March: 3.

Ericson, R. (2008) The state of pre-emption: Managing terrorism through counter law. In L. Amoore and M. de Goede (eds) *Risk and the War on Terror*. London: Routledge, pp. 57–76.

Ericson, R. and Haggerty, K. (1997) *Policing the Risk Society*. Oxford: Clarendon.

Foucault, M. (2009) *Security, Territory, Population: Lectures at the College de France 1977–1978*. Basingstoke: Palgrave Macmillan.

Frost, D. (2008) Islamophobia: Examining causal links between the state and race hate from below. *International Journal of Sociology and Social Policy*, 28(11): 546–60.

Hall, S., Crichter, C., Jefferson, T. and Roberts, B. (1978) *Policing the Crisis*. London: Macmillan.

Heath-Kelly, C. (2012) Reinventing prevention or exposing the gap? False positives in UK terrorism governance and the quest for pre-emption. *Critical Studies on Terrorism* 5(1): 67–85.

Hebenton, B. and Seddon, T. (2009) From dangerousness to precaution: Managing sexual and violent offenders in an insecure and uncertain age. *British Journal of Criminology* 49(1): 343–62.

Hillyard, P. (2009) The 'exceptional' state. In R. Coleman, J. Sim, S. Tombs and D. Whyte, (eds) *State, Power, Crime*. London: Sage: pp. 129–44.

Hudson, B. and Ugelvik, S. (2012) *Justice and Security in the 21st Century*. London: Routledge.

Kibbe, J. (2012) Conducting shadow wars. *Journal of National Security Law and Policy*, 5: 373–92.

Kundnani, A. (1999) *Spooked: How not to prevent violent extremism*. London: Commission for Racial Equality.

McCulloch, J. and Pickering, S. (2009) Pre-crime and counter terrorism: Imagining future crime in the war on terror. *British Journal of Criminology*, 49(5): 628–45.

McCulloch, J. and Pickering, S. (2010) Future threat: Pre-crime, state terror and dystopia in the 21st century. *Criminal Justice Matters*, 81: 32–33.

McGhee, D. (2010) *Security, Citizenship and Human Rights*. Basingstoke: Palgrave Macmillan.

McGovern, M. (2010) *Countering Terror or Counter-Productive?* Liverpool: Edge Hill.

Maras, H. (2013) *Counterterrorism*. New York: Jones and Burlington.

Miller, D. and Sabir, R. (2012) Counter-terrorism as counterinsurgency in the UK war on terror. In S. Poynting and D. Whyte (eds) *Counter-terrorism and State Political Violence*. London: Routledge: pp. 12–32.

Mlodinow, L. (2009) *The Drunkard's Walk: How randomness rules our lives*. London: Penguin.

Mythen, G. (2012a) Contesting the third space? Identity and resistance amongst young British Pakistanis. *British Journal of Sociology*, 63(3): 393–411.

Mythen, G. (2012b) No-one speaks for us: Security policy, suspected communities and the problem of voice. *Critical Studies on Terrorism*, 5(3): 409–24.

Mythen, G. and Walklate, S. (2006a) Communicating the terrorist risk: Harnessing a culture of fear? *Crime, Media, Culture: An International Journal*, 2(2): 123–42.

Mythen, G. and Walklate, S. (2006b) Criminology and terrorism: Which thesis? Risk society or governmentality? *The British Journal of Criminology*, 46(3): 379–98.

Mythen, G. and Walklate, S. (2008) Terrorism, risk and international security: The perils of asking what if? *Security Dialogue*, 39(2): 221–42.

Mythen, G. and Walklate, S. (2010) Pre-crime, regulation, and counter-terrorism: Interrogating anticipatory risk. *Criminal Justice Matters*, 81(1): 34–6.

Mythen, G., Walklate, S. and Khan, F. (2013) Why should we have to prove we're alright? Counter-Terrorism, risk and partial securities. *Sociology*, 47(2): 382–97.

O'Malley, P. (2010) *Crime and Risk*. London: Sage.

Pantazis, C. and Pemberton, S. (2009) From the old to the new suspect community. *British Journal of Criminology*, 49(1): 664–66.

Parker, A. (2013) *Speech by the head of MI5 to the Royal United Services Institute*. 8 October. Available at: www.rusi.org/events/past/ref:E5254359BB8F44 (accessed 25 January 2014).

Parmar, A. (2011) Stop and search in London: Counterterrorist or counterproductive? *Policing and Society*, 21(4): 369–82.

Poynting, S. and Mason, V. (2006) Tolerance, freedom, justice and peace: Britain, Australia and anti-Muslim racism since 11 September 2001. *Journal of Intercultural Studies*, 27(4): 365-91.

Prevent Strategy (2011) London: HMSO.

Runnymede Trust (2010) *Stop and Search Powers*. Available at: www.runnymede trust.org/events-conferences/econferences/ethnic-profiling-in-uk-law-enforcement/the-report/young-people-and-section-60/section-60-stop-and-search-powers.html (accessed 3 December 2013).

Salter, M. (2008) Risk and imagination in the war on terror. In L. Amoore and M. de Goede (eds) *Risk and the War on Terror*. London: Routledge: pp. 112–29.

Smith, G. (2012) Shoot-to-kill counter-suicide terrorism: Anatomy of undemocratic policing. In S. Poynting and D. Whyte (eds) *Counter-terrorism and State Political Violence*. London: Routledge: 33–48.

Spalek, B. (2008) *Reader in Ethnicity and Crime*. Buckingham: Open University Press.

Spalek, B. and Lambert, R. (2008). Muslim communities, counter-terrorism and counter-radicalization: A critically reflective approach to engagement. *International Journal of Law, Crime and Justice Studies*, 36 (4): 257–70.

Steinert, H. (2003) The indispensable metaphor of war: On populist politics and the contradictions of the state's monopoly of force. *Theoretical Criminology*, 7(3): 265–91.

Thiel, D. (2009) *Policing Terrorism: A review of the evidence*. London: The Police Foundation.

Thomas, P. (2010) Failed and friendless: The UK's 'preventing violent extremism' programme. *British Journal of Politics and International Relations*, 12: 442–58.

Thomas, P. (2012) *Responding to the Threat of Violent Extremism*. London: Bloomsbury.

Thomas, P. (2013) Preventing violent extremism under the coalition. *Public Spirit*. December Edition. Available at: www.publicspirit.org.uk/the-importance-of-local-context-for-preventing-extremism (accessed 23 January 2014).

Tombs, S. and Whyte, D. (2008) *Safety Crimes*. Cullompton: Willan.

UK National Security Strategy (2012) London: HMSO.

Vedby-Rasmussen, M. (2004) 'It sounds like a riddle': Security studies, the war on terror and risk. *Millennium – Journal of International Studies*, 33(2): 381–95.

Waddington, P., Stenson, K. and Don, D. (2004) In proportion: Race and police stop and search. *British Journal of Criminology*, 44: 889–914.

Zedner, Z. (2007) Seeking security by eroding rights: The side-stepping of due process. In B. Gould and L. Lazarus (eds) *Security and Human Rights*. Portland: Hart.

Zedner, L. (2009) *Security*. London: Routledge.

5

TERRORISM AND EXCLUSION

Risky subjects, suspect populations

If you see something, say something.

(Department of Homeland Security, 2010)

Introduction

In May 2013 people in the UK were presented with graphic media images of the attack that took place on serving soldier Lee Rigby in Woolwich, London. The rapidity with which the media labelled this a 'terrorist attack' was remarkable. This kind of response and the power of such labelling arguably contributed to, and fuelled, other headlines that followed in the wake of this event, such as 'Mosque attacked in Britain every three days since Lee Rigby's murder' (*International Business Times*, 2013). The murder of Lee Rigby occurred not long after the explosion of a bomb near to the finishing line of the Boston marathon on 15 April 2013, which killed three and injured over 250 people. The Boston marathon, as a global event, was widely reported in the media. In the immediate aftermath of these events the label 'terrorism' was resisted, though as more information came to light, the label 'terrorist' was deemed appropriate.

In each of the events referred to above, the role of the public was crucial both in the immediate response to what had happened to the victim(s) – and to the offenders in the case of the first example – as well as to the process of information gathering about the attacks themselves. Both events flag the importance of post-hoc eyewitness accounts for any investigative process and underlie the drive to actively involve the public in the management of terrorism – as echoed in the Department of Homeland Security's adage quoted above. This directive is not dissimilar to the UK government's calls for public vigilance to be found in their 'Preparing for Emergencies' document (see Mythen and Walklate, 2006). However, these two events and their coverage, in different ways, point to deeper structural issues that underpin the wider institutional and cultural drives inherent responses to them. Following on from some of the international issues addressed in Chapter 3 and the in-depth analysis of domestic responses to terrorism in Britain discussed in Chapter 4, in this chapter we wish to unravel some of the tensions that emerge when those deeper structural issues are brought to the surface. In so doing, it is important to develop an analysis that is sufficiently sensitive to comparative variations and similarities across different international contexts.

Of course, the quote taken from the Department of Homeland Security (DHS) puts to the fore the dilemma posed by terrorism for liberal societies discussed in Chapter 1: how to find a balance between civil liberties and the *appropriate* targeting of what is considered to be problematic behaviour in the maintenance of (State) security. The DHS is clear in its interpretation of seeing and saying. For them the focus is on *behaviour* not stereotypes. However this 'in principle' clarification does not necessarily translate into routine everyday practices either within the general population – as the headline from the *International Business Times* suggests – or perhaps more importantly among the professional organizations charged with implementing the policy of seeing and saying. Indeed, such policies themselves may equally reflect the reproduction of the unhelpful stereotypes discussed in Chapter 4. So, following on from this, unpacking the dilemma between civil liberties and the targeting of those thought to be problematic for civil liberties is of central importance for all societies who consider themselves to be embedded in the liberal democratic tradition. Against this backcloth, Hudson (2003: 74) remarks:

The balancing of rights has gone: the only rights that matter for most people are the safety rights of selves and loved ones. The sense of shared risk, shared responsibility has also gone: we cope with risk by a constant scanning of all with whom we come into contact to see whether or not they pose a threat to our security, and the only way we can operate this scanning is by adopting stereotypes of safe and risky kinds of people.

Hudson's observation leads us to reflect on how the practices around 'scanning' have been constructed, who is targeted by them, how such scanning is practised and what assumptions and challenges have become embedded in those practices. All of which enable a critical appreciation of what 'seeing and saying' entails. Following on from the data presented in Chapter 4, we wish to consider three elements integral to the process of 'seeing and saying': creating the suspected, targeting the suspected and making sense of the suspected. In the final section of this chapter we present the challenges posed by these responses for the 'suspected' themselves and by implication for the societies that have gone down this route in seeking security.

Creating the suspected

As earlier chapters have demonstrated, 11 September 2001 served as an important moment in terms of the ideational consolidation of binaries between the safe and the risky. It is worth remembering that, prior to 9/11, relatively little public attention was given to the activities of Al-Qaeda, though it is now evident that the Intelligence Services in the United States knew more than had been made publicly available (see Summers and Swann, 2011). Since this time, the Al-Qaeda network, and its cluster of associated terrorist inclined cells, have received almost permanent political and media exposure. For some historians and cultural commentators this activity is filling the vacuum left by the dissolution of the Cold War (e.g. Curtis, 2004; Oborne, 2006). As discussed in Chapter 3, the political line adopted by George W. Bush, Tony Blair and latterly in Britain by David Cameron embeds a reductivist construction of 'good' and 'evil'. This attempt to define opposing poles can be indexed to Joffe's (1999: 23) observations regarding the connections between blame and social fragmentation: 'In periods of crisis, when anxiety is raised, the out-group moves from being represented as mildly threatening, a challenge to the core values of the society, to being seen as the purveyor of chaos.' Of course in 2001, as Choudhury (2012) reminds us, Muslims were already at the forefront of political concern in the UK in the aftermath of the civil disturbances in the mill towns of the North West of England. These events contributed to a political narrative about the failure of multiculturalism and lack of community cohesion that required little pushing in the direction of rendering particular ethnic minority groups problematic. Consequently, in this 'Othering', Muslim minority groups have been systematically categorized as those to be feared. As Mythen *et al.* (2009: 740) note: 'while mundane risks have been attached to British Muslims as a collective, the profane risk of terrorism has been glued more firmly to young Pakistani males, thus cementing them as the risky other'. The extent to which such social labelling has produced wide political, policy and cultural ramifications is worthy of further discussion.

It should be remembered that, in the United States in particular in the immediate aftermath of 9/11, fear among the general public reached new heights. Forst (2011: 273) reports that members of the public:

> Bought millions of dollars worth of duct tape and gas masks, puzzled over the meaning of terror alert codes, and became extremely suspicious of men in turbans and women covering their heads with scarves. Four days after the 9/11 attack, a Sikh gas station owner, Balbir Singh Sodhi was shot and killed in Phoenix by a local resident who thought that Sodhi was a Muslim.

Despite the somewhat sweeping nature of Forst's comments, it is indubitably the case that certain policy responses have been driven by suspicion of the other (see Maira, 2009). After the 7/7 bombings in London, Tony Blair (2005), then British Prime Minister, made the following statement: 'This is a religious ideology, a strain within the worldwide religion of Islam, as far removed from its essential decency and truth as Protestant gunmen who kill Catholics or vice versa, are from Christianity.'

In these words we can observe the conflation of religion, violence and extremism and the construction of those to be suspected being given an unequivocal faith dimension. As elucidated in Chapter 4, these assumptions about dangerous faiths are inscribed in the highly maligned Prevent policy. Muslim minority groups become not only those not to be feared because of their ethnicity, they are also suspect because of their particular faith. It is this specific category of people about whom we should 'see and say'. These kinds of statements give political direction to a 'culture of suspicion' (Ericson, 2007) and the associated process of 'suspectification' (Hickman *et al.*, 2011). These processes and formations are harnessed not only politically but also in and by the media and in policy practices. Taken together, the constituent parts of this process afford the context in which the practices of targeting those suspected becomes both justified and justifiable. There is ample evidence to suggest that dominant media representations of Islam have dehumanized and demonized in equal measure, encouraging the public to accept a separation between safe and rational Western Christians and labile and risky Muslims. Chiming with the experiential narratives of Muslims detailed previously, Hickman *et al.* (2011: 17) comment that:

> The extensive coverage of the Muslim-related events, the focus on political and cultural issues, as well as the massive amount of coverage of the July bombings (which encompassed a question- ing of the place of Islam and Muslims in Britain) imply a deeply rooted and prevalent construction of Muslims as threatening in the British press.

In comparing the response to the IRA and Al-Qaeda, they suggest that:

> Whenever national security was at stake in the period under investigation, the government and parliament in office shared a

common self-understanding and appreciation of the role of state institutions, of the national interest, and of the control of violence. The urgent sense of risk and responsibility resulted in the passage of illiberal emergency measures couched in arcane references to a battle between good and evil. Despite divergences in political and ideological affiliation and the variable of time, Labour and Conservative governments similarly endorsed 'extreme' emergency measures in order to fight the 'extreme' methods of the terrorists.

(Hickman *et al.*, 2011: 13)

Given that dealing with the problems in Northern Ireland posed a continuous threat to security in Britain over four decades, it is no great surprise to find some continuity in political exaltations. Dominant security discourses exhibit perceptible continuities as the following quote illustrates: 'the most significant terrorist threat to the UK as a whole continues to come from Al Qaeda and those terrorist groups and individuals associated with it' (HM Government, 2011: 40, quoted by Choudhury, 2012: 29).

In the light of this ongoing continuity in political and media discourse around terrorism, there has been a resurgence of academic interest in the concept of 'suspect communities'. Hillyard's (1993) incisive analysis of the Prevention of Terrorism Act (1974) reminds us that under this legislation an individual is not a suspect because they are believed to have committed a specific offence. Rather, they become suspect because they are Irish. Thus:

In attempting to prevent the spread of political violence to Britain, anyone living in Ireland as well as anyone with an Irish background living in England can be seen as falling within a category of people who may legitimately be stopped. The Irish community as a whole can therefore be legally viewed as a suspect community.

(Hillyard, 1993: 33)

The striking parallels between the situation faced by Irish Catholics and British Muslims – in terms of labelling, suspicion, hostility and discrimination – are well captured by McGovern (2010) in a comparative qualitative study that brings to the surface a range of experiential similarities that cross the borders of faith. Revisiting Hillyard's concept, Pantazis and Pemberton (2009) suggest that the discriminatory practices evidenced against ethnic minority communities are resulting in a de facto dual system of justice not dissimilar to that experienced by those in Northern Ireland. Such a dual system of justice not only compromises democracy in the interests of security, in their view it also treats ethnic minority and Muslim groups as heterogeneous. Such a presumption provides the backcloth against which wider community relations are disrupted, assumptions about the process of 'radicalization' are made and permission to hate (such minority groups) is granted. While Greer (2010) has challenged this analysis both in relation to its evidential base and its conceptual efficacy – suggesting that there might be some mileage in talking about 'suspect locations' rather than suspect communities – there are deeper issues at play here that raise questions about how, who and why, the post 9/11 years have resulted in the perception of Muslim minority groups as being suspect.

The suspectification referred to above is evidenced by the bulk of sociological and criminological research undertaken among Muslim minority groups since 9/11. That work suggests that Muslims have been subjected to over a decade of intensified hostility. This has manifested itself in diffuse ways, from a rise in Islamophobic attitudes (Allen, 2010; Meer *et al.*, 2010; Poynting and Mason, 2007) to media stereotyping (Moore *et al.*, 2008), racially motivated violence (Allen and Nielsen, 2002; Frost, 2008) and inequitable counter-terrorism policing (Lambert, 2008; Mythen, 2008). Although ethnic minorities in Britain have long lived with the consequences of institutional racism, since 9/11 Muslim minority groups have persistently and pervasively been institutionally constructed as problematic and risky 'others'. Following the 7/7 bombings, this process of stigmatization accelerated further and impacted on young Muslim males in particular. As four of the men that committed the 7/7 attacks were British born Pakistanis, this demographic group has been regarded, particularly within media and intelligence circles, as the 'enemy within' (see Chalk, 2004; Evans, 2007). As David Cameron stated in 2011: 'the biggest threat that we face comes from terrorist attacks, some of which are, sadly, carried out by our own citizens'. It is important to note that while statements such as these reflect huge assumptions about who and what is problematic and why, the process of suspectification has not manifested itself in every country in the same way. These differences become more apparent when we consider how this 'suspect community' has been targeted.

Targeting the suspected

In most European countries the last decade or so has seen the introduction and/or extension of legislative powers designed to deal with the threat of terrorism. In some of those countries – Britain and France, for example – those legislative powers have historical continuity. In others continuities with the past are less obvious. In this part of this chapter we shall endeavour to document some of the differences and similarities across Europe in how terrorism has been targeted and what impact that has had. In all of the European countries referred to here it should be remembered that – legislative changes and the evidence of their impact notwithstanding – it is very difficult to directly compare the experiences of ethnic minority groups. France, for example, prohibits the collection of personal data, making estimates on the size of ethnic minority groups difficult – though it is estimated that Islam constitutes the second largest religious group in France standing at around 10 per cent. Sweden declared itself a multicultural society in 1975 and there are again no official statistics on faith, with estimates suggesting around 4.5 per cent of the population are Muslims. In Denmark 6.8 per cent of the population are Muslims (Lindekilde and Sedgwick, 2012). In the case of the UK, Choudhury (2012) notes:

> Muslims in Britain are ethnically diverse. Data from the 2001 census shows that three-quarters of Muslims (74 percent) are from an Asian ethnic background, predominantly Pakistani (43 percent), Bangladeshi (16 percent), Indian (8 percent) and other Asian (6 percent). Eleven percent of Muslims are from a White ethnic group, of which 4 percent are of White British

origin, and 7 percent from another White background, including Turkish, Cypriot, Arab and Eastern European. A further 6 percent of Muslims are of Black African origin, mainly from North and East Africa, particularly Somalia.

In citing this admittedly bald data we nonetheless already have some clues as to the kinds of problems faced by governments concerned to protect the State, preserve civil liberties and ensure that appropriately problematic behaviour is addressed. There are considerable gaps in knowledge about who, what and where might be 'problematic'. Of course, it is within these gaps that the problems associated with 'seeing and saying' can emerge. In the aftermath of 9/11 national policy responses emerged in a number of countries, some independent of Council of Europe resolutions, some using those same resolutions as the prompt and rationale. This has resulted in both parallel and distinct responses across Europe in targeting those deemed to be the suspects. Such responses have taken two forms: recourse to the legal framework (rendering particular behaviours illegal) and recourse to the policy framework (focusing on prevention of particular behaviours).

In Britain, the rafts of counter-terrorism legislation and policies associated with CONTEST are indicative of the setting in of the political imperative to 'think security' (see de Lint and Virta, 2004). However, this cue has also been taken up across countries and continents. Zedner (2009: 120) points out that – even in countries such as Italy, Germany and Spain with raised sensitivities to human rights as a result of recent experiences of authoritarian regimes – counter-terrorism measures have expanded markedly. Of course, what is perhaps of equal, if not more concern, is the question of who is most likely to be on the receiving end of the activities of the police and security services so armed with such a stringent legal framework. As was bottomed out in Chapter 4, the use of stop and search by the British police force, long subject to criticism (see, for example, Bowling and Phillips, 1998), has been but one aspect of the implementation of powers under terrorism legislation that has disproportionately targeted ethnic minorities. In general terms:

> The figures are stark: if you are a black person, you are at least six
> times as likely to be stopped and searched by the police in England
> and Wales as a white person. If you are Asian, you are around twice
> as likely to be stopped and searched as a white person.
>
> (EHRC, 2013: 5)

Though as the recent report from the EHRC (2013) intimates, there
has been some tightening of these practices. Recent statistics from
the Home Office published June 2013 indicate an overall reduction
in the number of stops and arrests under the terrorism legislation. What
the knock-on effect of this change has had on the use of other police
powers is too early to determine. However, it is evident that the issue
of (dis)proportionality does not only rear its head in the British context.
In Denmark, the introduction of the so-called 'Tunisian Law' in 2008
that affords 'tolerated residence' to individuals rather than deportation
– in essence a version of house arrest – and the introduction of
'inspection zones' in 2004 that 'allows the police to declare certain
public spaces to be 'inspection zones' for limited time periods, within
which the police can stop and search individuals for possession of illegal
weapons and explosives without any grounds for suspicion' (Lindekilde
and Sedgwick, 2012: 23), raise comparable questions to those pertinent
in Britain. The latter policy has resulted in large parts of Copenhagen
being designated as an 'inspection zone'; and has, as yet, not been legally
challenged. In France, the frequency of police checks has provoked
frustrations similar to those voiced in Britain. Camilleri (2012: 34) notes:

> To explain why descendants of immigrants of Muslim origin have
> a distinct mistrust for the police, it is necessary to take into account
> the frequency of contact these people have with the police force,
> especially in the form of police identity checks. Such identity
> checks have long been a source of controversy among young
> people from working class backgrounds, especially those of
> immigrant origin. Indeed, a 2009 OSI study based on *in situ*
> observations of such identity checks in Paris established that police
> controls often targeted young men that visibly belonged to
> ethnic minorities and who adopted 'youth' dress codes.

France has experienced several incidents of civil disturbance over the last decade or so in response to such tactics (see also Fassin, 2013). In Sweden there is evidence to suggest that, despite a formal State commitment to multiculturalism: '9/11 broke a positive trend in attitudes towards immigration and minorities' (Ramalingam, 2012: 14) with declining levels of trust becoming apparent between the police and ethnic minority groups. The situation in Germany seems less clear-cut, with evidence of discriminatory practices ambiguous, but also apparent support for an improved governmental response to the threat of terrorism nonetheless (Jesse and Mannewitz, 2012).

What is interesting in all of these responses, and the commentaries related to them, is that, on the whole, there is a paucity of research on the impact that these policy responses are having on the individuals and communities so targeted. What is also interesting is the primacy given to the legal framework in the first instance in all of these contexts, often supplemented by other 'counter-radicalization' strategies second. That said, in Germany, there seems to be a particular emphasis on political and social engagement as equal if not preferable to legal mechanisms (see Jesse and Mannewitz, 2012). In these multiple responses, much is presumed and said about the particular ethnic minority group seen to be the source of the problem, but much less said about other kinds of minority groups that may be equally prone to terrorist activity if, perhaps, differently motivated. In all of the examples cited above, the young Muslim male is both the subject and the object of the practices that follow on from the recourse to the law *whether or not* the particular country concerned has particular experience of terrorism promulgated by this particular group. In this respect, the incidents involving Anders Breivik in Norway in 2011 speak volumes about who is made to be a targeted suspect – by politicians, the media and consequently in the public imagination – and who is not (see Borchgrevink, 2013). The rapidity with which that event was attributed to Islamist terrorists in the media, only to be recanted very shortly afterwards, explicitly captures the social and cultural problematic that has become embedded here, pointedly not only in countries with prior direct experiences of terrorism. Putting the events in Norway in the frame serves as a reminder that there were, and are, a whole range of groups not considered terroristic because they do not possess the features that come under the radar of the Intelligence Services. Moreover, as Mullins and Thurman (2011: 47) point out about the activities of the FBI in America: 'because of the concern with international terrorism, the activities of [these] single issue groups has been virtually ignored'. Indeed a recent review of right-wing extremism in Europe indicates how little is known about the violent potential of such activities (Goodwin *et al.*, 2012). Being sensitive to the potentially wide range of sources for terrorist activity affords the opportunity to consider, in a little more detail, what kinds of justifications lie behind the targeting practices outlined above. What do these practices reveal about the sense being made of the 'suspected'?

Making sense of the suspected

As the previous discussion indicates, the targeting of those thought to be suspect has produced two procedural features: the reactive (characterized by law changing and law making activities) and the proactive (characterized by policies directed towards prevention). In practice while it is difficult to separate these features one from the other, they each share assumptions about how to make sense of the suspected. As flagged in Chapter 2, it should be remembered that the concept of terrorism is itself highly debated and different definitions will result in different ways of making sense of 'suspect' activities. Such sense making practices connect with different policy presumptions about the cause(s) of terrorism and the process of radicalization that is related to it. Our concern here will be to explore what has been made visible and kept invisible in the making of these connections. To this end, the discussion that follows will offer an overview of the different tendencies in sense making practices, particularly within criminology, and their relationship, or otherwise, with policy.

Much recent criminological endeavour has been preoccupied with comparing and contrasting terrorism with organized crime (see for example Findlay, 2008; Grabosky and Stohl, 2010). The appropriateness or otherwise of this endeavour is open to debate, if for no other reason than, as Hickman *et al.* (2011) observed, organized crime has not been subjected to the same suspectification. This is an observation that in and of itself raises questions about cause and effect. Such problems notwithstanding, it is possible to identify four tendencies in the search for aetiology: the 'lone wolf' approach, the strain theory approach, the subcultural approach and the structural approach. What follows is a brief summary of each of these tendencies.

The 'lone wolf' approach

The 'lone wolf' approach, as the label implies, focuses attention on the inherent characteristics associated with individual terrorists. In this approach the cause of terrorism lies within individual personality constructs or disorders. For example, Anders Breivik, as a white, blond-haired, Norwegian male from a middle class background, could not have differed more from dominant political conceptions of the kinds of individuals involved in terrorism. By engaging in a close reading of his manifesto and other sources of data, Billig and Stalne (2011) offer an analysis of Breivik and his actions that focuses attention on the relationship between his life experiences and his subsequent behaviour. His parents divorced when he was one year old and his father was absent for much of his adult life. This they suggest, along with a palette of crimogenic evidence, increased the likelihood of him becoming a criminal. Taken alongside a context in which his manifesto suggests he struggled with the tolerance of feminism and multiculturalism in wider Scandinavian society, this established a 'perfect storm of personal trauma and cultural double standards' (ibid.: 151). Thus, 'Breivik slaughtered fellow Norwegians whom he considered too tolerant of 'intruding' strangers, people who, according to him, had betrayed the national cause' (Simonsen, 2012: 203). These were people that he considered to be Marxists and/or multiculturalists, not Muslims. As Ian Burama (2011: 12) observes: 'different times produce different pathologies', but in recognizing those times, he goes on to suggest that 'this finally gave right-wing populists a cause with which to crash into the center of European politics' (ibid.). So, even the 'lone wolf' needs a suitable context in which to express himself. Away from the specificity of this particular incident, other work has looked to compare and contrast 'lone wolf' style far-right attacks with other kinds of far-right extreme violence. Notably Gruenewald *et al.* (2013) have pointed to the significance of mental instability/illness, military background, age and relationship status as distinguishing loners from other kinds of extremists. They suggest that combating this kind of attack, or what they call 'self-radicalization', carries the possibility for tailored preventive strategies based on intelligence sharing between the different relevant agencies. All of which returns us to the problems of risk and risk assessment commented on in Chapter 1. Interestingly, little work seems to suggest that the 'lone wolf' theory necessarily applies to the known terrorist activities that have been perpetrated by young Muslim men. This is largely a result of the fact that their commitment to suicide attacks means they cannot be subjected to interviewing and/or psychological analysis afterwards. Nevertheless, Pape (2006) argues that 95 per cent of suicide bombers also belong to or are affiliated with organizations. Such assertions notwithstanding, neither does the 'lone wolf' approach reasonably capture the question of faith. As was suggested earlier, in devising policy responses to terrorism, much has been assumed about faith as a driver for action. It is only from the videos and other materials left by 'suicide bombers' that it is possible to get a clear sense of their motivation. Listening to their voices raises some contradictions that jar with this 'lone wolf' thesis.

The strain theory approach

The strain theory approach to the causes of terrorism develops the work of Robert K. Merton and brings together psychology and sociology to focus attention on the relationship between the individual and the social conditions under which the individual may be propelled into criminal behaviour. Agnew (2010) has recently extended this conceptual framework to apply it to terrorism. He points to the importance of recognizing the 'collective strains' experienced by ethnic/religious/territorial groups and the extent to which such strains may, or may not, result in terrorism. He goes on to argue that there are a number of specific strains that are most likely to result in this outcome: when strains have a high impact, when they are seen to be unjust and when they are seen to be the result of powerful others 'with whom the members of the strained collective have weak ties' (Agnew, 2010: 136). He makes no claims for this theory to offer a complete explanation for terrorism, but does suggest that recognition of 'collective strains' and what might be called the resultant pressure points have important policy implications in ensuring that such pressure points are relieved. Failure to do so can contribute to furthering the strains experienced and thus furthering the potential for terrorist activity. Of course strain theory cannot account for why only a small minority of people exposed to such strains and/or material/cultural deprivations turn to violence as a response. In this respect, as an explanation, it faces the same dilemma as that faced by those of a more sociological tradition who draw attention to the search for identity that radical Islam is said to provide when living under conditions of persistent discrimination. Dalgaard-Nielsen (2010: 801) pointedly asks:

> What accounts for the difference between the minority, which reacts to the overall socioeconomic, political and cultural context, with violence and those who instead chose to become engaged in constitutional politics, those who remain apolitical, and those who seek meaning in an introspective religious movement?

It is at this juncture that the subcultural approach may have something to offer.

The subcultural approach

A variation of strain theory as derived from the work of Merton, the subcultural approach focuses attention on the extent to which shared values and understandings promote particular (criminal) behaviours. In the context of terrorism, focusing on subcultural values has been addressed by work that pays attention to the culture of violence thesis (see for example Mullins and Young, 2012) and work that draws attention to the relevance of the ideas about delinquent gangs popular in criminology during the 1950s and 1960s. Here the recent intervention of Cottee (2011) is worth noting. Cottee's work draws attention to the importance of both 'subcultural style' and structure in understanding the commitment to Jihadism. This shares some similarity with that approach to radicalization that Dalgaard-Nielsen (2010) calls the social movement approach. Both approaches accent the importance of social networks, personal bonds, and the construction of shared meanings and understandings about the world. They also have in common a commitment to listen to and engage with the voices of those sharing in these ways of thinking about the world. Such a commitment is seen to be important in understanding the social networks that exist between people, hence the subcultural approach. Cottee's interventions add a valuable contextual dimension to the work of Sageman (2007) who points to the fact that someone joining a Jihadist group does so already knowing an existing member of the group. This may well be a significant point of overlap between this kind of work and that focusing on the salience of the charismatic leader (see Dalgaard-Nielsen 2010: 807–8). It is evident that there may be much to learn from the subcultural/social movement or network approach in understanding what propels individuals into terrorist activity. However, caution needs to be expressed concerning how and under what conditions such networks result in violence, and the extent to which policy interventions themselves, in furthering experiences of discrimination, assist in the radicalization process, that is, in putting individuals in the frame for violence (Dalgaard-Nielsen 2010: 804).

Structural approaches

As might be imagined, structural approaches to the causes of terrorism focus attention on factors such as material deprivation, social inequality and disenfranchisement, though the evidence for and against the efficacy of these different variables is ambiguous. For example, many extremely impoverished Palestinians do not engage in political violence (Kreuger and Maleckova, 2003) while in some cases, it is those that are not socially deprived who do so (Post, 2007). The nineteen members of the so-called Hamburg Cell responsible for the 9/11 attacks were largely university educated and predominantly from what we would categorize as middle class family backgrounds (see Riedel,

2008). This suggests that it is mistaken to presume that material deprivation works in a simple and or straightforward manner. It is important to grasp the nettle that it is not always the poorly educated and/or the socially deprived who are capable of terrorist activities or who can be propelled into radicalization. Consequently, while much criminological and sociological theorizing (as discussed in Chapter 1) makes implicit and explicit assumptions about the nature of the impact of globalization and/or social inequality and its associated risks, when it comes to establishing empirical evidence as to the effect of such structural processes, as measured by socio-economic status, the outcome in respect of individual behaviour is ambivalent.

To summarize, there are a number of different explanations available to criminologists through which to make sense of what may drive people to engage in terroristic activity. While each has their relative strengths and weaknesses – and it is arguably prudent to view them as potentially complementary – it is important to note that they are each concerned with different levels of analysis – from the individual, to the cultural to the structural – making it difficult to assess their comparative value. Nonetheless, it should be noted that what they all have in common is a shared understanding of what and who the problem is. So they each align themselves, in different ways, with an inherently conservative criminological agenda. This is something that we shall return to in the conclusion; of particular interest for our discussion here are two issues. First, to what extent are these different perspectives reflected, if at all, in the policy responses directed towards the suspected. Second, and perhaps conversely, in the light of the evidence associated with each of these perspectives, to what extent have political, policy and media interventions contributed to the creation of the suspected. Taken together, a good question to ask might be: has this kind of work and the interventions that have followed contributed to the greater likelihood of terrorist behaviour and/or radicalization?

Contesting the suspected

The discussion above has drawn our attention to a number of processes. First of all the extent to which political and policy interventions alongside media coverage have created a particular section of the population, in Britain, America and other countries in Europe as the suspected. As a result of being created as the suspected, that same section of the population has become the target of discriminatory practices, invariably enshrined in or encouraged by law. At the same time, it is evident that while there are a number of different ways of making sense of the suspected, that is, making sense of what the drivers might be that would propel an individual, or a group of individuals, into violent action, the available evidence that underpins those different perspectives misses the explanatory mark. There are a number of reasons for this, but Borum (2013: 106) pinpoints one of great salience:

> Assuming that radicalisation is the key to understanding and predicting terrorism is a grave misapprehension. Investigators must be mindful that terrorism does not always follow a linear process where a vulnerable person is inducted into a particular ideology, and adherence to those ideas escalates until the individual inevitably is driven to commit acts of violence. Sometime terrorism evolves that way, but not often enough, perhaps, even to be considered 'typical'.

Such assumptions taken alongside the recourse to the legal response in targeting those deemed to be suspect appear to add a further dimension to the perception of discrimination felt by the groups so targeted (Change Institute, 2008) and thus exacerbates the potential for further violence and alienation. Such observations concur with Dalgaard-Nielsen's (2010) assertion that we actually know little about radicalization per se and, as a result, the kinds of policy responses referred to in this chapter and elsewhere in this book are liable to backfire. Why is this the case? Part of the answer lies in unpacking the domain assumptions on which the creating, targeting and making sense of the suspected has taken place. These assumptions, to use Sunstein's (2005) term, put blinders on our ability to make sense not only of particular terrorist events but also the experiences over the last decade and more of those who have been created as the suspects. Much of the above, as alluded to in the quote from Borum (2013), makes particular assumptions about the journey to becoming a radical.

The New York Police Department, for example, uses a model of radicalization that has four phases as an analytical tool (see Silber and Bhatt, 2007). Yet there does not appear to be a definition of radicalization on which all can agree, nor an identifiable journey that terrorists-to-be follow (see Kundnani, 2012). Nonetheless, assumptions about radicalization, and those most likely to become radical, embed particular views about the world that give space and voice to some – such as politicians, policy makers, newspaper editors and academics whom we could loosely group as the powerful – and affords little vocal space to those propelled to take violent action (in different ways, the powerless). In particular, it is the latter voices that are missing in political debate (see Mythen, 2012). One place in which to begin to fill this analytical gap is by engaging with the martyrdom videos of those who have committed terrorist acts.

In the martydom video made by Sidique Khan that we cited in Chapter 3, a clear indication is given of the 'elephants in the room' that none of the material cited above places centre stage. The pre-recorded videos made by the young British men responsible for the 7/7 attacks in London make frequent reference to the inaction of the West in defending Palestine against Israeli attacks, the illegal invasion of Iraq and the occupation of Afghanistan. Clearly, these driving motivations are less than convenient for the British government in that they introduce the idea that both State intransigence in the case of Palestine, and State violence in the case of Iraq and Afghanistan are important sources of grievance for young Muslims. The tendency of politicians and security officials to simply dismiss the actions of individuals such as Khan as the mindless actions of a monster fail to engage with the expressed values and opinions regarding British domestic and foreign policy of young men like Sidique Khan (see Gill, 2009: 155).

It follows then, if we are to render radicalization knowable, and subsequently preventable, it may well be important to start in a different place. This is not intended to imply that any of the factors or the policies discussed above are necessarily wrong, in and of themselves. However, it may be that the balance between the policy, the presumptions on which it is based, and the impact that it has, needs to be reconsidered. If we step outside of the contemporary blinders associated with those who are the suspected, we allow other prescient but less discussed issues in. The role of the State as transgressor, the emergence of the far right across Europe, alongside the experiences of Muslim converts (Moosavi, 2012), are all issues that might facilitate a much more meaningful and sensitive policy and cultural response to the management of politically motivated violence. With some imagination this becomes possible, but of course, to cast aside such blinders it is also necessary to attempt to break free of the shackles imposed by Northern theorizing (Connell, 2007).

Conclusion: the exceptional State or States of exception?

In this chapter we have traced the ways in which responses to those considered to be 'suspect' have been justified and rendered justifiable. In the process we have identified some lacunae, raised several unanswered questions and pointed to the assumptions on which much of the political, policy, media and academic work has been based. The end product – the suspectification of particular ethnic populations – is justified and explained by reference to the 'exceptional'. Thus, we, the public, are frequently reassured that – given the scale of the threat faced – the price paid by the few is in the interests of the many. The risks are exceptional, so exceptional responses become necessary. Yet, as time moves on, such exceptional powers can soon become normalized as accepted and acceptable security practices (see Zedner, 2009: 122).

Hillyard (2009: 142) reminds us in his analysis of State responses to political violence in Northern Ireland:

> Increasing use of a wide range of personnel in the exercise of informal control, intensified surveillance of the population, and the widespread shift away from the ordinary criminal law to the use of 'counter-terror' law are all essential elements of an exceptional state, the key element is the capacity to sanction and then condone widespread killings of its own citizens in an attempt to control Irish political violence. The implications for the 'war on terror' are far-reaching.

The validity and continued viability of this kind of response may well depend upon what is understood as constituting the exceptional. Out of the 'terrors of prevention' associated with the post 9/11 era, a productive discursive space has emerged in which critical legal scholars have been inspired by Agamben's (1995: 169) notion of the 'state of exception': 'The state of exception, which was essentially a temporary suspension of the rule of law on the basis of a factual state of danger, is now given permanent spatial arrangement, which as such nevertheless remains outside the normal order.' Scholars following this line of analysis have used this concept to point to the way in which, contemporarily, this notion of the exceptional has been used to create responses to threats that are neither legal nor non-legal – the continued existence of Guantanamo Bay is a good example of this. Whyte (2010: 150) reminds us that 'a state of exception is ultimately not a project of legal power, but a project of power'. He goes on to point out:

> In advanced capitalist societies, the state of exception has a range of simultaneous functions: as ideological or propaganda supports, as means of expanding or enhancing state security apparatuses, legitimizing colonial reach externally, and so on. But of those functions it is those that are connected to the preservation or deepening of a social order that continually seeks to expand its capacities for capital accumulation.
>
> (Ibid.)

Here the mutual economic advantages identified between the State and security industries discussed in Chapter 3 re-emerge. Our analysis clearly suggests that while material deprivation itself is difficult to evidence as a driver of radicalization, it is no coincidence that for all the societies referred to in this chapter (Britain, America, France, Sweden, Germany, Denmark), the suspected are invariably those at the lower end of the socio-economic pile, and in some societies lower than others. The 'exceptional' powers of the State have contributed to the construction of them as 'police property' – perhaps better read as 'State property' – without recognizing the embedded presumptions that such constructions entail, and with little heed to their impact. While there may be differences between States and thereby differences in the experiences that individuals thereby have – hence gradations of exceptionalism – the dilemmas posed by hegemonic State power excavated in Chapter 3, and the return to the sacred in the face of capitalism's crisis suggested in the introduction to this book, remain. As we shall see, this search for hegemonic power has adopted different rhetorical and policy devices in the face of the changing global economy: the search for resilience. Such differences, however, are more apparent than they are real as will become clear as the next chapter unfolds.

References

Agamben, G. (2005) *State of Exception*. Chicago, IL: University of Chicago Press.

Agnew, R. (2010) A general strain theory of terrorism. *Theoretical Criminology* 14(2): 131–54.

Allen, C. (2010) *Islamophobia*. London: Ashgate.

Allen, C. and Nielsen, J. (2002) *Summary Report on Islamophobia in the EU after 11 September 2001*. Vienna: European Monitoring Centre.

Billig, P. and Stalne, K. (2011) Learning from the unfathomable: An analysis of Anders Behring Breivik. *Integral Review*, October 7(2): 150–60.

Blair, T. (2005) Speech to Labour Party Conference. 16 July.

Borchgrevink, A. (2013) *A Norwegian Tragedy*. Cambridge: Polity.

Borum, R. (2013) Informing lone-offender investigations. *Criminology and Public Policy*, 12(1): 103–12.

Bowling, B. and Phillips, C. (1998) *Violent Racism: Victimization, policing and social context*. Oxford: Clarendon.

Burama, I. (2011) Europe's Turn to the Right. *The Nation*. 29 August–5 September: 11–12.

Camilleri, R. (2012) *Impact of Counter-Terrorism on Communities: France background report*. London: Institute for Strategic Dialogue.

Chalk, P. (2004) *Confronting the Enemy Within: Security intelligence, the police and counter-terrorism in four democracies*. Santa Monica, CA: RAND.

Change Institute (2008) *Studies into Violent Radicalization: Lot 2. The beliefs, ideologies and narratives*. London: Change Institute.

Choudhury, V. (2012) *Impact of Counter-Terrorism on Communities: UK background report*. London: Institute for Strategic Dialogue.

Connell, R. (2007) The northern theory of globalization. *Sociological Theory*, 25 (4): 368–85.

Cottee, S. (2011) Jihadism as a subcultural response to social strain: Extending Marc Sageman's 'Bunch of Guys' thesis. *Terrorism and Political Violence*, 23: 730–51.

Curtis, A. (2004) Fear gives politicians a reason to be, *The Guardian*, 24 September: 9.

Dalgaard-Nielsen, A. (2010) Violent radicalization in Europe: What we know and what we do not know. *Studies in Conflict and Terrorism*, 33(9): 797–814.

de Lint, W. and Virta, S. (2004) Security and ambiguity: Towards a radical security politics. *Theoretical Criminology*, 8(4): 465–89.

Department of Homeland Security (2010) Available at: www.dhs.gov/how-do-i/report-suspicious-activity (accessed 16 June 2014).

Equality and Human Rights Commission (2013) *Stop and Think Again*. London: EHRC.

Ericson, R. V. (2007) *Crime in an Insecure World*. Cambridge: Polity Press.

Evans, J. (2007) *Intelligence, Counter-terrorism and Trust*. London: Security Service.

Fassin, D. (2013) *Enforcing Order: An ethnography of urban policing*. Cambridge: Polity Press.

Findlay, M. (2008) *Governing Through Globalised Crime*. Cullompton, Devon: Willan.

Forst, B. (2011) Managing the fear of terrorism. In B. Forst, J. Greene and J. Lynch (eds) *Criminologists on Terrorism and Homeland Security*. Cambridge: Cambridge University Press, pp. 273–99.

Frost, D. (2008) Islamophobia: Examining causal links between the state and race hate from below. *International Journal of Sociology and Social Policy* 28(11/12): 546–60.

Gill, P. (2009) Intelligence, terrorism and the state. In R. Coleman, J. Sim, S. Tombs and D. Whyte (eds) *State, Power, Crime*. London: Sage, pp. 145–58.

Goodwin, M., Ramalingan, V. and Briggs, R. (2012) *The New Radical Right: Violent and non-violent movements in Europe*. London: Institute for Strategic Dialogue.

Grabosky, P. and Stohl, M. (2010) *Crime and Terrorism*. London: Sage.

Greer, S. (2010) Anti-terrorist laws and the United Kingdom's suspect Muslim community: A reply to Pantazis and Pemberton. *British Journal of Criminology*, 50: 1171–90.

Gruenewald, J., Chermak, S. and Freilich, J.D. (2013) Distinguishing 'loner' attacks from other domestic extremist violence: A comparison of far-right homicide incident and offender characteristics. *Criminology and Public Policy*, 12(1): 65–91.

Hickman, M., Thomas, L., Silvestri, S. and Nickels, H. (2011) *Suspect Communities? Counter-terrorism policy, the press, and impact on Muslim and Irish communities*. London: London Metropolitan University.

Hillyard, P. (1993) *Suspect Community: People's experience of the prevention of terrorism acts in Britain*. London: Pluto Press.

Hillyard, P. (2009) The 'exceptional' state. In R. Coleman, J. Sim, S. Tombs and D. Whyte (eds) *State, Power, Crime*. London: Sage, pp. 129–44.

HM Government (2011b) *Prevent Strategy, Cm 8092*. London: The Stationary Office.

Hudson, B. (2003) *Justice in the Risk Society: Challenging and reaffirming justice in late modernity*. London: Sage.

International Business Times (2013) Mosque attacked in Britain every three days since Lee Rigby's murder. 26 June.

Jesse, E. and Mannewitz, T. (2012) *Impact of Counter-Terrorism on Communities: Germany background report*. London: Institute for Strategic Dialogue.

Joffe, H. (1999) *Risk and the Other*. Cambridge: Cambridge University Press.

Kreuger, A. and Maleckova, J. (2003) Education, poverty and terrorism: Is there a causal connection? *The Journal of Economic Perspectives*. Autumn, 17(4): 119–44.

Kundnani, A. (2012) Radicalisation: The journey of a concept. *Race and Class*, 54(2): 3–25.

Lambert, R. (2008) Ignoring the lessons of the past. *Criminal Justice Matters* 73(1): 22–3.

Lindekilde, L. and Sedgwick, M. (2012) *Impact of Counter-Terrorism on Communities: Denmark background report*. London: Institute for Strategic Dialogue.

McGovern, M. (2010) *Countering Terror or Counter-Productive?* Liverpool: Edge Hill.

Maira, S. (2009) *Missing*. Durham, NC: Duke University Press.

Meer, N., Dwyer, C. and Modood, T. (2010) Embodying nationhood? Conceptions of British national identity, citizenship and gender in the veil affair. *The Sociological Review*, 58(1): 84–111.

Moore, K., Mason, P. and Lewis, J. (2008) *Media Images of Islam in the UK*. Cardiff: Cardiff School of Journalism, Media and Cultural Studies.

Moosavi, L. (2012) British Muslim converts performing 'authentic Muslimism', *Performing Islam*, 1(1): 103–28.

Mullins, C.W. and Thurman, Q. (2011) The etiology of terrorism. In B. Forst, J. Greene and J. Lynch (eds) *Criminologists on Terrorism and Homeland Security*. Cambridge: Cambridge University Press, pp. 40–65.

Mullins, C.W. and Young, J. (2012) Cultures of violence and terrorism: A test of the legitimating-habituation model. *Crime and Delinquency*, 58(1): 28–56.

Mythen, G. (2008) Sociology and the art of risk. *Sociology Compass*, 2(1): 299–316.

Mythen, G. (2012) Who speaks for us? Counter-terrorism, collective attribution and the problem of voice. *Critical Studies on Terrorism*, 5(3): 1–16.

Mythen, G. and Walklate, S. (2006) Communicating the terrorist risk: Harnessing a culture of fear? *Crime, Media, Culture: An International Journal*, 2(2): 123–42.

Mythen, G., Walklate, S. and Khan, F. (2009) 'I'm a Muslim, but I'm not a terrorist': Risk, victimization and the negotiation of risky identities, *British Journal of Criminology*, 49(6): 736–54.

Oborne, P. (2006) *The Use and Abuse of Terror: The construction of a false narrative of the domestic terror threat*. London: Centre for Policy Studies.

Pantazis, C. and Pemberton, S. (2009) From the old to the new suspect community: Examining the impacts of recent counter-terrorist legislation. *British Journal of Criminology*, 49: 646–66.

Pape, R. (2006) *Dying to Win*. New York: Random House.

Post, J.M. (2007) *The Mind of the Terrorist*. New York: Palgrave-Macmillan.

Poynting, S. and Mason, V. (2007) The resistible rise of Islamophobia: Anti-Muslim racism in the UK and Australia before 11 September 2001. *Journal of Sociology*, 43(1): 61–86.

Ramalingan, V. (2012*) Impact of Counter-Terrorism on Communities: Sweden background report*. London: Institute for Strategic Dialogue.

Riedel, B. (2008) *The Search for Al Qaeda: Its leadership, ideology and future*. Washington: Brookings.

Sageman, M. (2007) *Leaderless Jihad: Terror networks in the twenty-first century*. Philadelphia, PA: University of Pennsylvania.

Silber, M. and Bhatt, A. (2007) *Radicalization in the West: The homegrown threat*. New York: New York City Police Department.

Simonsen, K. (2012) Figuration of a cultural political crisis across Europe. *Environment and Planning D: Society and Space*, 30: 191–206.

Summers, A. and Swann, R. (2011) *The Eleventh Day: The ultimate account of 9/11*. London: Doubleday.

Sunstein, C.R. (2005) *Laws of Fear: Beyond the precautionary principle*. Cambridge: Cambridge University Press.

Whitaker, B. (2002) *Islam and the Media*. London: Central London Mosque.

Whyte, D. (2010) A fake law: The 'state of exception' and lex mercatoria in occupied Iraq. In W. Chambliss, R. Michalowski and R. Kramer (eds) *State Crime in the Global Age*. Uffculme: Willan Publishing, pp. 134–51.

Zedner, L. (2009) *Security*. London: Routledge.

6

MANAGING TERRORISM

From risk to resilience?

Abstract and malleable enough to encompass the worlds of high finance, defence and urban infrastructure within a single analytic, the concept of resilience is becoming a pervasive idiom of global governance.

(Walker and Cooper, 2011: 144)

Introduction

If risk was the policy and political hallmark of the first decade of the twenty-first century in relation to terrorism, as the second decade has unfolded, that same policy and political agenda is being increasingly informed by the concept of resilience. The purpose of this chapter is to consider the implications of this shift in policy focus by subjecting the concept of resilience, and what it implies for our understandings of terrorism, to critical scrutiny. Of course, this shift towards resilience has not occurred in a vacuum. It has arisen out of, and is connected to, the risk agenda. That agenda has been, and is, preoccupied with pre-emption and risk assessment, as discussed in Chapters 1 and 2. It is a preoccupation that has been concerned to reduce wider societal exposure to places, people and situations deemed 'risky'. In targeting the 'risky', assumptions have also been made in respect of who, what and where is *vulnerable* to terrorism as recounted in Chapters 4 and 5. In this way extant assumptions about vulnerability have provided the link that has facilitated the policy shift from risk to resilience. Hence this shift does not necessarily imply a policy break with the past but rather a reorientation within it (Furedi, 2008). This chapter will explore this policy shift and the assumptions it makes concerning what counts as resilience and who/what is considered to be resilient. In order to do this we will first explore the conceptual presumptions that link risk with vulnerability and resilience. Second, we shall detail the ways in which these presumptions have facilitated the policy shift to resilience: which might be termed 'resilience creep'. Next, using primarily British policy making as a case study, we shall reflect upon this policy turn and consider where it takes us in relation to managing the response to terrorism. These reflections enable us to make some observations about the tensions between this policy direction and the empirical evidence from real life experiences that suggest, when faced with catastrophe, human beings more often than not find themselves being cast as stoic 'heroes of the hour' (Furedi, 2004). Finally, and in conclusion, we consider what, other than the search for security, might be in train in this policy turn. Echoing the observations made in Chapter 3 we shall suggest that an underlying concern here is hegemonic power relations that seek to ensure the maintenance of the resilient State rather than a state of resilience in the State's subjects. First of all we offer some initial thoughts about the links between risk, vulnerability and resilience.

Risk, vulnerability and resilience

Misztal (2011) offers an overview of the wide-ranging definitions of vulnerability that exist across an equally wide-ranging set of scientific and social scientific disciplines. Our purpose here is not to be overly preoccupied with the debates that these wide-ranging definitions generate, but to offer an insight into how the interconnections between risk and vulnerability have facilitated the emergence of what might well be, in policy terms at least, signs of 'resilience creep'. In so doing, while it is important to note that the body is a common site of human vulnerability (*qua* Butler 2004) – no less so than when faced with violence(s) – vulnerability is also a social construct. Misztal (2011: 45–6) suggests, 'vulnerability is precipitated by and through the actions of others and to the extent that vulnerability has a reference to both the collective past and the future'. Thus, our understandings of what and/or who is vulnerable have a history and, by dint, significant *social* dimensions. Such social dimensions carry weight and meaning insofar as they assign select people, circumstances and places as 'vulnerable'. It follows then, that despite the equalizing presumptions of the risk society thesis recounted in Chapter 1, Moser (1998: 3) reminds us that 'the more assets people have, the less vulnerable they are'. This is a view further endorsed by Mythen's (2004: 140) concerns about the universal claims of the risk society thesis 'so long as class remains a fundamental indicator of vulnerability'. In chorus, Wilkinson (2010) suggests that the structural dimensions to risk and vulnerability are evident on a global scale – in particular in relation to exposure to major hazards such as drought and famine – given that the capacity to respond is severely limited by local economic potentialities. Against this backcloth of global/structural vulnerabilities, what Misztal (2011: 75) calls a 'second form of vulnerability' has emerged: 'the predicament of unpredictability'. This second form of vulnerability is marked by both an increasing awareness of the precarious nature of social life and a failure of 'the experts' to protect us against such precariousness – from the food we eat, to the jobs that may or may not be available to us, to how we experience our sense of identity or nationhood (see Valverde, 2011). Lupton (1999) suggests that the interconnections between risk, vulnerability and resilience embedded in this second form of vulnerability has popularized the view that exposure to harm has a negative impact on both social and psychological well-being.

Indexing risk, vulnerability and resilience with one another in this way has facilitated various applications of the precautionary principle in areas of policy making, including crime prevention and counter-terrorism. Such interlinking not only indicates a limited understanding of the nature of human agency and the capacity of organizations to respond to situations of risk/vulnerability, it also presumes a deficit model of human and organizational capacity in terms of the *management* of risk/vulnerability. According to Durodie (2004: 19), attitudes towards risk, vulnerability and resilience have shifted through time. 'Today,' he asserts, 'there is a widespread presumption of human vulnerability that influences both our discussions of disasters well before they have occurred, and that seek to influence them long after'. He contrasts this pessimism with earlier assumptions that 'on the whole . . . people were resilient and would seek to cope in adverse circumstances', a view that accords with the observations made by Furedi (2007). This negative precariousness characterizes what Bauman (2000) has called 'liquid modernity', a phase in which *nichtwissen*, or not-knowing (Beck 2009: 47), poses disconcerting questions for institutions and individuals alike (see Mythen and Walklate, 2013). The rising tide of this second form of vulnerability, concerned with the 'predicament of unpredictability' (Mizstal 2011), has prised open the door to policy related speak with a different orientation to that of risk. Enter resilience, on the back of pre-existing assumptions about risk and vulnerability. We discussed the problems associated with risk and risk creep in Chapter 1; here it is worth spending a little time considering what might be meant by resilience creep and how it intersects with vulnerability. First though a few comments about vulnerability.

According to Simon Green (2007), the concept of vulnerability has rarely been explored in its own right. In the context of criminology this may well be the case. Certainly, Misztal's (2011) coverage of the concept reaches well beyond criminology. Walklate (2011) has explored how different takes on vulnerability and risk lead to different positions in relation to resilience. She suggests three different, but parallel, ways in which these concepts can be understood: inherent, structural or experiential. Inherent vulnerability is intended to capture an appreciation of individual attributes. For example, Killias and Clerici (2000) suggest physical vulnerability contributes to the fear of crime and Pain (2003) has pointed to presumptions of physical vulnerability that fuel stereotypical views of the elderly, even though not all older people are frail. Such 'injurability' of the body (Butler, 2004: 34) captures one dimension of the experience of feeling vulnerable. For Sparks (1982), vulnerability is not physical, rather it is informed by those who are considered to be at risk and consequently can be harmed. Thus risk (from crime) and harm done (by crime) are equated with vulnerability (to crime) (Green, 2007). It is presumed that this relationship will determine who is the most vulnerable: thus alluding to patterns of *structural* vulnerability. Green's (2007) analysis does much to challenge the value of this relationship and, as Walklate (2011) has further commented, equating risk with harm conflates individual experience with group experience (and vice versa) as well as masking the processes that render some more readily visible as vulnerable victims than others. This is what Walklate (2011) refers to as experiential vulnerability. This version of vulnerability builds on the observation made by Das (2007: 6): 'to be vulnerable is not the same as to be a victim'. Walklate (2011) goes on to suggest that the conflation found within criminological understandings of vulnerability is transferred to criminological (and other) understandings of resilience with the resultant emphasis on negative precariousness. Noting again the work of Das (2007: 63) on the individual and collective responses to violence in the aftermath of the partition of India in 1947 and the massacre of Sikhs after the murder of Indira Ghandi in 1984, while human beings pose a threat and constitute a danger to each other, they are also a key source of hope for each other. Thus, precariousness does not always denote negativity. The grounded approach of Das (2007) – taken together with the analysis proposed by Walklate (2011) – implies a complexity to our understandings of vulnerability and resilience, not necessarily captured by the contemporary policy agenda.

Of course, Durodie (2004), quoted above, is referring to policy efforts by the British government to build resilience in the aftermath of 9/11. This was illustrated in a plethora of activity around disaster planning and preparedness (see Coaffee, 2006). This resilience planning embedded a range of assumptions about citizen involvement (Coaffee and Rogers, 2008a) and the reputational branding of safe places (Coaffee and Rogers, 2008b). In so doing it reflected presumptions of negative precariousness at the expense of recognizing what Siapno (2009) called 'everyday resilience'. Her intervention is noteworthy since it takes us away from *assuming* both that the individual is inherently vulnerable and that our capacity to respond to harms is limited. Her grounded analysis of responses to the tsunami in Aceh and East Timor – responses that included the support of family, friends and networks made during the crisis – offers a more sophisticated and nuanced understanding of people's responses to harm, risk and uncertainty. This approach, chiming with the work of Das (2007) and the observations of Moser (1998) referenced earlier, suggests a view of resilience that foregrounds assets rather than deficits. It stands in stark contrast to some academic presumptions regarding the ubiquity of the 'neurotic citizen' (see Isin 2004; Walklate and Mythen, 2010), media representations of a fearful public and many a governmental planning statement. It could be argued that the presumption of resilience deficit rather than asset has entered the policy door as it has become increasingly obvious that we know that we do not know: the inexorable recognition that presumptions of risk and associated risk assessments can and do fail us (see Fischhoff and Kadvany, 2011: 141). A presumption of resilience deficit prepares us for the impact of the unpredictable. A conceptual leap with this emphasis denies that resilience, along with risk and vulnerability, are concepts open to dispute and interpretation, and can be contested. If such denial is the case, what does resilience mean?

What does resilience mean?

According to the United States Department of Homelands Security:

> The term 'resilience' means the ability to prepare for and adapt to changing conditions and withstand and recover rapidly from disruptions. Resilience includes the ability to withstand and recover from deliberate attacks, accidents, or naturally occurring threats or incidents.
>
> (Presidential Policy Directive/ppd-21,
> 12 February 2013)

This kind of definition of resilience has become the standard trademark of numerous policy statements. Yet, as the quote from Walker and Cooper (2011) at the beginning of this chapter intimates, and the links between resilience and vulnerability that focus our attention on 'the second form of vulnerability' suggest, the ability 'to prepare for and adapt to' affords resilience an unpredictable edge. Given this edge, it is perhaps no great surprise to find a concept that is stretchy enough to 'work' in a range of different contexts. As an example of this stretchiness, the New American Foundation held a symposium entitled 'Defining Resilience' in 2012. They offered the following definition:

> The ability to bounce back, to absorb shocks, to persevere, to retain functionality over time, to endure, to adapt, to succeed, to survive, to sustain . . . so many verbs are conjured up by the term 'resilience.' Whether we're talking about our bodies, our minds, our communities, our institutions or our natural environment, the R-word provides a conceptual framework for designing a better tomorrow.

In this understanding the all-encompassing R-word not only carries a feel-good factor, it also facilitates a more optimistic view of the future. However, somewhat surprisingly, not much work has paid attention to how stretchy this concept can be.

Brand and Jax (2007) have offered a tenfold typology of resilience that draws a distinction between its descriptive and normative use, and Pendall *et al.* (2010) have explored the value of resilience as a social metaphor. Walker and Cooper (2011) have purposively explored the generality of resilience, Coaffee *et al.* (2009) have embarked upon a critical analysis of its role in processes of governance, and Lentzos and Rose (2009) have explored its differential deployment in relation to biosecurity. One way of making sense of the diverse uses to which this concept has been put is to identify some common themes in this work. In so doing it is possible to identify three uses of resilience: as an engineering concept, as a derivative of complex systems theory and as a metaphor. The first two of these uses have their origins in the ecological literature. The latter reflects its more recent political use. It will be of value to say a little about each of these themes in turn.

In ecology in the 1950s, the dominant view of nature presumed that after a shock or disruption, natural processes were driven by a search for equilibrium: to repair and return to some pre-existing state. This reflected an understanding of resilience that Holling (1973) referred to as the 'engineering definition'. This definition assumed that the time it took to return to a stable state equated with the ongoing persistence of the system:

the 'bouncebackability factor'. This is close to the dictionary definition of resilience. However, Holling (1973) was at pains to point out that this engineering definition reflected a rather limited understanding of the natural world. In a similar vein, Berkes (2007) suggested that the presumption of stability, embedded in ecosystem management, neglected the fact that 'much recent research supports the view that ecosystems are inherently unpredictable, and not stable or equilibrium centred' (ibid.: 286). Gunderson and Holling (2002) developed this view of ecosystems and in so doing introduced an understanding of resilience that is now associated with complex systems theory.

In this work Gunderson and Holling (2002) talk of a state of 'panarchy': a complex, cyclical interrelationship between natural systems and human systems. The definition of resilience presumed here foregrounds an understanding that centres a cyclical process of adaptation to change. Such a cyclical process involves growth, accumulation, restructuring and renewal, not that dissimilar from the kinds of processes that might be associated with a system of capital accumulation. These connections come to the fore in Walker and Cooper's (2011: 147) analysis of the genealogy of resilience and it is to features of this use of resilience that we shall return later in this chapter.

The third theme found in definitions of resilience is the metaphorical. For example, Pickett *et al.* (2004: 72) suggest that, notwithstanding the 'fuzziness' of resilience, 'it proves useful as metaphors are intended to offer novel ways of thinking about and understanding complex phenomena and, particularly to reveal new connections and insights across seemingly disparate conceptual paradigms'. This is an understanding endorsed by Brand and Jax (2007). They reason that this metaphorical use of resilience, as a 'boundary object', facilitates cross-disciplinary and interdisciplinary discussion. Further, Coaffee *et al.* (2009) suggest the versatility of resilience as a metaphor, a 'floating signifier' (ibid.: 111), has facilitated the transference of its use from complex systems theory through to policy and practice (see also Rogers 2011: 54).

Walklate *et al.* (2013) offer a typology of resilience that catalogues seven layers to it (from the individual, familial, communal, institutional, national, regional to the global) that stands as testimony to the work that this concept can do, and has done, in policy. In this sense Davoudi (2012) is correct to assert that resilience has become a bridging concept between the natural and social sciences. So, alongside these different thematic elements in definitions of resilience, available social science literature on the *evidence for* resilience provides another layer of complexity to our understanding of this concept. From that literature it is possible to assert that resilience captures more than resistance or survival and more than preoccupations with risk or safety. Gilligan (2000: 37) defines resilience as 'the capacity to do well despite adverse experience'. Indeed, much research on resilience has been focused on 'the dynamic process whereby individuals show adaptive functioning in the face of significant adversity' (Schoon 2006: 6). In order to identify resilience Schoon (2006: 8) states:

> It has to be established whether the circumstances experienced by individuals do in fact affect their chances in life. If there is no association between the experience of adversity, access to resources and opportunities, and consequent adjustment, the phenomenon of resilience would be a mere chance event, a random occurrence.

Much empirical work on resilience has focused on the way in which age and developments over the life-course are important variables in producing such positive outcomes (see Bouvier, 2003; Kearon *et al.*, 2007; Layler, 1999; Ungar, 2004) with a good deal of attention being paid to the relationship between the life chances of the socially disadvantaged and the likelihood of educational achievement. In reviewing a wide range of empirical work on resilience, Schoon (2006) observes there has been a shift from thinking about resilience as an individual attribute (a disease model) to focusing on the social conditions that promote it. Resilience, in other words, like vulnerability, has both individual and social dimensions. Moreover, as with vulnerability, resilience is not measured directly but only in relation to risk from and exposure to adversity and rather like vulnerability conflates individual resilience with group resilience and reflects a tendency to gloss experiential resilience entirely.

From this literature Walklate *et al.* (2012) suggest it is possible to differentiate social psychological/sociological, from what they call 'whole life' approaches to resilience, which, when taken together, offer a picture in which 'resilience is multi-layered and multi-facetted. There are resiliences rather than a unitary, uniform understanding of resilience' (Walklate *et al.*, 2013: 12). In their typology of resilience each of the different layers of resilience provoke different policy possibilities that may act in concert or resist one another. However, at the same time it should be noted that:

> Human beings also endeavour to deliberately impact upon and change their lives and the lives of others, and it is within these processes of deliberation that we find slippage between these states and resilience and the work that politicians and policy makers want this concept to do.
>
> (Walklate *et al.*, 2012: 192)

This complex conceptual lineage endows resilience with plasticity and arguably it is this quality that enables it to be harnessed in State response to contemporary security challenges as an ideological device as much as a practical one. Furedi (2008: 648) reminds us that:

> The absence of an agreed definition of resilience need not necessarily be a problem. It can often serve as prelude to a debate that can lead to conceptual clarity. It is, however, a problem when such a widely used concept and policy objective is used in a taken-for-granted manner, since there is a danger that it will play the role of a cultural metaphor rather than an analytical concept. The absence of a self-conscious engagement with the analytical status of the concept means that it works mainly as a rhetorical idiom used to signify the desirability of managing risks.

Thus, it is perhaps productive to subject the policy turn that has been built on this concept to critical scrutiny and ask the questions: how did we get here and what kind of work can this conceptual/policy turn do?

Resilience and 'resilience creep'

As the discussion above intimates, resilience is not new to the social sciences. However, there has been a rather muted interest in it until relatively recently, particularly within criminology. For example, half a century ago Taylor (1960) highlighted the relationship between resilience and institutionalization for prisoners and Day (1964) subsequently considered the resilience of young offenders. More recent work has indexed resilience to disrupted families and criminal behaviour (Haas *et al.*, 2004; Juby and Farrington, 2001; Stattin *et al.*, 2004), crime prevention (Hayden *et al.*, 2007), vulnerability and repeat victimization (Winkel *et al.*, 2003), female desistance from crime (Rumgay, 2004), young people's resistance to criminal behaviour (Murray, 2008) and the durability of illegal drug networks (Bouchard, 2007). However, perhaps quickened by a string of terrorist attacks in Madrid, London, Mumbai, Stockholm and Utoya, the search for 'resilience' has upped its pace. This search carries with it significant implications for the criminological agenda and raises some vital questions concerning who this quest is actually for and what it is about. In the same way that 'risk creep' has proved a problem for research and policy making, criminologists might justly be concerned about resilience creep.

O'Malley (2011: 12) points out that in the wake of 9/11, the turn to resilience is not characterized by specificity but by its conceptual capacity to demand preparedness for *any* catastrophe. He goes on to suggest that such catastrophes become 'challenges', and the aim is not simply recovery from disaster, but to develop the capacity to 'thrive' (ibid.: 11). This understanding of preparedness for any catastrophe can be illustrated by what happened in Britain in the immediate aftermath of 9/11. The fuel protests of September 2000, the floods in the autumn of 2000, the foot and mouth outbreak of February 2001 and the firefighters strike in November 2002 are referred to by Cole (2010) as the four Fs. The cumulative effect of these occurrences put to the fore the necessity to rethink questions of civil security in general and carried implications for responding to terrorism in particular. As Coaffee (2006) notes, these domestic emergencies resulted in resilience becoming embedded in the Civil Contingencies Act (2004) and other emergency planning policies.

So, in contrast to the post-9/11 language of risk that characterized responses to terrorism, the tenor of this policy shift placed much more attention on the notion of social responsibility: a search for collective resilience. This generalized shift to preparedness required the public to assist the State in securing resilient economies and infrastructures through collective vigilance and endeavour. Of course, there is nothing novel in the invitation of the State to citizens to be alert and active against threats. Garland's (2001) conceptual intervention of 'responsibilisation' captures much of this kind of drive in relation to crime and crime control (see also Findlay, 2008 and Simon, 2007). So, the groundwork was already in place for strategies of responsibilization to reach out into other aspects of everyday life. There is nothing particularly unique to Britain in this policy shift. The Australian National Strategy for Disaster Resilience (2009) reflects similar concerns. It states:

> The whole-of-nation Strategy recognises the important roles we all play in achieving a more resilient Australia. The priority outcomes in the Strategy call on all individuals, organisations and governments to actively play their part. Involvement means realizing the potential of all parties to build their resilience to disasters, and supporting and influencing these outcomes. You and your organisations need to consider how to support participation within your community. Governments, through adopting and supporting the Strategy, will review existing policies and instruments (not limited to the traditional emergency management sector), with a view to incorporating disaster resilience outcomes through all government operations.

A case study presented by Gal (2011: 6) from the National-Resilience Project at the Israeli National Security Council adds some weight to the value currently placed on national resilience. His findings suggest that 'during the time of the Second Intifada, under a prolonged period of daily suicidal attacks causing hundreds of casualties, the Israeli society demonstrated a relatively high level of national resilience'. This study is particularly interesting since it clearly intimates that bad things can and do happen – in some contexts on a routine daily basis – but this does not mean that such negative precariousness is necessarily debilitating. This is a point to which we shall return.

In Britain and arguably elsewhere, resilience creep has taken on a particular flavour. If we situate this turn to resilience within the government's 'Big Society' agenda, it is possible to discern tangible links between an ostensibly political agenda, largely driven by economic cost cutting and a wide-ranging resilience policy stance. The more the State is able to responsibilize citizens, community groups and third sector agencies to develop contingency plans and to develop strategies to manage threats, the less of this work has to be done centrally. Simultaneously, such processes belie the entrepreneurial undertones that this kind of policy shift engenders (see O'Malley, 2011). However, when we examine this policy turn against the academic narratives on resilience referenced above, not only do we become sensitive to the kind of definition of resilience that is being adopted, we are also alerted to the extent to which those policies may or may not resonate with empirical evidence that points to inherent, structural and experiential resilience. In other words, there are *resiliences* rather than one uniform or unitary sense of resilience.

British resilience or resiliences of Britain?

Coaffee *et al.* (2009: 110) inform us that the expressed desire to build resilience has been commonly used as a 'modus operandi of governance underpinning domestic emergency'. Illustrative of this modus operandi and citing Edwards (2009), they go on to suggest that UK disaster management policy frames resilience in terms of the capacity of an individual or community to withstand or recover from adversity: the engineering definition. This 'bouncebackability' (Coaffee *et al.*, 2009) take on resilience is tempered in later policies insofar as it recognizes that for individuals resilience is not constant: 'they need to be able to assess their proximity or vulnerability to these risks and use this as a motivation to act and be prepared' (Cabinet Office, 2011c: 11). However, the marriage between resilience, risk and vulnerability, commented on above, is self-evident. Further, the United Kingdom Strategic National Framework On Community Resilience defines resilience as, 'communities and individuals harnessing local resources and expertise to help themselves in an emergency, in a way that complements the response of the emergency services' (Cabinet Office, 2011c: 11). Within this document four different types of community are identified: (i) geographical, (ii) interest, (iii) circumstance and (iv) supporters. All of these different communities are exhorted to enable, remove barriers, facilitate dialogue, raise awareness and work towards a shared framework to increase resilience against threats. Here we have evidence of the presumption of resilience deficit (in communities in particular) that flies in the face of what it is that is actually known about how individuals and communities work and respond in times of emergency (see, *inter alia*, Durodie, 2004; Furedi, 2007; Wessely, 2005).

Alongside policy statements such as these, and in conjunction with the Civil Contingencies Act (2004) and the National Risk Register of Civil Emergencies (see Cabinet Office, 2012), there is 'emergency preparedness' guidance at a local level on the most severe potential threats to the UK including 'malicious attacks' – meaning terrorism of various kinds – and 'natural disasters'. This follows on from the non statutory guidance accompanying the Civil Contingencies Act (2004) that formally addressed opportunities for national and local responses to emergencies. Here, resilience is defined as the 'ability of the community, services, area or infrastructure to detect, prevent, and, if necessary to withstand, handle and recover from disruptive challenges' (HM Government, 2010: 330). Thus, local and national resilience is to be maintained in 'local resilience areas', under the guidance of 'local resilience forums' comprising those considered to be the appropriate coordinated responders (police, fire, local authorities) under the Civil Contingencies Act (2004). This macro policy development was thought to bring together all aspects of the disaster cycle: preparedness, response, recovery and mitigation (see Coaffee *et al.*, 2009).

In reviewing this policy the government established a Critical Infrastructure Resilience Programme that offers an assessment of Britain's resilience capabilities and guidance for how resilience can be fostered by industry, emergency services and government departments working together to maintain and improve essential services in the event of a 'natural hazard' (Cabinet Office, 2011b: 12). Herein we are reminded that resilience is also dependent upon a well-designed infrastructure, organized emergency services and contingency planning from businesses (Cabinet Office, 2011a). Hand-in-hand with this the UK has also set in train a Community Resilience Programme as a part of its Strategic National Framework on Community Resilience (SNFCR). This 'invites individuals and communities to prepare themselves in the event of an emergency and provides examples of how to do so' (Cabinet Office, 2011c: 3). Of course, in the foreground of such policies is the assumption that communities lack the ability to be resilient and without the involvement of the State remain vulnerable to impending risk, or 'disruptive challenges' (Furedi, 2008). Within this Strategic National Framework – as indicated in the Sector Resilience Plans for Critical Infrastructure 2010/2011 aptly named *Keeping the Country Running: Natural hazards and infrastructure* – it is evident that it is the terrorist threat (redefined in resilience policy as 'malicious attacks') that has been fore-grounded. It is this threat that informs the distribution of people and resources in the implementation of these policies (Coaffee *et al.*, 2009; Cole, 2010). This, despite the fact that the government's own register of risks actually puts pandemic influenza and coastal flooding as higher and as more severe threats than terrorism (Cabinet Office, 2012; Cole, 2010). The prioritization of 'malicious attacks' over flooding or pandemic influenza is interesting, particularly if we consider the relative economic costs of these different threats/challenges. For example, the Cabinet Office (2011b) itself noted that not only are natural hazards now a priority risk for the UK, they are also expensive. The summer floods of 2007, for instance, cost the economy and critical infrastructure £4 billion and £674 billion respectively, not to mention the reputational organizational damages suffered in its aftermath. There were similar if perhaps larger scale economic consequences suffered in the United States post Hurricane Katrina. Yet despite these real economic consequences, there is still an emphasis on the threat from terrorism prevailing in both countries. The question remains: why? In order to begin to frame an answer to this question it will be necessary to situate these policy preoccupations with resilience within the policy agenda that is geared more specifically to the prevention of terrorism.

As Chapter 4 has demonstrated, the preventive strategy in respect of terrorism is articulated in the British context, primarily through the CONTEST agenda. This is presently in its third iteration, pre-dates SNFCR and has four strands: Pursue, Prevent, Protect and Prepare. In its most recent form, the joins between CONTEST, SNFCR and the National Risk Register can be easily discerned. CONTEST priorities set for 2011–15 are to:

- continue to build generic capabilities to respond to and recover from a wide range of terrorist and other civil emergencies;
- improve preparedness for the highest impact risks in the National Risk Assessment;
- improve the ability of the emergency services to work together during a terrorist attack;
- enhance communications and information sharing for terrorist attacks.

The links and contradictions with the SNFCR are evident here – especially in relation to the government's own assessment of potential threats in the National Risk Register. Since 9/11 – and more pointedly since 7/7 in case of the UK – Muslim minority groups have been consistently constructed in policy as 'risky' others and represented as a threat to national stability (see Abbas, 2011; Mythen *et al.*, 2012). These are the individuals and groups against whom the (assumed non-Muslim) public must be *collectively* resilient since they have been constituted as both external and internal threats to security.

As detailed in Chapters 4 and 5, the introduction of the Terrorism Act (2000) permitting stop and search powers to be used without cause for suspicion has not only proven to be ineffectual in terms of apprehending potential terrorists but has also been highly detrimental to community relations (Sharp and Atherton, 2007; Thiel, 2009). Thus, somewhat paradoxically, the strategic targeting of young Muslims for section 44 searches has led to the development of a range of personal and collective 'resilient' techniques and strategies to avoid harassment, defuse tension and resist risk labelling (see Mythen *et al.*, 2013). Insofar as the 'safe' population are exhorted by the State to be vigilant and resilient against Islamic extremists, empirical evidence suggests that moderate Muslims finding themselves constructed as 'risky' are forced to develop resilience to and against surveillance, intrusion, questioning and the casual racism of other members of the public. Thus, institutional fears about worst-case scenarios, reflected in the statements from the CONTEST strategy above, overlaid with presumptions around whom it is we need to be resilient from, have arguably been used as an ideational prop for the loss of liberty for (some) individuals. This may ironically provoke the 'law of inverse consequences', where the risk that is apparently being managed actually becomes heightened by the repressive activities of the State. Moreover, in terms of resilience policies, what we have also exemplified here are the tensions between resilience as presumed and resilience as experienced, and the unintended consequences that result when the former ignores the latter.

If we return to the questions posed by Brand and Jax (2007) – resilience from what, to what, with what – we can forge connections between the policy turn to resilience and the earlier policy preoccupation with risk. There is (at least) one remarkable feature of continuity between the two: the focus on Muslim minority groups. This focus, of course, endorses the continuing significance attached to the 9/11 moment, and other similar moments, that have followed in its wake. However, its reinforcement in the policy turn to resilience not only flies in the face of empirical evidence surrounding individual and community resilience in times of disaster – some of which was evident at the 9/11 moment itself – it also serves to hide the deeper structural concerns that are arguably embedded here. So, if we consider the underbelly effects of these political and policy narratives of resilience, another layer of resilience comes into view: one that is not preoccupied with the engineering definition of resilience, nor one simply using resilience as an ideological metaphor, but one that comes closest to that proposed by Gunderson and Holling (2002) in their complex systems theory. This version of resilience is more than a reflection of politicians' anxieties (Furedi, 2008). It is neither concerned with individuals, communities nor institutions but is concerned to support and maintain the State as resilient. Thus, in the perpetual prioritization of the terrorism, now dressed up as 'malicious threats', we can discern a deeper preoccupation. This deeper preoccupation draws our attention to a concern with the resilience of the State. This is more than a metaphorical concern, though that use serves important ideological purposes: it has real consequences. Those consequences, intended and unintended, form an important link between the unpacking of the processes of suspectification discussed in Chapter 5, with the perpetuation of those processes, over and through time, discerned here. They lead us to reflect upon the suspect nature of this policy turn to resilience, in and of itself.

Suspect people, suspect communities or suspect policies?

So far in this chapter we have located the emergence of the policy turn to resilience within the policy precursor of risk and we have noted that an important bridge between these two concepts has been presumptions about vulnerability. Interestingly, despite a wealth of empirical evidence that suggests otherwise, the policy turn to resilience has done little to challenge the assumptions made about who or what is considered to be vulnerable and why. These conceptual parameters remain unchallenged. So, for example, the capacity of individuals and communities not to panic but to cooperate in times of disaster has largely been sidelined (Wessely, 2005). Moreover, perhaps more significantly, the presumption of resilience deficit (suggested above) denies how it is that individuals, communities, institutions and nations get on with the 'challenges' they face on a routine daily basis, resilience policies notwithstanding. There are numerous empirical examples that document these capacities. Rather than being 'incapacitated by fear' (Furedi 2004: 19), community relations can and do, especially in economically deprived communities, foster the conditions for the maintenance of resilience (Innes and Jones, 2006). For example, the work of Eggerman and Panter-Brick (2010: 78) points to the way in which cultural norms and values in highly deprived areas of Afghanistan 'function as both an anchor for resilience and an anvil of pain'. They go on to suggest that 'strong religious faith [iman] and individual effort [koshesh] are values that structure a *discourse of resilience* in the face of adversity' (ibid.: 81, emphasis in the original).

These remarks are not intended to imply, neither do they mean, that resilience is uncontested. Harrison (2012: 13) usefully reminds us that the concept of community resilience 'conflates how people see themselves or are seen as members of different communities while living in the same place'. Moreover, Mason and Pulvirenti (2013) go on to suggest that some aspects of such contestation may be 'papered over' by professionals in the interests of collective safety especially in the context of domestic violence. In other words, community resilience may look different dependent upon an individual's subject position in their community. It may also look different depending upon one's global/geographical position alongside what kind of issue is of concern. Debates around resilience and climate change for example can have a different shape and form depending upon access to global resources and geographical position. This then acts as yet another pertinent juncture to be reminded of Connell's (2007) observations on Northern theorizing. At the level of the individual, those subjected to the policies outlined here do not necessarily respond in the way policy might want or predict. The potential for a diverse range of individual and community responses is supported in the comparative work of Hickman *et al.* (2011) and the qualitative work of Mythen (2012). Indeed, Mythen goes on to suggest that, as a result of feeling that they are made to *choose* an identity as a result of the types of policy interventions that cast non-compliance as aberrance, young Pakistani males may be inclined to adopt a renewed commitment to Islam as a means of anchoring self-identity.

These observations suggest that there are tensions between different kinds of knowledges (about resilience and what it means), and the viability of those knowledges as a basis for action. As with risk, in which it is possible to discern different knowledge bases that inform policy, research and practice (see Walklate and Mythen, 2011), so too with resilience. Put simply, we can track and trace a policy narrative, an academic narrative and a 'real life' narrative about resilience. Although the points at which these narratives of resilience align are few and far between, the overarching narratives of risk and resilience do coincide, and where they do so it is in relation to, as noted by Davoudi (2012: 299), those situations when 'we cannot consider resilience without paying attention to issues of justice and fairness in terms of both the procedures for decision-making and the distribution of burdens and benefits. In short, who is to be included and excluded from "resilience(s)"?'

Thus, our discussion points to a common denominator in the policy agendas of risk and resilience. Those who are included and/or excluded as having the capacity for, or lacking the capacity for, resilience are the same as those deemed risky: the Muslim minority. There is then a symmetrical relationship between those considered suspect, those considered risky and those against whom we must be resilient. There is little recognition that the policies contribute to this symmetry and are, by implication, themselves suspect. We have suggested that these policies are reliant, not on evidence, but on political assertion. Such an assertion serves the interests of the kinds of inclusive and exclusive practices that contribute to the maintenance of the State. In particular the exclusive practices – those deemed suspect and/or who need resilience enhancement – reflect the kind of 'Othering' commented on by Bauman (2006) and Young (2007) discussed in Chapter 1. They have the distinct qualities of not only maintaining the State but also feeding the fears and insecurities that underpin the maintenance of the State. Here we can observe not only liquid fears (Bauman 2006) but also liquid resilience. This kind of resilience has an inherent plasticity and a hermeneutic stretchiness. It is the kind of resilience that can be harnessed by dominant social groups, central in the processes of resilience definition. These are the groups, who are also, coincidentally, those central to the risk defining processes. As asserted in Chapter 3, the political manipulation engaged in by the Bush and Blair regimes around the 'war on terror'/'war against terrorism', stands as an incontrovertible case in point (see also Mythen and Walklate, 2006; Simon, 2007).

To summarize: given the impact that the events at the turn of the twenty-first century produced, alongside the responses deemed appropriate to deal with such events, some continuity between the past and the present in relation to those deemed 'problematic' to the Westocentric world is hardly surprising. Moreover the presumed Occidentalism in both the conception and the application of the policies with which we have been concerned above is also hardly surprising. However, both inevitably result in the denial of other interpretations of how to be prepared for catastrophe and both also assist in masking the deeper preoccupation of this policy turn to resilience: that of maintaining a resilient State.

Building States of resilience or reproducing the resilient State?

Notwithstanding one's view of the legitimacy of the responsibilization of citizens around security generally, the preceding discussion has documented an important contextual change since 9/11 and the policies that followed in the wake of those events. While for Britain and America in particular (but also other European States) counter-terrorism remains a strategic priority, it does so in a context in which public sector services alongside military services face severe budgetary constraints as many Westocentric states grapple with the fallout of the 2008 banking crisis. Against this economic backcloth it is easy to see how and why resilience has risen up the policy agenda in the shape and form that it has. To offer a crude analysis of these changes, while risk required the allocation of significant State resources, resilience is rather more cost-effective. It incites individuals, families and communities to 'do-it-yourself', albeit with steers from the State. Within this policy 'imaginary' (Carlen, 2008), the resilience with which such policies are actually concerned is the resilience of the State. Thus, it is possible to argue that the policies discussed above speak to 'an imagined political community' (imagined in this case by politicians) in which the State engages in:

> Hegemonic projects that seek to reconcile the particular and the universal by linking the nature and purposes of the State into a broader – but always selective – political, intellectual, and moral vision of the public interest, the good society, the commonweal or some analogous principle of societalization.
>
> (Jessop, 2002: 42)

Such projects function in support of the 'neo-liberal imaginary of each subject being the entrepreneur of oneself' (O'Malley, 2011: 13); on the one hand responsibilized as individual citizens and on the other hand having their efforts harnessed as part of a resilient community response to the 'disruptive events' of terrorism and natural hazards.

Thus, in the shadows of this policy take on resilience lurks the silhouette of the State: not an ideologically or economically deterministic or determined State, but one that works expediently in such a way as to ensure that institutions and organizations selectively engage in activities that they subsequently become bound by. In Althusserian terms, this search for resilience, and the exhortations for citizens and communities to *be* resilient, makes appeals to individuals who are 'always-already' exposed to dominant ideas and impacted by ideological forces (Althusser, 1970). In a similar vein, Aradau (2010) observes that however disruptive a catastrophic event might prove to be, the capitalist system ultimately preserves its identity. It does not, as the disparaging phrase goes, waste a good crisis. She remarks 'while the CIA conjure images of a spiritual caliphate, we will still have Amazon.com' (2010: 7). Echoing Walker and Cooper's (2011) analysis of Gunderson and Holling's complex systems theory of resilience, we are reminded that the public good of resilience is preserved in the interests of not just the State, but the capitalist State. This is not intended to imply that there may, or may not, be other beneficiaries in the process of 'building' resilience. Such benefits may range from communities receiving investments to both public and private sector organizations making gains from their involvement in such initiatives. All of these interest groups may benefit from this resilience moment. Indeed politicians and policy makers may invoke the concept of resilience metaphorically to ensure public support for policy. However – especially under times of economic constraint – this metaphorical use belies underlying economic and ideological interests. It also belies those practices that align suspect communities and suspect individuals with those who are resilient deficient and against whom the 'rest of us' need to build resilience, all on the back of policies, themselves suspect since they bare little relationship with the evidence. This 'fostering of resilience', as Aradau and Van Munster (2011: 46) have observed, is the 'goal of preparedness'. The question is, on what basis is this preparedness being constructed? They go on to suggest that it is rooted in a 'politics of catastrophe'.

Conclusion: moving towards a 'politics of catastrophe'?

In this chapter we have tried to unpack and problematize the concept of resilience. We began with three definitions of resilience: as an engineering concept, as a derivative of complex systems theory and as a metaphor. We have explored these takes on resilience against contemporary policy initiatives, using the United Kingdom as our case study, which assume that the building of resilience requires the active engagement of not just individuals, but communities, charities, businesses and the emergency services. Yet, in translating the concept of resilience into policy, it has been possible to discern tensions between those policy presumptions, what resilience actually means and what is known about how it is manifested. We have also observed symmetry between those defined as risky and those against whom we must be resilient, which becomes evident in the use and application of resilience in relation to counter-terrorism measures. This exploration has suggested that much more is at stake here than building individual, community or national capacity to deal with adverse incidents. We have argued that there is a need to recognize not only that the concept of resilience is socially constructed but also that it is being harnessed in the survival of the State and that such practices can have different forms in different contexts (see Walklate *et al.*, 2012). This is made possible not only by the State sketching threats that are 'out there', and invoking ways in which citizens should respond to them, but also through consolidation of the kind of 'what if' thinking described in earlier chapters embedded in the shift from risk to resilience that we have discussed here. In this way resilience has been mobilized to activate citizens to be resilient from threats that range from managing 'suspect communities' to responding to natural hazards. Simultaneously, this policy directive serves to drive forward underlying economic and political agendas, perhaps not on the cheap, but certainly with a lighter touch from the State and a larger input from the community.

In subjecting resilience to such critical scrutiny, we have been concerned to pinpoint what is missing from how this concept, and the policies that have been derived from it, have been constructed. As Williams and Drury (2009: 296) postulate:

There are many myths about disasters. The first and most enduring is that crowds panic. A second is that people are inevitably immobilized by fear. A third is that chaos occurs within responding agencies. Research shows that panic is rare. Many people who are directly involved are the first to take action. Often, disasters create unity and improve inter-agency cooperation.

As we have argued, the capacity of individuals and communities to 'keep calm and carry on' has been sidelined. Indeed, government policy makers have largely ignored academic narratives that show resilience to be a variable and highly contested concept. It should be remembered that resilience is not an objective condition, nor an immutable state that individuals or communities can arrive at through working together. Rather, there are multiple resiliences that manifest themselves in different contexts and conditions. This point is well made in the work of Siapno (2009) who, drawing on Castillo's (2003) 'repertoire of traditional resources of resilience' on the nature of 'everyday resilience' discusses the impact of forcible displacement experienced in East Timor after the tsunami. She states that: 'Unintended consequences that are not soul destroying and crippling, but enable slow recovery, resiliency, and having the capacity to make whole again – healing – that which has been destroyed, albeit, with tiny, small steps' (Siapno, 2009: 60).

These findings are evocative of those of Eggerman and Panter-Brick (2010) cited earlier. An appreciation of such 'repertoires of resilience', meaningfully engaged in and meaningfully understood, would be of value whether we are talking about surviving a large-scale hurricane, managing the aftermath of a bomb attack, circumnavigating over-zealous counter-terrorism, or trying to measure well-being and resilience in local communities. Indeed the findings of the work of Mythen et al. (2013) and Mythen (2012) would point to the efficacy of such an understanding. This kind of understanding might facilitate a better appreciation of the contradictions posed by a decade preoccupied with terrorism particularly for those targeted by such preoccupations.

However, it is also important to be mindful that within the spectrum of unexpected and everyday resiliences, constructed in circumstances beyond individuals' own choosing, is also where the search for the resilient State may take its greatest toll. Gaillard (2010: 227) has noted in reflecting on the relationship between policy development and climate change: 'the gap is wide. Closing it will require huge efforts from all those involved, and will definitely require much more than the metaphorical use of concepts such as vulnerability, capacity and resilience'. Focusing on counter-terrorism, security and resilience policy, we can observe a similar gap and, as with climate change, those who are least able to deflect or resist the policy logic may well be those that pay the greatest price for it. Aradau and Van Munster (2011) sagely note that, within the context of economics, when catastrophe strikes the insurance companies ensure that the propertied remain propertied. Indeed, in their view, catastrophe, and the associated politics driven by uncertainty, 'challenge capitalisms commitment to the security of the future' (ibid.: xxx). Within such politics, not only is what is shattered, but what can be also becomes problematic. Anderson (2010) points out that liberal democracies are increasingly centred on preparedness, pre-emption, precaution combined with resilience. Hence they are rooted in anticipation of not just the next catastrophe but *the* catastrophe. The one from which there will be no return. Against this backcloth:

> The question at issue is not whether one chooses vulnerability or resilience as the norm or defining condition of individuals and their community. Rather, the problem is the representation of resilience as merely an antidote to a prior problem. Down-sizing the status of resilience to a secondary role also indicates that far from being natural it is perceived as a reaction that needs to be stimulated from the outside. If resilience is depicted as a kind of cultural pain-relief to a community suffering from an illness, it will lack any organic relationship to society.
>
> (Furedi, 2008: 657)

It is this lack of an organic relationship to society that we have demonstrated in this chapter; the consequences of which are being met, resisted and paid for by those communities in which the political wish, it would appear, is for the exact opposite. While it is evident that much of the underlying ethos of the policy agenda under discussion here has relied upon 'the political manipulation of public fears. The legislative frenzy that has followed since 2001 has necessitated a state of perpetual fear to be manufactured and sustained' (Pantazis and Pemberton, 2012: 664). As they go on to observe, these politics are also corrosive with effects that 'will continue to erode our fundamental civil liberties for the foreseeable future' (ibid.: 665). In this sense, in the search for anticipatory policies, it may be that liberal democracies have already paid at least some of the price.

In conclusion, there may well be more than a politics of catastrophe at stake. If we return to the questions posed by Connell (2007) and Aas (2012) posited in the introduction to this book, if the geography of such anticipatory practices continues to be framed in isolation from other ongoing global threats, then there is perhaps a higher price to pay for the relative stability of the Western world. No wonder then that Bell (1979) presaged a return to the sacred.

References

Aas, K. (2012) The earth is one but the world is not: Criminological theory and its geopolitical divisions. *Theoretical Criminology*, 16(1): 5–20.

Abbas, T. (2011) *Islamic Radicalism and Multicultural Politics*. London: Routledge.

Althusser, L. (1970) *Lenin and Philosophy and Other Essays*. New York: Monthly Review Press.

Anderson, B. (2010) Preemption, precaution, preparedness: Anticipatory action and future geographies. *Progress in Human Geography*, 34(6): 777–98.

Aradau, C. (2010) The myth of preparedness. *Radical Philosophy*, 161 May/June: 2–7.

Aradau, C. and Van Munster, R. (2011) *Politics of Catastrophe: Genealogies of the unknown*. London: Routledge.

Australian National Strategy for Disaster Resilience (2007). Available at www.ag.gov.au/cca (accessed 15 April 2014).

Bauman, Z. (2000) *Liquid Modernity*. Cambridge: Polity Press.

Bauman, Z. (2006) *Liquid Fear*. Cambridge: Polity Press.

Beck, U. (2009) *World at Risk*. Cambridge: Polity Press.

Bell, D. (1979) *The Cultural Contradictions of Capitalism*. 2nd edn. London: Heinemann.

Berkes, F. (2007) Understanding uncertainty and reducing vulnerability: Lessons from resilience thinking. *Natural Hazards*, 41: 283–95.

Bouchard, M. (2007) On the resilience of illegal drug markets. *Global Crime*, 84: 20–32.

Bouvier, P. (2003) Child sexual abuse: Vicious circles of fate or paths to resilience? *The Lancet*, 361: 446–7.

Brand, F.S. and Jax, K. (2007) Focusing the meaning(s) of resilience: Resilience as a descriptive concept and a boundary object. *Ecology and Society*, 12(1).

Butler, J. (2004) *Precarious Life*. London: Verso Books.

Cabinet Office (2011a) *A Summary of the Sector: Resilience plans for critical infrastructure 2010/2011*. London: Cabinet Office.

Cabinet Office (2011b) *Keeping the Country Running: Natural hazards and infrastructure*. London: Cabinet Office.

Cabinet Office (2011c) *Strategic National Framework on Community Resilience*. London: Cabinet Office.

Cabinet Office (2012) *National Risk Register of Civil Emergencies*. London: Cabinet Office.

Carlen, P. (2008) Imaginary penalties and risk crazed governance. In P. Carlen (ed.) *Imaginary Penalities*. Cullompton: Willan, pp. 1–25.

Castillo, F.A. (2003). Bamboo or Molave: Limits of resilience and implications for post-conflict work. Paper presented to the conference on the Negotiation of People's Health Rights, Cagayan de Oro City, Philippines, pp. 1–13.

Coaffee, J. (2006) From counter terrorism to resilience. *The European Legacy*, 11(4): 389–403.

Coaffee, J. and Rogers, P. (2008a) Rebordering the city for new security challenges: From counter-terrorism to community resilience. *Space and Polity*, 12 (1): 101–18.

Coaffee, J. and Rogers, P. (2008b) Reputational risk and resiliency: The branding of security in place-making. *Place, Branding and Public Diplomacy*, 4 (3): 205–17.

Coaffee, J., Wood, D. and Rogers, P. (2009) *The Everyday Resilience of the City*. London: Palgrave.

Cole, J. (2010) Securing our future: Resilience in the twenty-first century. *The RUSI Journal*, 155(2): 46–51.

Connell, R. (2007) The northern theory of globalization. *Sociological Theory*, 25(4): 368–85.

Das, V. (2007) *Life and Words: Violence and the descent into the ordinary*. Berkeley, CA: University of California Press.

Davoudi, S. (2012) Resilience: A Bridging Concept or a Dead End? *Planning Theory and Practice*, 1(2): 299–333.

Day, M.J. (1964) An adventure experiment with boys on probation. *British Journal of Criminology*, (4)5: 486–91.

Durodie, B. (2004) The limitations of risk management: Dealing with disasters and building social resilience. *Tidsskriftet Politik*, 8(1): 16–21.

Edwards, C. (2009) *Resilient Nation*. London: Demos.

Eggerman, M. and Panter-Brick, C. (2010) Suffering, hope and entrapment: Resilience and cultural values in Afghanistan. *Social Science and Medicine*, 71: 71–83.

Findlay, M. (2008) *Governing Through Globalised Crime*. Cullompton: Willan.

Fischhoff, B. and Kadvany, J. (2011) *Risk: A very short introduction*. Oxford: Oxford University Press.

Furedi, F. (2004) Heroes of the Hour. *New Scientist*, 8 May, p. 19.

Furedi, F. (2007) From the narrative of the Blitz to the rhetoric of vulnerability. *Cultural Sociology*, 1(2): 235–54.

Furedi, F. (2008) Fear and security: A vulnerability-led policy response. *Social Policy and Administration*, 42(6): 645–61.

Gal, R. (2011) Social resilience in times of protracted crises: An Israeli case study. Paper presented to Inter-University Seminar on Armed Forces and Society, symposium on National Resilience, Chicago, October.

Gaillard, J.C. (2010) Vulnerability, capacity, and resilience: Perspectives for climate and development policy. *Journal of International Development*, 22: 281–92.

Garland, D. (2001) *The Culture of Control*. Oxford: Polity.

Gilligan, R. (2000) Adversity, resilience and young people: The protective value of positive school and spare time experiences. *Children and Society*, 14: 37–47.

Green, S. (2007) Crime victimisation and vulnerability. In S. Walklate (ed.) *Handbook on Victims and Victimology*. London: Routledge, pp. 91–118.

Gunderson, L.S. and Holling, C.S. (eds) (2002) *Panarchy: Understanding transformations in human and natural systems*. Washington, DC: Island Press.

Haas, H., Farrington, D., Killias, M. and Sattar, G. (2004) The impact of different family configurations on delinquency. *British Journal of Criminology*, 44(4): 520–32.

Harrison, E. (2012) Bouncing Back? Recession, resilience and everyday lives. *Critical Social Policy*, 33(1): 97–113.

Hayden, C., Williamson, T. and Webber, R. (2007) Schools, pupil behaviour and young offenders: Using postcode classification to target behaviour support and crime prevention programmes. *British Journal of Criminology*, 47(2): 293–310.

Hickman, M., Thomas, L., Silvestri, S. and Nickels, H. (2011) *Suspect Communities? Counter-terrorism policy, the press, and impact on Muslim and Irish Communities*. London: London Metropolitan University.

HM Government (2010) *Non Statutory Guidance Accompanying the Civil Contingencies Act (2004)*. London: Stationary Office.

Holling, C.S. (1973) Resilience and the stability of ecological systems. *Annual Review of Ecology and Systematics*, 4: 1–23.

Innes, M. and Jones, V. (2006) *Neighbourhood Security and Urban Change*. York: Joseph Rowntree Foundation.

Isin, E. (2004) 'The Neurotic Citizen', *Citizenship Studies*, 8(3): 217–35.

Jessop, B. (2002) *The Future of the Capitalist State*. Cambridge: Polity Press.

Juby, H. and Farrington, D. (2001) Disentangling the link between disrupted families and delinquency. *British Journal of Criminology*, 41(1): 22–40.

Kearon, A., Mythen, G. and Walklate, S. (2007) Communicating the terrorist threat: Public perceptions of government advice. *The Security Journal*, 20(2): 77–95.

Killias, M. and Clerici, C. (2000) Different measures of vulnerability and their relation to different dimensions of fear of crime. *British Journal of Criminology*, 40(3): 437–50.

Layler, K. (1999) Street children: A comparative perspective. *Child Abuse and Neglect*, 23(8): 759–70.

Lentzos, F. and Rose, N. (2009) Governing insecurity: Contingency planning, protection, resistance. *Economy and Society*, 38: 230–54.

Lupton, D. (1999) *Risk*. London: Sage.

Mason, G. and Pulvirenti, M. (2013) Former refugees and community resilience: Papering over domestic violence. *British Journal of Criminology* advance access, 401–18.

Misztal, B. (2011) *The Challenges of Vulnerability: In search of strategies for a less vulnerable social life*. London: Palgrave-Macmillan.

Moser, C. (1998) The asset vulnerability framework: Assessing urban poverty reduction strategies. *World Development*, 25(1): 1–19.

Murray, C. (2008) Conceptualising young people's resistance to offending as active resilience. Advance access *British Journal of Social Work*. Doi:10.1093/bjsw/bcn115.

Mythen, G. (2004) *Ulrich Beck: A critical introduction to the risk society*. London: Pluto Press.

Mythen, G. (2012) No-one speaks for us: Security policy, suspected communities and the problem of voice. *Critical Studies on Terrorism*, 5(3): 409–24.

Mythen, G. and Walklate, S. (2006) Criminology and terrorism: Which thesis? Risk society or governmentality? *British Journal of Criminology*, 46(3): 379–98.

Mythen, G. and Walklate, S. (2013) Risk, nichtwissen and fear: Searching for solidity in liquid times? In M. Davis, (ed.) *Liquid Sociology*. Aldershot: Ashgate, pp. 139–56.

Mythen, G., Walklate, S. and McGarry, R. (2012) States of resilience and the resilient state. *Current Issues in Criminal Justice*, 24(2): 185–204.

Mythen, G., Walklate, S. and Khan, F. (2013) Why should we have to prove we're alright?: Counter-terrorism, risk and partial securities. *Sociology*, 47(2): 382–97.

O'Malley, P. (2011) Security after risk: Security strategies for governing extreme uncertainty. *Current Issues in Criminal Justice*, 23(1): 5–16.

Pain, R. (2003) Old age and victimisation. In P. Davies, P. Francis and V. Jupp (eds) *Victimisation: Theory, research and policy*. London: Palgrave, pp. 61–79.

Pantazis, C. and Pemberton, S. (2012) Reconfiguring security and liberty: Political discourses and public opinion in the new century. *British Journal of Criminology*, 52(3): 651–67.

Pendall, R., Foster, K. and Cowell, M. (2010) Resilience and regions: Building understanding of the metaphor. *Cambridge Journal of Regions, Economy and Society*, 3(1): 71–84.

Pickett, S.T., Cadenasso, M.L. and Grove, J.M. (2004) Resilient cities meaning models and metaphor for integrating the ecological socio-economic and planning realms. *Landscape and Urban Planning* 69: 369–84.

Rogers, P. (2011) Development of a resilient Australia: Enhancing the PPRR approach with anticipation assessment and registration of risks. *The Australian Journal of Emergency Management*, 261: 54–8.

Rumgay, J. (2004) Scripts for safer survival: Pathways out of female crime. *Howard Journal*, 43(4): 405–19.

Schoon, I. (2006) *Risk and Resilience: Adaptations in changing times*. Cambridge: Cambridge University Press.

Sharp, D. and Atherton, S. (2007) To serve and protect? The experiences of policing in the community of young people from black and other ethnic minority groups. *British Journal of Criminology*, 47(1): 746–63.

Siapno, J.A. (2009) Living through terror: Everyday resilience in East Timor and Aceh. *Social Identities*, 15(1): 43–64.

Simon, J. (2007) *Governing Through Crime*. Oxford: Oxford University Press.

Sparks, R. (1982) *Research on Victims of Crime: Accomplishments, issues, and new directions*. Rockville, MD: US Department of Health and Human Services.

Stattin, H., Romelsjo, A. and Stenbacka, M. (2004) Personal resources as modifiers of the risk of future criminality. *British Journal of Criminology*, 37(2): 198–223.

Taylor, A. (1960) The effects of imprisonment. *British Journal of Criminology*, 1(1): 64–9.

Thiel, D. (2009) *Policing Terrorism: A review of the evidence*. London: Police Foundation.

Ungar, M. (2004) A constructionist discourse on resilience: Multiple contexts, multiple realities among at risk children and youth. *Youth and Society*, 35(3): 341–65.

Valverde, M. (2011) Questions of security: A framework for research. *Theoretical Criminology*, 15(1): 3–22.

Walker, J. and Cooper, M. (2011) Genealogies of resilience: From systems ecology to the political economy of crisis adaptation. *Security Dialogue*, 42(2): 143–60.

Walklate, S. (2011) Reframing criminal victimisation: Finding a place for vulnerability and resilience. *Theoretical Criminology*, 15(2): 179–94.

Walklate, S. and Mythen, G. (2010) Agency, reflexivity and risk: Cosmopolitan, neurotic or prudential citizen? *British Journal of Sociology*, 62(1): 45–62.

Walklate, S. and Mythen, G. (2011) Beyond risk theory: Experiential knowledge and 'knowing otherwise'. *Criminology and Criminal Justice*, 11(2): 99–114.

Walklate, S., Mythen, G. and McGarry, R. (2012) States of resilience or the resilient State? *Issues in Crime and Criminal Justice*, 24(2): 185–204.

Walklate, S., Mythen, G. and McGarry, R. (forthcoming) Searching for resilience: A conceptual excavation. *Armed Forces and Society*.

Wessely, M. (2005) Victimhood and resilience. *New England Medical Journal*, 356 (6): 558–60.

Winkel, F., Blaauw, E., Sheridan, L. and Baldry, A. (2003) Repeat victimisation and vulnerability for coping failure: A prospective examination of a potential risk. *Psychology, Crime and Law*, 9(1): 87–95.

Wilkinson, I. (2010) *Risk, Vulnerability and Everyday Life*. London: Routledge.

Williams, R. and Drury, J. (2009) Psychosocial resilience and its influence on managing mass emergencies and disasters. *Psychiatry*, 8(8): 293–6.

Young, J. (2007) *The Vertigo of Late Modernity*. London: Sage.

CONCLUSION

(Re)orienting criminology

> How can it be that we think we are safe? We think we can be safe
> when we leave a billion people to struggle literally for their daily
> survival; the poorest billion for whom every day is a fight to secure
> enough nutrients . . . how can this be safe?
>
> (Sachs, 2007: 2)

Throughout the course of the book we have emphasized what we see
as the contradictions of terrorism. That is, contradictions in terms of
the processes by which acts, processes and groups are labelled, but also
in terms of the regulation and management of terrorism. In bringing
to the surface some of the contradictions that arise in the construction,
regulation and practice of terrorism we have sought to stress that there
are important messages for criminology and criminologists to take
heed of. As Hall and Winlow (2012: 2) point out, criminology has
historically been slow to respond to crises in a fast-changing world and
has been rather stuck in outdated frameworks and modes of analysis.
In this concluding chapter we hope to convince you, the reader, that
there is much for criminology to embrace, or at least think about
embracing, as the discipline evolves and matures in the twenty-first
century. However, before we outline what we would see as areas ripe
for sustained excavation, it is important to step back and think laterally
and reflexively. For criminology to justify the label 'critical', there is

a need to challenge the domain assumptions that we both inherit and create. This is more than a trifling task, as Bourdieu and Wacquant (1992: 251) proclaim:

> There is no risk of overestimating difficulty and dangers when it comes to thinking the social world. The force of the pre-constructed resides in the fact that, being inscribed in both things and minds, it presents itself under the cloak of the self-evident which goes unnoticed because it is, by definition, taken for granted.

Thus, the task is both steep and broad. It entails reflecting on what is assumed, whose voice counts within the discipline, which conceptual agendas are preferred and what is muted or silenced (see Connell, 2007; Aas, 2012). So, where do we begin?

One place from which to move forward would be by returning to the issues raised in Chapter 1. Here we mapped the turn to risk and considered the influence of risk on criminology, as both a uniform and a unifying concept (O'Malley, 2006). In this chapter we also documented the rising concern with the precarious nature of being, as found in the work of Bauman (2006). Yet we also flagged up a hermeneutic gap in terms of appropriate sensitivity to and understanding of *experiences* of risk and *feelings* of (in)security in contemporary society. The conflation between individual experience and collective experience, implicit in the criminological embrace of these concepts, puts blinkers on how we might theorize, and thereby better understand the subjective conditions that people live through. At present, a conflation between risk and security as theoretical objects of study and habituated sensory experiences can be discerned not only within the academy, but also in policy and practice. It is a conflation that has become easily transferred and embedded in the recent policy turn to resilience as we saw in Chapter 6. For us, a distinct reluctance to explore grounded lived experiences of risk and (in)security leads us to encourage rather than see the limits of the search for 'biographical solutions to systemic problems' (Bauman, 2000: 2–3). Moreover, starting from the (imagined) object rather than the subject constrains the development of a more nuanced criminological vision. To give one illustration of this, perhaps the fear of crime debate might not appear so conceptually sterile if its parameters were shifted to think about security in the round – as multilayered and multifaceted – inclusive of diverse voices and sensitive to disparate geographical conditions. Of course, pushing at the boundaries of the fear of crime debate in this way demands a reoriented criminological imagination. This reorientation is one that matters in respect of methodology as well as method (see Young, 2011). It is important to note, as Carlen (2012: 28) reminds us, that:

> Although academic criminology as a profession is quite properly divided in regard to values, methodologies and politics, resistance to governmental attempts to erode the professional ideals of autonomy and independence in knowledge production is in the collective interests of criminology, criminologists and all their diverse publics.

Yet we also need to acknowledge that the tools and methods which we as criminologists use are far from neutral. As Carlen infers, our discipline is constituted by diverse constituencies who make competing knowledge claims (see Garland, 2001: 24; O'Malley, 2006). So how does a discipline with diverse knowledge claims and diverse constituencies respond to the kinds of questions posed in the preceding chapters? What might comprise a 'criminological imagination' (*qua* Young, 2011) in such circumstances?

Criminology: taking in culture, politics and economy

In many respects, the issues discussed in the preceding chapters return us to some rudimentary criminological questions. In this book we have drawn attention to these questions by asking you, the reader, to reflect on who and what has been defined as risky, criminal and dangerous since 9/11. What exactly has the '9/11 effect' (Roach, 2011) resulted in for whom? What underlying power relationships have produced these effects? Who has been listened to in the process and what has been done on the basis of that listening? These questions are all pertinent for a criminologist since it is beyond doubt that terrorism in all its myriad guises 'counts' as criminal behaviour.

We have argued here that a tight focus on visible and tangible social harms such as terrorism enables the State to set the security agenda and to prioritize some threats over others. As Jackson (2005: 92) notes, for citizens in the West the risk of being killed in a terrorist attack 'ranks somewhere near the risk of being killed by DIY accidents or lightning strikes'. In Chapters 3, 4 and 5 we posited that the prioritization of terrorism both socially and economically has immediate consequences for particular sections of society. Further, the unintended nature of some of those consequences impact upon us all. In our view, this means that we should not only elucidate but also confront the material State violence embedded in the pitching of this ideational compromise (see Coleman *et al.*, 2009: 14). In this regard, there is much to be learned from the past and the unfortunate litanies of draconian counter-terrorism regulation (see Hillyard, 2009: 143; McGovern, 2010). Criminology has both the tools and the knowledge to provide the foundation for that learning. If we are to maintain the social relevance of the discipline, then terrorism enacted by non-State or State actors has to be one of its central concerns. For the criminological imagination to thrive, a broader consideration of security needs to be embraced, one that considers security *in the round* and recognizes the place of terrorism within the full palette of social harms in society. To this end, the recent wave of excessive legislation and over regulation around terrorism should act as a spur, rather than a reason to retreat from debate under the expedient auspices that the subject matter 'belongs' to other (sub)disciplines such as politics, peace studies and international relations. Geopolitical conflicts of interest involving violence, and ideological contests and struggles over power, should not be seen as beyond the analytical ambit of criminology. On the contrary, we would argue that the porous nature of borders and the globalization of crime and violence mean that such issues need to be situated at the centre rather than the margins of criminological inquiry. The corollary implication of this is that if criminology continues to place primary emphasis on the local, national and the empirically quantifiable, it risks becoming something of a 'zombie discipline' that continues to function according to its own partially outmoded traditions rather than recognizing structural transformations, engaging with prescient global issues and building research agendas that scrutinize injustices, harms and inequalities. In order to engage with global issues in a way that avoids reifying the metropole (Connell, 2007), the very concepts, debates and data we use must be subjected to scrutiny, alternative frames of reference must be developed and our interpretations reconsidered (see Keim, 2010). In so doing we need to embrace rather than shy away from ambiguity and to observe rather than conceal the grey areas. Where issues of security and conflict are concerned, the lines of distinction are often much finer than we are encouraged to believe. This brings to mind Jean Paul Sartre's reflections on his role in resisting the Vichy regime in France. Sartre is said to have remarked that he would have to decide whether to be a philosopher or a bomb-maker (Martin, 2012: 304).

Returning to our conceptual starting point, the unprecedented nature and the profound effects of policies and processes of securitization have led to terrorism being cast by some thinkers as the emblem of a dangerous and volatile age. Beck (2002), for instance, has alluded to the modern world as a 'terroristic world risk society', while Borradori (2003) recounts the unsettling experience of living in 'a time of terror'. Insofar as the problem of terrorism should not be belittled, we maintain that it is but one of a range of harms that cause injury and death in the world today. Although media, political and academic attention has gravitated towards terrorism, global social problems such as drought, poverty, malnutrition and disease continue to take lives by the thousand each and every day. In the context of an uneven and divided world, our primary objective in this book has been to ask why terrorism has become such a fundamental concern and to illuminate the contradictions that arise in the treatment of terrorism as a social problem.

We began the book with an explanation of the origins of the title. Bell's (1979) analysis of the dilemmas faced by liberalism was our catalyst. His searching analysis put to the fore the tensions between liberalism's demand for compromise in the interests of civitas alongside the expectations of freedom in Western capitalist society. He states:

> Liberalism accepts the tension of the public and the private, the
> dual roles of person and citizen, individual and group. The ques-
> tions are: how to find common purposes, yet retain individual
> means of fulfilling them; and how to define individual (and group)
> needs and find common means of meeting them. Can these tasks
> be accomplished in a society where 'interest' alone rules?
>
> (Bell, 1979: 279)

While Bell's analysis focused on the cultural, as the quote above
indicates, he was not wont to lose sight of the economic. Neither
have we. In considering the counter-terrorism security drive we have
drawn attention to the importance of economic relationships both in
sustaining the business of terrorism and in generating the (economic)
interests of (various) States. If we step back from the substantive
practices with which we have been concerned and place those practices
within a broader economic framework, it is not only possible to
discern their role in sharper focus, it is also possible to better formulate
the connections between them.

In Chapter 1 we reviewed the various responses discernable to the
problem of not-knowing. There we argued that the institutional
responses to this problem reflected the drive to keep the body politic
safe. We suggested that institutions are, in many respects, bound to do
this under conditions of *nichtwissen*, but particularly bound to within
the wider socio-economic framework of a neoliberal regime. As Fox-
Piven (2010: 111) astutely observes, the political project of domination
remains central under neoliberal economic regimes, however conceived.
Within the velvet glove resides a fist of iron. In Chapter 5 we assessed
the extent to which the neoliberal project has informed institutional
preoccupations in different geographical locations, underscoring the
extent to which it has taken hold in most Western States. It is important
to add the coda that the disciplinary aspects of the neoliberal regime
are only likely to increase as austerity measures bite and are likely to
take their greatest toll on those defined as risky: the suspected. This is
a common experience for the already socially excluded: the 'growing
global surplus population rendered structurally irrelevant' (Hallsworth
and Lea, 2011: 142). What Bauman (2004) calls the 'wasted' coexist

in the context of flexible capitalism in which crime has become a 'master theme' (Feeley, 2003: 126). We suggested some time ago that an aspiration to 'govern through terrorism' could be discerned within the security management policies of Western governments such as Britain and America (Mythen and Walklate, 2006). In our view, this tendency has only intensified over the last decade. While widespread concerns have been raised in the UK by civil rights campaigners, academics and journalists about the effects of anti-terrorism legislation on fundamental democratic freedoms and liberties, basic legal rights such as the right to a fair trial, privacy, asylum and free movement have been curtailed with recourse to the exceptionality of the terrorist threat (see Zedner, 2009). This is a pattern that has historically repeated itself. As Newman (2004: 91) states, 'there is always a violence at the heart of every form of political and legal authority'. In thinking security, the architecture of the neoliberal project involves spotting people who 'do not fit' (Bauman, 2002: 132). What is particularly interesting in all of this is what Jessop (2010: 338) might call, 'complexity reduction'. This concept refers to an everyday problem faced by human beings. Insofar as we are unable to grasp a full understanding of the world and all its nuances at one and the same time, we select and give meaning to some aspects of the world over others. However, while we all engage in this practice, some of those meanings carry greater weight than others. 'Complexity reduction' neatly returns us to the work of Bell (1979) quoted in the introduction, in relation to the caveat regarding the search for simplistic explanations. Here, Jessop advises us to think a little more deeply about the problem of simplification. He encourages us to think about the ways in which all kinds of practices, including those of policy, have been, and are impacted upon by the turn to the cultural in the social. In his analysis the cultural is not as a separate sphere, but one that is intimately connected with and to political economy. Thus, Jessop (2010) is particularly interested in how and under what cultural conditions specific visions and representations take root in preference over others, especially in the context of crisis:

> Relatively successful economic imaginaries presuppose a substratum of substantive economic relations and instrumentalities

as their elements. Conversely, where an imaginary has been successfully operationalized and institutionalized, it transforms and naturalizes these elements and instrumentalities into the moments of a specific economy with specific emergent properties. This process is mediated, as indicated above, through the interaction among specific economic imaginaries, appropriately supportive economic agents – individual or collective – with appropriate modes of calculation and behavioral or operational dispositions, specific technologies that sustain and confirm these imaginaries (e.g. statistics, indexes, benchmarks, records), and structural constellations that limit the pursuit of contrary or antagonistic imaginaries, activities, or technologies.

(Jessop, 2010: 346)

His use of the imaginary in this context comprises much more than the imaginaries of professionals engaged in criminal justice practice. However, it is certainly connected to those 'risk crazed practices' observed by Carlen (2008), particularly given its emphasis on appropriate supporting technologies that limit alternative ways of thinking. Further, Jessop's observations set the context within which the more specific comments made about terrorism by Aradau and Van Munster (2012: 106) can be understood: 'preparing for the next attack effaces the surprise and contingency of the social by privileging the imaginary of legal responsibility and economic survival over other sociopolitical relations'. As we observed in Chapters 3 and 5 – and as Fox-Piven (2010) reminds us – neoliberalism is just another phase of capitalism but a phase of capitalism with arguably a particular characteristic: complexity reduction that privileges the cultural belying the continued centrality of the economic. So, if we look to the continuities within capitalism rather than focusing on the fragility and discontinuity of this present moment we might well get a better feel for the risks and dilemmas of contemporary times alongside the risks and dilemmas for contemporary criminology.

In thinking about the continuities, it is no coincidence that old-fashioned 'police property' (Lee, 1981) invariably includes the young, the unemployed and those from ethnic minority groups. These are also the sections of society who have suffered as work has become deregulated and as labour has become more insecure. In the context of austerity measures, they are those most likely to be both the subject and the object of such measures, as well as the least materially able to manage the consequences. There is nothing particularly new about this (e.g., Fox-Piven and Ohlin, 1971). As the gap between rich and poor grows ever bigger, not just in relation to wealth but also in relation to all forms of 'well-being', including life expectancy, these are the stark consequences of neoliberal capitalism. Consequently, there is a symmetrical relationship between those least likely to be preoccupied with the liquid anxieties of the age – since their preoccupations have always been with work, food and shelter – and those most likely to be the targets of institutional preoccupations, since they constitute the other, the wasted, those to be feared. In this respect there is some similarity here between the argument presented in this book and that offered by Hallsworth and Lea (2011). However, the processes underpinning this symmetrical and symbiotic relationship are, as Wacquant (2009) suggests, doubly political. They are a product of institutional actors *and* rest on a presumption that 'we have a life in common'. It is our contention that if we do have a life in common, that life is most pronounced in the realm of the economic.

Many commentators have revisited the work of Polanyi (1957–2001) in order to make sense of the contemporary malaise of capitalism. Polanyi's concept of a 'double movement' suggested that market capitalism shifted in the face of resistance to protect people and society from its worst excesses. However, despite some conceptual play with the notion of a 'double move' in anticipating terrorism (see Aradau and Van Munster, 2012: 106), Polanyi's concept has been found wanting in grasping both the complexity and the lived reality of the present moment. Fraser (2013) offers one way to fill this gap in Polanyi's work, developing the notion of a 'triple movement'. Centring a number of puzzling questions for contemporary times, such as for example, why do political elites fail to tackle out of control markets and why do we not observe the presence of *united* counter-hegemonic social movements, her analysis suggests that it is necessary to take account of the power of emancipation. While recognizing that this in and of itself adds further complexity to our ability to make political sense of the contemporary world, it does add to our sense-making practices of the role of the cultural. For Fraser (2013: 132), there can be 'no emancipation without some new synthesis of marketization and social protection'. Without which, she wryly observes, billions of people across the world become abandoned since they 'rightly understand that there is something worse than being exploited – namely, being counted as not worth exploiting' (ibid.). Bell (1979: 282) might say, 'people become more equal so that they can be *treated* equally'. For our analysis, such cultural expectations belie the contradictions inherent in the compromises made with liberty in the interests of security. Throughout the book we have sought to argue that the demand for security should not and cannot come at the expense of justice (see Hudson and Ugelvik, 2012: 8). Furthermore, we have restated the need to recognize that 'terrorism' comes in many hues. History shows that what Zizek (2013: 124) calls 'defensive violence' is not only justifiable, but sometimes *required* for emancipation to be achieved, as demonstrated through the struggle against Apartheid in South Africa and the uprisings ongoing in the Middle East. The contradiction between the cultural expectation of emancipation and the material experience of exploitation has profound consequences. At the present analytical juncture, enter the not so ghostly presence of neoliberal capitalism. However, within even that ghostly presence, whether we are discussing risk, resilience or security, there are other available imaginings (O'Malley and Bougen, 2008). How does criminology imagine these imaginings?

Advancing the criminological imagination?

It would be remiss to end without an appreciation of the work of Jock Young. In *The Criminological Imagination*, Young (2011) completed the third part of a trilogy of books. The first text, *The Exclusive Society* (1999) dealt with the cultural transformations that have accompanied the embrace of late modernity. The second, *The Vertigo of Late Modernity* (2007), addresses the apparent inexorable rise of insecurities associated with the processes of inclusion and exclusion. In the third and final book he presents us with a wide-ranging critique of the kind of criminological work, and its science, that has underpinned the political and policy processes that were a constituent part of the changes documented in the first two books. In volume three, Young invites us to reconsider the seminal work of C. Wright Mills in making sense of the criminological involvement in the 'science of othering' documented in the other two volumes, most notably Mills' observations on the dangers of abstracted empiricism. Here Young is centrally preoccupied with the 'bogus of positivism'. Much of this critique is directed towards the 'most influential criminology generated by the most atypical society' (Young, 2011: 80). Young argues that the influence of this 'fetishism with numbers' not only takes its toll on what is considered to be acceptable criminological work but also rests on unsound assumptions about social reality. The toll taken by the 'bogus of positivism' is equally pertinent to victimology (Walklate, 2008). Implied in the critique developed by Young, and among the ironies for a critical criminology that he goes on to outline, are the problems with which our book began: Northern theorizing (Connell, 2007) and its associated presumptions of Occidentalism (see Cain, 2000), coupled to the problems of geography and voice as commented on by Aas (2012). Inserting these interventions into Young's analysis, affords the possibility of adding two further ironies to those listed by Young for critical criminology: knowledge is universal–knowledge is context bound, the state is absent–the state is central (Walklate, 2012 *qua* Young, 2011: 215).

Young (2011: 275) states, 'those who would seek to marginalize critical criminology fail to comprehend its purchase on the grain of social reality'. Here we would add, even when we do not particularly like what it is that such a social reality is saying to us. It is imperative that we speak the unspoken and give voice to the unpalatable if we are to recognize the power of the 'et ceteris paribus' clause embedded within hegemonic epistemologies (see de Sousa-Santos, 2007; Mythen and Walklate, 2013). Such epistemologies are a feature of the 'bogus of positivism' within criminology. Yes, there have been some gains for some people as a result of the power of positivism. This might be unpalatable, but it is nevertheless a reality. However, if criminology after Young is to be a moral enterprise then it is as important as ever to challenge the Occidentalism of positivism and make explicit the ironies embedded in much of contemporary criminology's world view. This means developing an intellectual agenda along theoretical, as well as empirical, lines in such a way that the contributions that criminology makes can be both factually solid, but also conceptually grounded and theoretically challenging. This is why the issues debated in this book are of crucial concern for a discipline that aspires to be politically relevant and socially present.

References

Aas, K. (2012) The earth is one but the world is not: Criminological theory and its geopolitical divisions. *Theoretical Criminology*, 16(1): 5–20.

Aradau, C. and Van Munster, R. (2012) The time/space of preparedness: Anticipating the next terrorist attack. *Space and Culture*, 15(2): 98–109.

Bauman, Z. (2000) *Liquid Modernity*. Cambridge: Polity Press.

Bauman, Z. (2002) *Society Under Siege*. Cambridge: Polity Press.

Bauman, Z. (2004) *Wasted Lives*. Cambridge: Polity Press.

Bauman, Z. (2006) *Liquid Fear*. Cambridge: Polity Press.

Beck, U. (2002) On world risk society, *Logos*, 1 (4): 1–18.

Bell, D. (1979) *The Cultural Contradictions of Capitalism*. London: Heinemann.

Borradori, G. (2003) *Philosophy in a Time of Terror: Dialogues with Jurgen Habermas and Jacques Derrida*. Chicago, IL: University of Chicago Press.

Bourdieu, P. and Wacquant, L. (1992) *An Invitation to Reflexive Sociology*. Chicago, IL: University of Chicago Press.

Cain, M. (2000) Orientalism, Occidentalism and the Sociology of Crime. *British Journal of Criminology*, 40(2): 239–60.

Carlen, P. (2008) Imaginary penalties and risk-crazed governance. In P. Carlen (ed.) *Imaginary Penalities*. Cullompton, Devon: Willan, pp. 1–25.

Carlen, P. (2012) Criminological knowledge: Doing critique, doing politics. In S. Hall and S. Winlow (eds) *New Directions in Criminological Theory*. London: Routledge, pp. 17–29.

Coleman, R., Sim, J., Tombs, S. and Whyte, D. (2009) Introduction. In R. Coleman, J. Sim, S. Tombs and D. Whyte (eds) *State, Power, Crime*. London: Sage, pp. 1–19.

Connell, R. (2007) The northern theory of globalization. *Sociological Theory*, 25(4): 368–85.

de Sousa-Santos, B. (2007) *Another Knowledge is Possible: Beyond northern epistemologies*. London: Verso.

Feeley, M. (2003) Crime, social order and the rise of neo-conservative politics. *Theoretical Criminology*, 7(1): 111–30.

Fox-Piven, F. (2010) A response to Wacquant. *Theoretical Criminology*, 14(1): 111–16.

Fox-Piven, F. and Ohlin, C. (1971) *Regulating the Poor*. New York: Pantheon Books.

Fraser, N. (2013) A triple movement? Parsing the politics of crisis after Polanyi. *New Left Review* (May–June): 119–32.

Garland, D. (2001) *The Culture of Control: Crime and social order in contemporary society*. Oxford: Oxford University Press.

Hall, S. and Winlow, S. (2012) Introduction: The need for new directions in criminological theory. In S. Hall and S. Winlow (eds) *New Directions in Criminological Theory*. London: Routledge, pp. 1–14.

Hallsworth, S. and Lea, J. (2011) Reconstructing Leviathan: Emerging contours of the security state. *Theoretical Criminology*, 15(2): 141–58.

Hillyard, P. (2009) The exceptional state. In R. Coleman, J. Sim, S. Tombs and D. Whyte (eds) *State, Power, Crime*. London: Sage, pp. 129–44.

Hudson, B. and Ugelvik, S. (2012) *Justice and Security in the 21st Century*. London: Routledge.

Jackson, R. (2005) *Writing the War on Terrorism: Language, politics and counterterrorism*. Manchester: Manchester University Press.

Jessop, B. (2010) Cultural political economy and critical policy studies. *Critical Policy Studies*, 3(3–4): 336–56.

Keim, W. (2010) The internationalization of social sciences: Distortions, dominations and prospects. In *International Social Science Council World Social Science Report: Knowledge divides*. Paris: UNESCO Publishing, pp. 169–70.

Lee, J.A. (1981) Some structural aspects of police deviance in relations with ethnic minority groups. In C. Shearing (ed.) *Organisational Police Deviance*. Toronto: Butterworth, pp. 49–82.

Martin, A. (2012) *The Boxer and the Goalkeeper: Sartre versus Camus*. London: Simon & Schuster.

McGovern, M. (2010) *Countering Terror or Counter-Productive?* Liverpool: Edge Hill.

Mythen, G. and Walklate, S. (2006) Criminology and terrorism: Which thesis? Risk society or governmentality? *British Journal of Criminology*, 46(3): 379–98.

Mythen, G. and Walklate, S. (2013) Risk, nichtwissen and agency: Keeping the self solid in liquid times? In M. Davis (ed.) *Liquid Sociology: Metaphor in Zygmunt Bauman's writings on modernity*. Aldershot: Ashgate, pp. 139–56.

Newman, S. (2004) Terror, sovereignty and law: On the politics of violence. *German Law Journal*, 5(5): 569–84.

O'Malley, P. (2006) Criminology and risk. In G. Mythen and S. Walklate (eds) *Beyond the Risk Society*. London: McGraw-Hill, pp. 43–59.

O'Malley, P. and Bougen, P. (2008) Imaginable insecurities: Imagination, routinisation and the government of uncertainty post 9/11. In P. Carlen (ed.) *Imaginary Penalities*. Cullompton: Willan, pp. 26–44.

Polanyi, K. (1957–2001) *The Great Transformation*. Boston, MA: Beacon Press.

Roach, K. (2011) *The 9/11 Effect: Comparative counter-terrorism*. Cambridge: Cambridge University Press.

Sachs, J. (2007) Bursting at the seams. *Reith Lecture 1*. BBC: London.

Wacquant, L. (2009) *Punishing the Poor*. London: Duke University Press.

Walklate, S. (2008) What can International Criminal Victimisation Surveys tell us about women's diverse lives? In M. Cain and A. Howe (eds) *Women, Crime and Globalisation*. Oxford: Hart Publishing, pp. 201–14.

Walklate, S. (2012) Review of *The Criminological Imagination* by Jock Young. *Criminology and Criminal Justice*, 12(1): 106–8.

Young, J. (1999) *The Exclusive Society*. London: Sage.

Young, J. (2007) *The Vertigo of Late Modernity*. London: Sage.

Young, J. (2011) *The Criminological Imagination*. Cambridge: Polity.

Zedner, L. (2009) *Security*. London: Routledge.

Zizek, S. (2013) *Demanding the Impossible*. Cambridge: Polity.

INDEX